SERVANTS OF GLOBALIZATION

SERVANTS OF GLOBALIZATION

Women, Migration and Domestic Work

RHACEL SALAZAR PARREÑAS

STANFORD UNIVERSITY PRESS

Stanford, California

Stanford University Press
Stanford, California
© 2001 by the Board of Trustees of the
Leland Stanford Junior University

Original printing 2001
Last figure below indicates year of this printing:
10 09 08 07 06 05 04 03 02 01

Printed in the United States of America

To the courageous immigrant women in my family,
my mother, Cecilia Salazar Parreñas, and
aunts, Leticia Salazar Yap and Eva Salazar Pagunsan

CONTENTS

ACKNOWLEDGMENTS

I could not have written this book without the generous support of many individuals. First and foremost, I am grateful to the women who participated
in this study. Not only did they provide sparse energy and time, but they also
shared with me life stories that were emotionally difficult for them to recall.
Without their cooperation, this book would not have been possible.

This book began as a dissertation project for the Department of Ethnic
Studies at the University of California at Berkeley. I benefited immensely
from the guidance and wisdom provided by my chair, Evelyn Nakano Glenn.
She continuously challenged my thinking with her keen ability for posing
the most difficult questions. Since acting as my undergraduate thesis advi-
sor, she has mentored my academic development in all of its different stages.
Arlie Hochschild went far beyond the call of duty as a reader. By challenging and pushing me to analyze emotions, she directed me to look at migration not only as a social process but also as an experience. I owe a great deal to
Trinh T. Minh-ha, who introduced me to the world of poststructuralist theories. Finally, Raka Ray and Michael Omi helped me organize my thoughts
and ideas about this project. I am grateful to all of them for sharing their
ideas and expertise with me.

Many friends and colleagues closely read different parts of the manuscript
and lent valuable criticism and suggestions for improving the text. I am most
grateful to Maria Bates, Karen Brodkin, Julianna Chang, Viet Nguyen, and
Catherine Ramirez. I also benefited from comments shared by Pierrette
Hondagneu-Sotelo, Josh Kun, Pei-Chia Lan, Juana Rodriguez, Mary Ryan,
Min Zhou, and my fellow students in my spring 1998 dissertation writing
class.

Discussions with many other individuals also helped me process the ideas
that came into this book, including Rafael Alarcón, Amalia Cabezas, Charlotte Cote, Nicole Hickman, David Hernandez (who helped reformulate my
title), Fred Jamili, Amy Lonetree, Miguel Martinez, Jerry Miller, Celine Pa-

rreñas, Rolf Parreñas, Eric Porter, Roberta Saccon, Erika Shuh, Serena Satyasai, Frehiwot Tesfaye, and Laura Verallo Rowell. A special thanks goes to my friends Sherry Apostol and Manuel Ocampo for providing me with much appreciated breaks in the field, as well as timely retreats from writing, and to Malou Babilonia for ensuring that I had the optimal writing environment.

The earliest version of this book was written during the sixteen months that I met regularly with Charlotte Chiu, Angela Gallegos, and Mimi Motoyoshi. I am grateful for their friendship, encouragement, and advice. These women saw me through writing the very first to last sentence of my dissertation.

For graciously allowing me to take time off to complete this manuscript, I thank my colleagues at the University of Wisconsin–Madison. I received support from different institutions in various stages of this project. I am grateful to the Department of Ethnic Studies, Graduate Division, and Graduate Opportunity Fellowship Program at the University of California, Berkeley; National Science Foundation Graduate Research Fellowship; Department of Anthropology at University of California, Los Angeles; Babilonia Wilner Foundation; and University of California President's Postdoctoral Fellowship Program.

I could not have found a better editor than Laura Comay, whose commitment, support, and understanding of my goals for this project pushed me through the revision process. I would also like to thank Jonathan Okamura and the anonymous readers of this manuscript for their helpful suggestions. The skillful copyeditor Robert Burchfield also strengthened this manuscript.

I thank my family: Shari Carpenter, for her incredible confidence in my work and the encouragement and emotional support that she gave me during the early stages of this project, and Stephen Carpenter, for his companionship and comfort during most of the time that I worked on this book. My sisters Celine, Rhanee, Cerissa, Juno, Aari, and Mahal also provided much encouragement. They are my greatest source of motivation. My brother, Rolf, and my parents, Florante and Cecilia, also provided support.

Throughout the writing process, my friend Jennifer Lee gave me much encouragement, inspiration, laughter, and welcome distraction. This book benefits from our many conversations and exchanges of ideas. From short and long distances, my good friend Fernando Gaytan listened to me endlessly ramble on about this project. This book owes a great deal to his patience and confidence. The comfort of knowing that I could always turn to him sustained me through the most difficult times.

Finally, I dedicate this book to my mother, Cecilia Salazar Parreñas, and my aunts, Leticia Salazar Yap and Eva Salazar Pagunsan. The struggles that they have undergone as immigrant women underscored my need to do this project.

R.S.P.
Berkeley, California

SERVANTS OF GLOBALIZATION

Migrant Filipina Domestic Workers in Rome and Los Angeles

Diwaliwan, a glossy monthly magazine published in Hong Kong, caters to Filipino/a migrant workers around the globe. While pictures of Philippine movie stars and "Ms. Diwaliwan" monthly beauty contest winners usually grace the front page of the magazine, the most striking image on the cover is the notation of the price in the Hong Kong dollar, Australian dollar, Canadian dollar, Japanese yen, Italian lire, Spanish peseta, and at least a dozen other currencies. While the widespread circulation of *Diwaliwan* points to the existence of the Filipino/a diaspora, the magazine's contents reveal some aspects of its readership.[1] This magazine periodically covers issues concerning overseas domestic work. This is because the majority of Filipina migrants scattered all over the globe are domestic workers.

The outflow of women from the Philippines and their entrance into domestic service in more than 130 countries represent one of the largest and widest flows of contemporary female migration (Tyner, 1999). Filipino women are the quintessential service workers of globalization. As Nigel Harris states, "Filipinas are everywhere, a genuine labor force—maids gossiping and smoking on their day off in downtown Hong Kong or Singapore, working Japanese farms, running the duty-free shops of Bahrain, cleaning most of the world's cities from London to São Paulo" (1995: 15). According to nongovernmental organizations in the Philippines, there are approximately 6.5 million Filipino migrants. Since the early 1990s, women have composed more than half of deployed Filipino migrant workers (Asis, 1992). Of these women, two-thirds are employed in domestic service (Tolentino, 1996). By definition, domestic workers are employees paid by individuals or families to provide elderly care, childcare, and/or housecleaning in private homes.

This study enters the world of migrant Filipina domestic workers by comparing their experiences of migration and settlement in the two cities with the largest populations of Filipino migrants in Italy and the United States: Rome and Los Angeles (King and Rybaczuk, 1993; U.S. Census, 1993). I focus my study on Italy and the United States first because they are the two most popular destinations of Filipino migrants in Western countries. Second, the Philippines has particular colonial ties to both countries. As suggested by migration systems theory, migration streams are not randomly selected but instead emerge from prior links established through colonialism or preexisting cultural and economic ties (Castles and Miller, 1998). While the United States maintains enormous economic dominance in relation to the Philippines, Italy indirectly enjoys cultural dominance through the institution of the Roman Catholic Church. Third, contemporary Filipino migration flows to these two countries did not originate in a formal recruitment policy as they did for most other destinations of Filipino overseas laborers (for example, Hong Kong and Saudi Arabia). The movements of domestic workers into these two countries are for the most part informal streams that are not monitored by the state. In Italy, migrant women from the Philippines, Cape Verde, and Peru are concentrated in domestic service (Andall, 1992). In the United States, domestic work has been an occupation historically relegated to women of color and immigrant women (Dill, 1994; Glenn, 1986; Rollins, 1985; Romero, 1992). Notably, however, Filipina migrants are not concentrated in domestic service in the United States labor market.

My study looks at the politics of incorporation of migrant Filipina domestic workers. It does not concentrate solely on domestic work as an occupational issue. Instead, I view the experiences of migrant Filipina domestic workers through the lens of four key institutions of migration—the nation-state, family, labor market, and the migrant community. Within each institution, I examine a particular process of migration. Accordingly, they are (1) the outflow of migration, (2) the formation of the migrant household, (3) the entrance into the labor market, and (4) the formation of the migrant community.

In conducting a cross-national study, I found that migrant Filipina domestic workers in Rome and Los Angeles encounter similar issues of migration within each of the institutional processes that I set out to analyze. They experience partial citizenship vis-à-vis the nation-state. In terms of the family, the majority of women in both cities maintain transnational households. As such, they share the pain of family separation. In both cities, many of them perform domestic work with a college education in hand. From this they share the experience of contradictory class mobility or an inconsistent social status in the labor market. Finally, they encounter both social exclusion and feelings of nonbelonging in the formation of the migrant community, albeit from different sources—in Rome from the dominant society and in Los Angeles from middle-class members of the Filipino migrant community. Still, in both cities they face alienation from other migrants. My examination of institutional processes focuses on these four issues, which I refer to as *dislocations,* meaning the positions into which external forces in society constitute the subject of migrant Filipina domestic workers. My analysis of dislocations illustrates their process of constitution and the means by which migrant Filipina domestic workers resist (attempt to eliminate) or negotiate (attempt to mitigate) the effects of these dislocations in their everyday lives. From this perspective, the experience of migration is embodied in dislocations.

The formation of parallel dislocations among migrant Filipina domestic workers in different geographical settings came as a surprise. Because they face remarkably different "contexts of reception" in Rome and Los Angeles, I expected to find a larger degree of variation in their experiences. In *Immigrant America,* a pivotal overview of the politics of immigrant incorporation into the United States, Alejandro Portes and Rubén Rumbaut (1996) establish that experiences of migration shift and differ according to local "contexts of reception." The "context of reception" charts the migrant's path of incorporation well beyond his or her control. This context is shaped by a combination of various features, most important of which are government policies; labor market conditions, including patterns of "ethnic typification"; and the constitution of the ethnic community (Portes and Rumbaut, 1996: 86).

This study's underlying question asks, why do migrant Filipina domestic workers in cities with different "contexts of reception" encounter similar dislocations?[2] The answer lies mostly in their shared role as low-wage laborers in global capitalism. As such, this study provides a "cross-national comparison" to emphasize the similarities engendered by globalization among the low-wage migrant workers demanded in the economic centers of global capitalism (Portes, 1997). My discussion foregrounds the position and shared experiences of migrant Filipina domestic workers as the global servants of global capitalism. These shared experiences of dislocations are the tropes of alliance among them. That is, they may draw cross-national alliances on the basis of these dislocations and consequently perceive themselves as part of a global

community of workers dislocated into low-wage labor by the economic turmoil caused by global restructuring in the Philippines.

Filipino Migrants in Rome and Los Angeles

The "contexts of reception" for Filipino migrants in Rome and Los Angeles
are distinct in many ways. First, the histories of Filipino migration into Rome
and Los Angeles differ, with the former beginning not until the 1970s and
the latter beginning as early as the 1900s with the arrival of highly selected
government scholars (*pensionados*) soon after the colonization of the Philippines by the United States in 1898 (Espiritu, 1995). The different migration histories of these two host societies are not surprising considering that
Italy has historically been a country of emigration. Only recently, in the
1970s, did it noticeably become a country of immigration. Thus, in contrast
to the United States, which has had long-standing policies on migration,
Italy did not implement a comprehensive migration policy until 1987 (Pugliese, 1996).

Second, the demographic characteristics of these Filipino migrant communities are remarkably different. For example, while 70 percent of Filipino
migrants in Italy are women, their gender composition in the United States
is more balanced. Third, the politics of immigrant incorporation are differentiated by the basis of citizenship in the United States and Italy. The jus soli
(right by birth) is the basis of citizenship in the United States, while it is the
jus sanguinis (right by descendence) in Italy. Consequently, migrants can be
granted permanent residency in the United States but can only be temporary
residents of Italy.

Finally, the ethnic typification of Filipinos in the labor markets of Rome
and Los Angeles varies tremendously. In Rome, 98.5 percent of Filipinos are
in domestic work (Venturini, 1991). In Los Angeles and the rest of the United
States, contemporary Filipino migration can more or less be described as a
professional stream (Portes and Rumbaut, 1996). However, similarities in labor market conditions do exist between Rome and Los Angeles. Both labor
markets demand a pool of cheap labor to fill the need for low-wage service
jobs (Cohen, 1992; Sassen, 1988). In Rome, foreign diplomats, state officials,
and the presence of Italian cinema increase the demand for low-wage service
workers. In Los Angeles, low-wage migrant workers are needed to fill jobs in
decentralized industries of electronics and garment and furniture manufacturing as well as the formal and informal service sectors that cater to highly

specialized business professionals in the city (Bozorgmehr et al., 1996; Sabagh, 1993). Despite the typification of migrant Filipinos as professionals in the United States, a sizable contingent of them can be found performing low-wage service jobs not only in private homes but also in hotels, airports, and other establishments.

ROME

While Filipino migration into Italy officially began in the 1970s, Filipino migrants did not become a visible presence in Rome until the 1980s. Accounting for the large informal stream of migrants, Filipino officials in Rome believe that by 1995 more than 200,000 Filipinos had settled in Italy, with slightly less than half of them in Rome. A fairly recent event, this migration stream has been distinguished by its unidirectional flow of labor market incorporation into the informal low-wage service sector. Hence, this ethnic community, one comprised mostly of women, inhabits a very constrained niche in the Italian labor market.

As a receiving state, Italy is far more restrictive than the United States. Yet it has granted amnesty to undocumented migrants more consistently and generously, for example, awarding it in 1987, 1990, and 1995. In Italy, legal migrants hold a *permesso di soggiorno* (permit to stay), which grants them temporary residency. With its length of stay extending to seven years, residence permits for most Filipino migrants are renewable contingent on the sponsorship of an employer, the regular employment of the migrant, and finally the continual filing of income tax by the employer/s. Though the residence permit, with very few exceptions, generally restricts the labor market activities of migrants to domestic work, it grants them access to social and health services and rights to family reunification with spouses and children under the age of eighteen (Campani, 1993a). Notably, these rights were not bestowed on migrants until the implementation of the 1989/90 Martelli Law (Soysal, 1994).[3]

Even though Italy has historically been a country that sent workers to industrial centers of Northern Europe, the recent wave of immigration did not result in compassionate understanding among Italians (Ancona, 1991; Bonifazi, 1992; Montanari and Cortese, 1993; Veugelers, 1994). Instead, it has led to increasing sentiments of nationalism and xenophobia. A 1991 survey conducted by the Institute for Statistical Research and Analysis of Public Opinion in Italy indicates that "61% of respondents think that immigration brings 'only or mainly disadvantages'" to Italian society (Bonifazi, 1992: 29). This reflects an increase of almost 18 percent from a survey carried out in 1989. Immigration is in fact considered not only a social problem by most Italians but also an issue of political debate, as shown by the rise of the Northern League, whose campaign platform includes hostility against migrants (Ruzza and Schmidtke, 1996).

LOS ANGELES

In contrast to their counterparts in Italy, Filipino labor migrants settled in Los Angeles as early as the 1920s.[4] Prior to World War II, low-skilled male workers composed the majority of the relatively small number of Filipinos in the United States, which in 1965 only reached a population of 200,000 (Hing, 1998). Filipinos were mostly agricultural workers in rural areas, but a few settled in urban areas such as Los Angeles, where they provided low-wage service labor, for example, as cooks and domestic workers (Melendy, 1974).

The reconstitution of this community composed primarily of never-married single men came in 1965.[5] The 1965 Immigration Act drastically changed the composition of the Filipino population with the direct recruitment and immigration of skilled workers, specifically professionals and technicians demanded in the fields of science, engineering, and health, and their subsequent use of family reunification preference categories for the migration of kin (Reimers, 1985). Since 1970, the rate of Filipino migration has surpassed those of all other Asian ethnic groups. In fact, Filipino contemporary migration to the United States is second in size only to the Mexican migration flow (Portes and Rumbaut, 1996).

As the Filipino population throughout the United States diversified in terms of gender, region of origin, and level of education and grew in size exponentially, so did the Filipino community in Los Angeles. Filipinos now represent the second largest Asian American group in the country with a population exceeding 1.4 million (U.S. Census, 1993). They are the largest Asian American group in California and the second largest, next to the Chinese, in Los Angeles County. In 1990, there were 219,653 Filipinos living in Los Angeles County (Ong and Azores, 1994a: 104).[6] Like most other Asian ethnic groups in the United States, most Filipinos are immigrants. In 1990, 64 percent of Filipinos in the United States were born in the Philippines (U.S. Census, 1993). In Los Angeles, the foreign-born comprise 76 percent of the Filipino population (Ong and Azores, 1994a).

In contrast to Rome, where Filipino migrant workers are relegated to domestic work in a split labor market blatantly segmented by race and nationality, Filipinos in Los Angeles benefit from the civil rights struggles of the 1960s. They have more opportunities and occupy more varied positions in the labor market. Though often categorized as professionals, Filipino migrants do in fact also end up filling semi- and low-skilled occupations. A skilled worker may settle for semiskilled employment because of restrictive measures against foreign-trained professionals.[7] A survey of a random sample of persons issued visas from Korea and the Philippines in 1986 shows that 60 percent "of all professional and technical workers experienced downward mobility after entry" (Lowell, 1996: 360). While Koreans counteract this downward trend by turning to small-business entrepreneurship, Filipinos use their English-language skills and seek wage employment. Migrant Filipinos arguably fare worse. A turn to wage employment means that they do not develop an ethnic enclave that cushions newcomers in the community. The self-employment rate among Filipinos according to the 1990 federal census is only thirty-two per thousand, the lowest among all migrant ethnic groups (Portes and Rumbaut, 1996). In contrast to Koreans, they neither benefit from an ethnic enclave that stimulates economic mobility in the community nor have a niche that offers jobs with skills acquisition in ethnic entrepreneurship. Instead, Filipinos are split between the haves and the have-nots in the wage labor market.

We can speculate that the large flow of medical professionals from the Philippines partially initiated the entrance of Filipina migrants into domestic work. Considering nursing home facilities as well as private homes, the Filipino Worker's Center of Los Angeles estimates that Filipinos comprise the largest number of providers of elderly care in Los Angeles. This is not surprising considering that the Philippines is one of the largest sources of medical workers in the United States (Ong and Azores, 1994b). With knowledge of available jobs saturating networks in the community, migrant Filipinos have developed an "immigrant niche" in nursing (Waldinger, 1996). Without doubt, Filipina migrants can be found in its various levels, from registered nurses to licensed vocational nurses and certified nursing aides. This niche funnels information regarding elderly care into the community.[8]

As in Italy, xenophobia mars the incorporation of migrants into the United States (Portes and Rumbaut, 1996). This is perhaps most true in California, where in 1995 voters, fueled by the belief that immigrants burden the economy and drain government services, supported the state referendum Proposition 187, which bars undocumented immigrants from any tax-supported benefits including education, health, and social services (Martin, 1995). Anti-immigrant sentiments in California are targeted primarily against Latino migrants. In Italy, the same can be said of African migrants.

In summary, Rome and Los Angeles offer migrant Filipinos starkly different "contexts of reception." The starkest difference comes in government policies—migrant Filipina domestic workers in Rome are limited to temporary visas, but in Los Angeles they qualify for permanent residency. In fact, domestic workers qualify for the labor certification program that grants residency to migrants whose skills amend the labor shortage in the United States labor market. The demographic composition of the community is also strikingly different, with the one in Los Angeles occupying diverse sectors of the labor market and the other in Rome concentrated solely in domestic work.

Due to the greater integration of Filipino migrants in the United States, it is not surprising that fewer women enter domestic work in this country than in Italy. For this same reason, I anticipated greater differences between domestic workers in Rome and Los Angeles. For example, I expected to find a greater number of women maintaining complete family units in Los Angeles and a lesser number of educated women in domestic work. The varying degrees of integration in these two countries led me to question why domestic workers in Rome and Los Angeles share some experiences. What structural factors propel two distinct groups of Filipina low-wage workers into parallel trajectories? What does the emergence of similarities between them, in spite of their different contexts, imply about the process of globalization?

Why a Cross-National Perspective on Migrant Filipina Domestic Workers?

Despite their large number and wide dispersal, there is still very little academic discussion on the status of migrant Filipina domestic workers. With the exception of Philippine-based publications, existing works include the book-length studies of Nicole Constable (1997) and Abigail Bakan and Daiva Stasiulis (1997c) and articles by the aforementioned scholars as well as by Giovanna Campani (1993a, 1993b), Dan Gatmaytan (1997), Patricia Licuanan (1994), James Tyner (1994, 1999), and Brenda Yeoh et al. (1999).

In contrast to other studies, I present a comparative study of migrant Filipina domestic workers. The insights contained in other studies, however, allowed me to expand my methodological scope. Anthropologist Nicole Constable's (1997) study *Maid to Order in Hong Kong*, for example, offers an exemplary reading of the contradictions in the daily lives of migrant Filipina domestic workers in Hong Kong. Using a Foucauldian lens, Constable examines the dialectic relationship between discipline and resistance in the lives of migrant Filipina domestic workers, and she shows that their strategies of resistance at times involve conforming to the disciplining imposed upon them by the state, recruitment agencies, and employers. The collection of essays edited by Abigail Bakan and Daiva Stasiulis (1997c), *Not One of the Family*, reinforces the conclusion that the occupational issues of migrant domestic workers extend to the level of the nation-state. They demonstrate that political and social inequalities structure the incorporation of migrant domestic workers into Canada, where they are subject to restrictive temporary visas that require live-in employment and leave them vulnerable to unregulated employment standards.

A comparative study extends the discussions that have been initiated by these scholars. Heeding the call of Alejandro Portes (1997) for more "cross-national comparisons" in the analysis of international migration, a comparative study of migrant Filipina domestic workers contributes to a broader understanding of the significant variables molding their incorporation as migrant workers into the host society. Moreover, a comparative perspective is a tool for studying how similarities emerge in two different settings.[9] By limiting my comparison to domestic workers, I can achieve a feasible study that draws out similarities and differences in experiences across nations.

Another reason I chose to conduct a comparative study is to underscore the emergence of not just a labor migration outflow but a labor diaspora as the particular result of global restructuring vis-à-vis the Philippines. Migrant Filipina domestic workers are the servants of globalization. If, as Ulf Hannerz reminds us, "the contemporary work of globalization involves the globalization of work" (1996: 99), how is a localized occupation such as domestic work globalized? Global restructuring refers to the economic reconstitution triggered by transnational corporatism and postnational finance capitalism (Reich, 1991; Sassen, 1994, 1996b, 1996c). By resulting in a heightened demand for low-wage service labor in global cities, where there is a concentration of highly specialized professionals (for instance, accountants and business consultants), global restructuring engenders multiple migration flows of female workers entering domestic work and consequently results in the globalization of this occupation.

Calling forth a comparative study of migration, globalization requires a shift from a unilocal to multilocal perspective in the analysis of economic activities. A comparative study ensures that a focus on the local does not overlook the global (Mufti and Shohat, 1997). With the relocation of production in globalization, the decline in manufacturing activities in Pittsburgh, for example, can no longer be understood without the simultaneous consideration of manufacturing activities in other localities, such as export processing in Mexico and informal manufacturing in New York. Though not constituting a traceable relocation such as production activities, low-wage service labor—such as domestic work—should also be understood in a multilocal perspective to emphasize the expansion of reserve armies of cheap labor with the formation of a (low-wage) labor diaspora and the demands for low-wage service workers by the economic bloc of postindustrial nations.

Hence, by showing the emergence of similarities among migrant Filipina domestic workers in different contexts, this study brings to the forefront the significance of their shared position in the global economy. Despite the differences in the particularities of their destinations, migrant Filipina domestic workers do fulfill a similar economic role in globalization. In both Rome and Los Angeles, they are part of the low-wage service workforce of the economic bloc of postindustrial nations. With this in mind, we can see more clearly that a cross-national perspective allows us to truly situate migration flows in globalization and its corresponding macrostructural trends.

Finally, I conduct a comparative study so as to situate the lives of Filipino Americans in a diasporic instead of a domestic perspective (Wong, 1995).[10] A turn toward a diasporic perspective follows the trajectory established by Lisa Lowe (1996) in *Immigrant Acts* of placing the analysis of Asian American experiences in an "international context," one that is mindful of the construction of Asian American subjects in the globalization of the economy, the foreign policies of the United States, and the resulting migration of Koreans, Southeast Asians, and Filipinos from the wars and foreign presence of the United States in Asia. Extending Lowe's contention that post-1965 Asian immigration to the United States is a result of colonization, I wish to point out that United States colonialism in the Philippines resulted not only in a migration flow to the United States but also in a labor diaspora that far transcends this country in its geographic scope. The economic turmoil caused by United States colonialism and the subsequent presence of institutions such as the World Bank in the Philippines have led to a migration flow the world over. Notably, the diaspora in which I categorically situate migrant Filipinos is not based on the notion of an essential allegiance among them but instead is based on their particular position as migrant workers in the global economy.

The large contingent of Filipino labor migrants to the United States is conceivably part of a larger outflow of a hierarchical labor diaspora from the Philippines. Professionals, semiprofessionals, and low-wage workers make up this diaspora. Moreover, the presence of Filipina domestic workers in the midst of the more visible professional migrants in the United States points to this country's inclusion in the Filipina domestic worker diaspora. Indeed, a large number of undocumented Filipina women in the United States end up in domestic work (Hogeland and Rosen, 1990). The case of the United States invites an assessment of the larger structural forces and migrant institutions that propel a distinct subgroup of Filipinas into domestic work. Thus, I situate the experiences of Filipina domestic workers in a diasporic terrain, one that cannot be understood without the simultaneous consideration of the experiences of their counterparts in other countries. The Filipino labor diaspora is conceivably composed of one labor force in the global economy. By making this point, I do not mean to imply that migrant Filipina domestic workers or Filipino labor migrants have the same experiences the world over. As I show in Chapter 2, the Filipino labor diaspora is segmented by gender and class. Despite my seemingly contradictory findings, I do maintain that experiences in this diaspora are differentiated by social, political, legal, historical, and economic contexts of incorporation. Yet by drawing out existing similarities in their experiences, I wish to move toward finding a cross-national coalitional ground for the Filipino diasporic subject.

Filipinos in Globalization: An Imagined Global Community of Filipina Domestic Workers

As political economist Saskia Sassen states, "International migrations are produced, they are patterned, and they are embedded in specific historical phases" (1993: 97). The contemporary outmigration of Filipinas and their entrance into domestic work is a product of globalization; it is patterned under the role of the Philippines as an export-based economy in globalization; and it is embedded in the specific historical phase of global restructuring. The global economy is the stage that migrant Filipina domestic workers in Rome and Los Angeles have entered in their pursuit of the accumulation of capital. Considering that they perform the same role on the same stage (but in different places) for the same purpose, the emergence of similarities between them becomes less surprising despite the different contexts of their destinations. *Ben Anderson*

The existence of an "imagined (global) community," using Benedict Anderson's conceptualization of the nation, reinforces the presence of similarities in their lives.[11] The imagined global community of Filipina migrants emerges, in part, from the simultaneity of their similar experiences as domestic workers across geographic territories. A Filipina domestic worker in Rome may "imagine" the similar conditions faced by domestic workers in Singapore, London, and Kuwait. Notably, they are only able to conceive of a global community because of the existence of shared interests and practices among them.[12]

The dislocations that are constituted in their labor migration are these shared experiences. As such, they are the premise of their community and from which they carve a symbolic transnational ethnic identity as Filipino diasporic subjects. Dislocations, or "narratives of displacement," as Stuart Hall refers to them, are the conjunctures or specific positionings of subjects in social processes (Hall, 1988, 1991a, 1991b). As mentioned, the dislocations of migrant Filipina domestic workers include partial citizenship, the pain of family separation, the experience of contradictory class mobility, and the feeling of social exclusion or nonbelonging in the migrant community.

In a series of essays on cultural identity, Stuart Hall formulates a notion of ethnic identity that is based on the process of subjectivity and the conjunctures that emerge from the subject's positioning in multiple axes of domination (Hall 1988, 1991a, 1991b). Dislocations represent conjunctures from which migrant Filipina domestic workers develop a cross-national allegiance. This conjuncture-based identity works against the notion of an essential unified self, in other words a Cartesian subject whose origin is its actual self (Hall, 1988). Instead, identity is an ongoing "process of identification" in the context of history and society (Hall, 1991a: 15). It is based on the effects of systems of inequality on the subject. Hence, dislocations are neither essential nor exclusive to migrant Filipina domestic workers but instead emerge from the specificities and conjunctures in their location in the political economy of globalization and its corresponding institutional processes. The sharing of these dislocations enables the formation of an imagined global community.

Yet this imagined global community does not emerge solely from the sharing of experiences but comes from, borrowing the words of social theorist Michel de Certeau, the creation of continuously traveled "bridges" across geographic territories ("frontiers") in migration. As Arjun Appadarai (1996) notes, imagination is not a fantasy that can be divorced from actions. This imagined global community is constituted by circuits like those identified by anthropologist Roger Rouse as tying together sending and receiving communities of migration into a singular community through the "continuous circulation of people, money, goods, and information" (1991: 14) or what anthropologists Linda Basch, Nina Glick-Schiller, and Christina Szanton Blanc (1994) refer to as "transnational social fields" in their seminal study on transnationalism, *Nations Unbound*.[13]

Migrant Filipina domestic workers maintain transnational projects that connect the Philippines to various geographical locations. For example, ethnic goods circulate from the Philippines to the United States, other countries of Asia, the Middle East, and Europe. However, these webs are not restricted to a binary flow that is directed solely to and from the Philippines. Tangible and imagined links also weave the multiple migrant communities that make up the Filipino labor diaspora more closely together. Instead of just a transnational community, these links forge the creation of a global community.

In the case of the Filipino diaspora, circuits function multinationally. First, the circulation of goods occurs in a multinational terrain. In Europe, for instance, ethnic goods circulate to connect multiple Filipino migrant communities with their shipment from the Philippines to the United Kingdom and only then to other European nation-states. Moreover, multinational ethnic enclave businesses have sprouted with franchises of remittance agencies in Europe, Asia, the Middle East, and North America. Philippine bank-sponsored remittance centers such as Far East Bank-SPEED and PCI Bank compete with carriers such as LBC across continents. Although money does not usually circulate between migrant communities, remittance agencies represent collective locations among geographically distanced migrant workers.

In addition, transnational family ties of migrants are not limited to the Philippines. Intimate decisions involved in family maintenance transcend multiple borders. The families of the following handful of women vividly show that migration creates multinational households in various forms, an observation previously made by Khandelwal (1996) regarding contemporary Indian migrant families. Vanessa Dulang, a single woman who followed two of her sisters to Rome in 1990, is the seventh of eleven siblings who decided to work abroad, as two of her sisters and brother live in Kentucky while an older brother navigates to different countries as a seaman. The youngest among her siblings, Ruth Mercado works in Rome while her oldest sister is a barmaid in Switzerland, her brother a tricycle driver in Manila, and her other sister cares for the elderly in Saudi Arabia. Her retired parents stay in the Philippines, where they depend on the remittances sent by their daughters from three different nations. A trained nurse, Gloria Diaz works as a domestic worker in Rome, while her oldest sister works as a nurse in the United States and another sister as a nurse in Manila. A domestic worker in Los Angeles, Dorothy Espiritu had previously worked in Saudi Arabia, during which time her oldest daughter began working in Japan and another daughter in Saudi Arabia. Finally, there is the family of Libertad Sobredo, a domestic worker in Los Angeles. Her nine children are either working outside of the Philippines, in Saudi Arabia and Greece, or pursuing their college degrees in Manila. These families exemplify the formation of a multinational, and not just binational, household structure among Filipino labor migrants. The interdependency among members of multinational families results in the circulation of money from multiple countries to the Philippines, where economically dependent family members usually reside. Accentuating the experience of a multinational family, Libertad Sobredo, for example, usually deals with family crises occurring across the Pacific in the Philippines by making transatlantic phone calls to her eldest son in Greece.

Finally, magazines that cater to Filipino labor migrants provide additional solid evidence of a circuit that links the multiple migrant communities of Filipinos across the globe. The distribution of the monthly publications *Tinig Filipino* and the aforementioned *Diwaliwan* in more than a dozen countries signifies the presence of a diasporic community from which these magazines profit and which in turn is perpetuated by their circulation of information (to say the least) across geographic borders. As print language created the "imagined community" of the nation in the 1800s, it now provides a tangible link connecting geographically dispersed migrant Filipina domestic workers. A vehicle for creating the notion of a global community and instilling "in the minds of each . . . the image of their communion" (Anderson, 1983: 6), *Tinig Filipino* aptly describes itself as the "Linking Force Around the World."

In contrast to its competitor *Diwaliwan*, which frequently covers "showbiz" news in the Philippines and mostly features short stories, *Tinig Filipino* offers its readers a forum for dialogue as overseas workers themselves write most of the articles published in the magazine. As such, this magazine is arguably a gateway to the world of its primary audience of migrant Filipina domestic workers. Titles of articles reflect some aspects of the social realities that these migrant workers face and at the same time reveal some of the dislocations that they encounter in migration. While the title "I Want to Go Home But Where Is Home?" suggests the jagged process of settlement in migration, the title "The American Dream" tells of the construction of the United States as the ideal destination of migrant Filipinos, a legacy of the colonial relationship between the United States and the Philippines. Other titles address family and work related issues. For example, the title "Isang Kontrata Na Lang Anak" (One more contract, my child) insinuates the recurrence of family separation in migration. Readers' high level of educational attainment is also revealed by the common use of the English language in writings by domestic workers and frequent references to canonical literary figures, such as William Shakespeare and Elizabeth Barrett Browning. Imagine my surprise when I encountered a Shakespearean quote, "Our doubts are traitors and make us lose the good we oft might win, by fearing to attempt." Though first surprised, I soon realized that these quotes simply reflected the high level of education among migrant Filipina domestic workers. Thus, instead of being surprised, I was left to imagine that there are Filipina domestic workers all over the world relaxing from the physical challenges of their daily routines and relieving themselves of their mentally stifling duties by reading literary texts of the Western canon.

The significance of *Tinig Filipino* is that it enables workers—isolated domestic workers—to reach each other cross-nationally and cross-continentally. In *Tinig Filipino*, the global community comes together on the platforms of particular "narratives of displacement," neither essential nor exclusive narratives but narratives that are prominent within this historical moment. At the same time, it is the existence of narratives of displacement that gives *Tinig Filipino* an avid readership. These narratives are the basis of coalition and solidarity in the labor diaspora, a coalition that has great potential for extending to other groups of migrant workers.

This study centers on the narratives of displacement, or dislocations, of migrant Filipina domestic workers. I explain their experience of migration by mapping out the dislocations that they encounter in migration and that serve as the basis of their identity as Filipino diasporic subjects in this age of late capitalism and globalization. In the process, I also explain how these dislocations form and are contested. In doing so, I address the question of why migrant Filipina domestic workers in host societies with different "contexts of reception" have similar experiences. As I will show, the answer rests largely on their positioning in globalization as part of the secondary tier labor force of the economic bloc of postindustrial nations.

Methodology

My research is based primarily on tape-recorded and fully transcribed open-ended interviews that I collected with domestic workers in Rome and Los Angeles for a period of ten months between June 1995 and August 1996. More than four months in Rome gave me ample time to collect forty-six in-depth interviews with Filipina domestic workers. The interviews ranged from one-and-a-half to three hours in length. I also collected ten in-depth interviews with male domestic workers so as to examine the gendered determinants of migration and settlement in Italy. In addition, I conducted tape-recorded interviews with various community leaders and public figures (for example, Filipino religious clergy, elected officers of the Filipino feminist group and hometown associations, and the disc jockey of the Filipino radio show). I collected an unsystematic sample of research participants by using chain and snowball referrals, but I made sure to diversify my sample by soliciting research participants in numerous community sites such as churches, parks, and plazas.

In Rome, I enhanced the data provided by the in-depth interviews with a short survey of a nonrandom sample of 301 Filipino domestic workers— 222 women and 79 men. Two young Filipina domestic workers whom I had befriended assisted in the collection of the survey data. The survey consisted of questions on biographical data, such as year of migration, legal status, and the frequency and amount of remittances. The surveys were conducted at three churches and three main public locations where Filipinos gather during their day off. These gathering sites are located in four different districts of Rome. The main reason I conducted the survey was to compensate for the absence of government statistics on Filipinos in Italy.

I also conducted participant-observation in the community, which entailed the following: regularly attending church services and after-church activities; attending informal get-togethers during days off in apartments, as well as more formal get-togethers like weddings, birthdays, and christenings; hanging out in plazas and parks with Filipinos on their day off; spending many hours at employers' homes with domestic workers and assisting them with their work; and, finally, observing and volunteering at Life-Asper, a community organization that legally assists Filipinos with labor contracts and obtaining legal documents.[14]

In Los Angeles, I collected a smaller sample of twenty-six in-depth interviews with Filipina domestic workers that also range from one-and-a-half to three hours in length. From various informants, I heard of only two Filipino men working as domestic workers and decided that their extremely small number made them negligible to my study. Tapping into the community began with the network of my mother's friends and relatives. To diversify my sample, I posted flyers in various businesses—restaurants and remittance centers in downtown Los Angeles. Two women who later referred me to many other women responded to the flyers. Interestingly, more women (twenty) called not to be interviewed but to find jobs. Phone messages left on my machine were descriptions of the type of job that they preferred—usually the companionship of an elderly person. Utilizing networks of the domestic workers, the sample of interviewees was collected unsystematically through a snowball method, as I did in Italy. Nonparticipant-observation provided a gateway to the Filipino community of Los Angeles, as I attended meetings of community groups, the occasional parties given by community organizations, and the more frequent parties given by individual families, and I spent time with domestic workers at their own and their employers' homes.

In Los Angeles, five respondents who had agreed to be interviewed later backed out, telling me they did not have time because they were too busy with work or telling me that they just could not do it. Most of them felt guilty, I believe, as they all apologized profusely and offered to refer me to their friends. I suspect that their legal status had a lot to do with their decision to withdraw because a few of them repeatedly asked me to explain the purpose of my research and to verify that the research was truly confidential. In contrast, I could not accommodate all of the women and men who volunteered to be interviewed in Rome. This is not to say that I did not have to solicit research participants. In Rome, I struggled to represent as many community centers and locales in my sample of participants as possible.[15]

In Los Angeles, interviews were conducted in English or Tagalog with frequent interspersions of Tag-lish (Tagalog-English). In Rome, most of the interviews were conducted in Tagalog and then translated into English. Research participants themselves decided on which language to use in the interview. In Rome, I was soon informed of the protocol of language use that I needed to follow. I had to initiate conversations in Tagalog instead of English so as not to be mistaken for a snob who wanted to distinguish her higher-class status. At the same time, it was equally rude of me not to respond in English to those who chose to speak to me in this language. As a guest of the community, I learned that I had to wait for members to initiate the language in which I should converse with them.

My efforts to speak Tagalog were cause for amusement in Rome. While I grew up in Manila until the age of twelve, I no longer had a strong command of Tagalog after having spent years in the United States and never having returned to the Philippines. In Rome, I found myself once again familiarized with my native language. By the time I was ready to leave Rome, many of the people I had interviewed commented on how my Tagalog had improved dramatically from the choppy Tag-lish that they had heard during my first month in the field.

In contrast to my interviewees in Los Angeles, many of the women interviewed in Rome insisted that I use their real names, asserting that they were neither embarrassed about their personal lives nor their work as domestic helpers. Although they may feel betrayed that I have not complied with their request, I have decided to follow academic convention and use fictitious names for all of my interviewees for their and my own protection.[16]

In summary, the in-depth interviews consist of open-ended questions about the life history of subjects. The women tell their own stories about their migration, family, community relations, and work experiences. The interviews provide a rich source of data from which to understand the experiences of the women in the four key social processes of migration that I have set out to analyze.[17]

Characteristics of the Samples

In this section, I compare the characteristics of the samples collected in Rome and Los Angeles. The variables considered are type of domestic work, age, marital status, region of origin, legal status, duration of settlement, and educational attainment.[18]

The women whom I interviewed perform three types of domestic work: housecleaning, elderly care, and childcare, none of which emerged as a dominant job in either city. A more salient pattern did emerge among their living arrangements. In Los Angeles, most of them are "live-in" workers who stay with the employing family throughout the weekday and return to their own home only on the weekend. For instance, only four "live out" of the employing family's home.[19] This contradicts the trend toward day work found among Latina domestics in the United States (Romero, 1992). In contrast, the women in Rome can more or less be divided equally between live-in and "part-time" workers, which is the term that Filipino day workers use to describe themselves.[20] For the most part, providers of elderly care tend to be live-in workers.

As expected, differences exist between the two groups of women in this study. For example, the median age of domestics in Los Angeles is fifty-two, which is much greater than the median age of thirty-one for the women in Rome. They also come from different regions of the Philippines, with many women in Rome originating from Southern Luzon provinces and in Los Angeles from the Visayas. However, there are more similarities between them than differences. For instance, most are legal residents of their respective host societies. In Rome, thirty of forty-six interviewees have a renewable *permesso di soggiorno*, while fifteen of twenty-six interviewees in Los Angeles are permanent residents of the United States.[21] Many are also recent migrants who entered their respective destinations in the early 1990s (see Table 1).

In both cities, they are also mostly mothers with a fairly high level of educational attainment. Contrary to the popular belief that Filipina domestic workers are usually young and single (CIIR, 1987), my study shows a larger number of married women. In Los Angeles, only five of twenty-six interviewees are never-married single women, while in Rome, less than half of the women I interviewed (nineteen) are never-married single women. Women with children living in the Philippines constitute a greater portion of my sample in both Rome and Los Angeles: twenty-five of forty-six in Rome and fourteen of twenty-six in Los Angeles. Based on the women's median age, we can assume that in Rome the children are fairly young and those in Los Angeles are older.

Because they perform jobs that are considered "unskilled," domestic workers are often assumed to lack the training needed for higher-status jobs in the labor market. In the case of Filipina domestics in Italy and the United States, the prestige level of their current work does not in any way reveal their level of educational training (see Appendix A and Table 2). Most of my interviewees had acquired some years of postsecondary training in the Philippines. In Rome, my interviewees include twenty-three women with college degrees, twelve with some years of college or postsecondary vocational training, and seven who completed high school. In Los Angeles, my interviewees include eleven women with college diplomas, eight with some years of college or postsecondary vocational training, and five with high school diplomas.

Even with a high level of educational attainment, Filipino women migrate and enter domestic work because they still earn higher wages as domestic workers in postindustrial nations than as professional workers in the Philippines (see Appendix A and Table 3). In Rome, part-time workers receive an average monthly wage of 1,844,000 lira (U.S.$1229), live-in workers 1,083,000 lira (U.S.$722), and providers of elderly care 1,167,000 lira (U.S.$778).[22] After taking into account the additional cost of living for part-time workers, there is just a slight difference in salary between the three types of domestic workers. In Los Angeles, Filipina domestic workers receive a weekly instead of a monthly salary, which is an arrangement that they prefer as it results in higher earnings. Providers of elderly care receive on average a salary of $425 per week, and live-in housekeepers and childcare providers receive on average $350 per week. Wages of domestic workers in

Rome and Los Angeles are significantly higher than those that they had received in the Philippines. Among my interviewees, the average monthly salary of women who had worked in the Philippines during the 1990s was only U.S.$179.

The Organization of the Book

This book examines the experiences of migrant Filipina domestic workers through the lens of the dislocations that they confront in migration and settlement. As such, the book is organized around the institutional processes in which these dislocations form. In my discussion of each dislocation, I illustrate the process of its constitution, its impacts on the lives of migrant Filipina domestic workers, and how these women in turn resist and negotiate the dislocation.

Providing a theoretical overview, Chapter 1 explains the analytic approaches that I utilize to identify the dislocations of migration. I use three theoretical approaches, two of which are established approaches in migration studies: the macrostructural and intermediate level of analysis to the study of migratory processes. The third approach utilizes poststructural theories in the humanities and is what I call the analysis of migration from the level of the subject.

In Chapters 2 and 3, I analyze the social process of the outflow of migration. Chapter 2 examines the dislocation of partial citizenship, which is the subject positioning of migrant Filipina domestic workers vis-à-vis the nation-state at both ends of the migration spectrum. In Chapter 3, my query into the lives of migrant Filipina domestic workers moves to the question of why they migrate. While the political economy of global capitalism unquestionably dictates the flow of migration, it does not do so single-handedly. This chapter presents the process by which gender inequalities in both receiving and sending states also control the migration of Filipina domestic workers. My discussion shows that their migration constitutes an international division of reproductive labor, which refers to the three-tier transfer of reproductive labor among women in sending and receiving countries of migration.

Chapters 4 and 5 examine the formation and maintenance of transnational families in global restructuring. Chapter 4 establishes the family to be a milieu of dislocation, specifically of the pain of family separation, and Chapter 5 examines how migrant Filipina domestic workers cope with this dislocation. Chapter 6 interrogates the social process of the entrance and performance of domestic work and maps relations of power, both personal and nonpersonal aspects, between domestics and employers. The deconstruction of power relations reveals the dislocation of contradictory class mobility.

Chapter 7 examines the Filipino migrant communities of Rome and Los Angeles. This chapter shows that Filipina domestics in these two cities share the localized dislocation of nonbelonging. For women in Rome, nonbelonging results from their curbed integration in Italian society—socially, physically, and economically. For women in Los Angeles, nonbelonging is generated not by the host society but by the host community, as it results particularly from class disparities in the middle-class-centered Filipino migrant community of Los Angeles.

Returning to the initial research questions, the concluding chapter underscores the significance of macrostructural determinations of migration. In this final chapter, I explain why similarities exist between Filipina domestic workers in Rome and Los Angeles.

The Dislocations of Migrant Filipina Domestic Workers

Filipina domestic workers face four key dislocations in migration: partial citizenship, the pain of family separation, contradictory class mobility, and non-belonging. In this chapter, I explain how I identify these dislocations by using three levels of analysis—macrostructural, intermediate, and subject level—to lay out the theoretical foundation of my study.

Two dominant approaches are used to explain the processes of migration. The macroapproach documents macroprocesses that control the flows of migration and the labor market incorporation of migrants (Sassen, 1988). One of the best-known macrostructural approach is the world-system model. The second method, an intermediate level, centers its analysis on institutions (for example, households and social networks) to document social processes of migration and settlement (Massey et al., 1987). Social processes by definition are processes shaped by the interplay of structures and agency. Offering equally valid but different perspectives on the processes of migration, these two approaches neither contradict nor oppose one another. For example, both criticize the traditional microlevel approach to the study of migration from the level of the individual for disregarding structural determinants of migration and settlement (Pedraza-Bailey, 1990).

Another way of examining migratory processes is from the level of the subject. This perspective examines how migrants are situated in social processes of migration and how migrants in turn navigate through these constitutive processes. Analyzing migration from the level of the subject does not retreat to the widely critiqued analysis of migration from the level of the individual because the theoretical conception of a subject differs from that of an individual. In contrast to the "free will" ascribed to an individual, a subject is not free reigning but instead is "something at the behest of forces greater than it" (Smith, 1988: xxxiii). Joan Scott writes: "They are not unified, autonomous individuals exercising free will, but rather subjects whose agency is created through situations and statuses conferred on them. Being a subject means being 'subject to definite conditions of existence, conditions of endowment of agents, and conditions of exercise'" (1992: 34). In other words, subjects cannot be removed from the external forces that constitute the meanings of their existence. At the same time, agency is not denied in this conception. Instead, in this view agency is enabled and limited by the structures that constitute subjects.

The three levels of analysis that I utilize in this study reveal different aspects of migratory processes. The macrolevel approach clarifies our understanding of the structural processes that determine patterns of migration and settlement. The intermediate level of analysis documents the institutional transformations and shifts in social relations that are engendered in migration. Finally, the subject level approach broadens our understanding of migratory experiences by examining the positionings of migrants within institutional processes.

Globalization and the Macrolevel of Analysis

As I noted, globalization is a framework that needs to be considered in order to achieve a complete understanding of the local (Dirlik, 1996; Grewal and Kaplan, 1994; Kearney, 1995). Anthropologist Michael Kearney defines globalization as "social, economic, cultural and demographic processes that take place within nations but also transcend them, such that attention limited to local processes, identities, and units of analysis yields incomplete understanding of the local" (1995: 548). Sassen further qualifies that globalization "is not an encompassing umbrella" (1998: 3). Instead, it operates in specific institutional and geographical contexts and thereby reaches the "most molecular elements in society" (Foucault, 1980: 99). Globalization, through its corresponding macroprocesses, shapes the subject formation of migrant Filipina domestic workers and the position of these subjects in institutions (Dirlik, 1996; Grewal and Kaplan, 1994; Ong, 1999; Sassen, 1998). We need to thus consider macroprocesses to understand the dislocations of migration. These macroprocesses include the formation of the "global city" (Cohen, 1992; Sassen, 1988, 1994, 1996c, 1996d), the feminization of the international labor force (Sassen, 1988, 1996a), the "opposite turns of nationalism" (Sassen, 1996b), and the formation of an economic bloc of postindustrial nations (Reich, 1991; Sassen, 1993).

As firmly established in the literature on migration, global capitalism functions through and maintains an overarching world-system that organizes nations into unequal relations and creates a larger structural linkage between sending and receiving countries in migration (Portes and Walton, 1981; Sassen, 1984; Zolberg, 1983). Migrants are "part of the ongoing circulation of resources, both capital and labor, within the boundaries of a single global division of labor, that is between a dominant core and a dependent periphery" (Friedman-Kasaba, 1996: 24). In the case of the Philippines, this division of labor emerges in the direct recruitment of its citizens to provide labor to more advanced capitalist nations in Europe, the Americas, Asia, and the Middle East (Battistella and Paganoni, 1992). One can arguably look at the destinations of migrant Filipina domestic workers as an economic bloc that solicits lower-wage labor from less advanced nations in the global economy.

Contributing an insightful theoretical framework on the position of women in the global economy, Sassen (1984, 1988) establishes a structural link between the feminization of wage labor and globalization. According to Sassen, globalization simultaneously demands the low-wage labor of women from traditionally Third World countries in export-processing zones of developing countries and in secondary tiers of manufacturing and service sectors in advanced capitalist countries (Sassen, 1984).[1] The case of women in the Philippines provides an exemplary illustration. While Filipino women comprised 74 percent of the labor force in export-processing zones by the early 1980s (Rosca, 1995), they constituted 55 percent of the migrants by the early 1990s (Asis, 1992).

Under the global capitalist system, the penetration of manufacturing production in developing countries directly leads to socioeconomic restructuring in advanced capitalist countries such as Italy and the United States. First, the manufacturing production that remains in these latter countries (such as garment, electronics, and furniture) must compete with low production costs in developing countries. This results in the decentralization and deregulation of the few remaining manufacturing jobs in these nations (Sassen, 1996c).

Second, multinational corporations with production facilities across the globe, by and large, maintain central operations in new economic centers, or "global cities" (Sassen 1994), where specialized professional services (for example, legal, financial, accounting, and consulting tasks) are concentrated.

Examples of such cities in the United States and Italy are New York, Los Angeles, Miami, and Milan. The rise of these geographic centers in which decision making in the operation of overseas production takes place demands low-wage service labor to maintain the lifestyles of their professional inhabitants. For the most part, immigrants, many of whom are female, respond to these demands (Sassen, 1984).[2]

Another macroprocess that corresponds with global restructuring is the "opposite turns of nationalism" (Sassen, 1996b). One turn has already been described, that is, the "denationalization of economies." The other turn is the "renationalization of politics," which refers to increasing sentiments of nationalism. In postindustrial nations, renationalization partially results from the use of immigrants as scapegoats against the economic displacement faced by middle-income workers in the deindustrialization of the economy (Sassen, 1996b; Ong, 1999). An apt example of renationalization at work is the "orientalization" of Asians in the United States as shown by the campaign contribution crises that recently plagued the Democratic Party (Ong, 1999). While the denationalization of economies causes the renationalization of politics, the former also overturns or at the very least eases the impacts of the latter. An example is the selective incorporation of foreign-born skilled workers, an adjustment allowed by state regimes to maximize the benefits of global capitalism (Ong, 1999).

Macroprocesses in globalization provide the condition for the subjection of migrant Filipina domestic workers. As such, the questions directing this study can be reformulated around these macroprocesses to emphasize their centrality in the formation of dislocations. How does the opposite turn of nationalism situate migrant Filipina domestic workers in various institutional settings? How do the feminization of the labor force and the relegation of these women to low-wage service work in postindustrial nations situate them in the global labor market? Finally, how does the rise of the "global city" place them in a contradictory position in the family and community?

As this study intends to show, these macroprocesses impose dislocations on migrant Filipina domestic workers. To provide an introductory synopsis, the opposite turns of nationalism, for instance, consigns them to the position of partial citizenship in host societies with their rejection as citizens by the renationalization of politics and acceptance as low-wage workers by the denationalization of economies. Another example is the demand for their labor in globalization and its corresponding macroprocess of the feminization of the labor force; this predicament relegates them to low-wage service work regardless of their level of educational attainment and thereby leads to their contradictory class mobility. Finally, their concentration in "global cities" promotes the formation of transnational households and consequently results in the dislocation of the pain of family separation as the low wages of domestic work cannot cover the high costs of raising a family in the geographic centers of global capitalism.

Intermediate Level of Analysis

Studies that apply an intermediate level of analysis to the examination of migration diverge from those using a macrostructural level of analysis by recognizing agency in their systematic view of migratory processes. At the same time, they build from and depend on these latter studies for the structural context of their discussions about institutional and social processes. By amending the conspicuous absence of agency in the macrolevel approach, various intermediate level studies have been able to expand the scope of our understanding of migratory processes (Pedraza, 1994). They address questions that macrolevel discussions cannot answer, for example, those concerning the constitution of migration flows, such as why migration flows are concentrated in specific communities, why they persist after the initial causal factors of migration have eroded, and why there is a specific gender and class constitution to migration (Grasmuck and Pessar, 1991; Hondagneu-Sotelo, 1994).

In this approach, migrants are shown to respond to larger structural forces through the manipulation of institutions (for instance, social networks) in the creation of migrant communities, in the maintenance of migration flows, or in easing and securing one's social and labor market incorporation upon settlement. These are a few examples of the social processes captured in the intermediate level of analysis. Notably, the development of the intermediate level of analysis by Douglas Massey and his colleagues (1987) has led to the further expansion of migration studies in the areas of transnationalism and gender studies. Studies in these areas have returned the favor by theoretically advancing the intermediate level of analysis in their consideration of social relations in institutional and social processes of migration (Hondagneu-Sotelo, 1994; Kibria, 1993). As they have significantly advanced the field of migration studies, I turn to the two burgeoning areas of transnationalism and gender studies to look at how this approach directs us to the identification of dislocations.

TRANSNATIONALISM

In this age of globalization, migrants no longer inhabit an enclosed space, as their daily practices are situated simultaneously in both sending and receiving communities of migration (Rouse, 1991). As such, they can now be conceived of as "transmigrants," meaning "immigrants whose daily lives depend on multiple and constant interconnections across international borders and whose public identities are configured in relationships to more than one nation-state" (Glick-Schiller et al., 1995: 48). This category moves us beyond the long-standing binary construction of settlement in migration studies that is split between migrants (temporary settlers) and immigrants (permanent settlers).

Just as globalization "installs itself in very specific structures," transnational processes do not supersede but instead are embedded in the institution of the nation-state (Sassen, 1998: 3; Guarnizo and Smith, 1998; Ong, 1999). Numerous studies have shown a variety of ways that "transnational processes are anchored in" nation-states (Kearney, 1995: 548). For instance, transnationalism functions along juridical territories (Ong, 1999). Moreover, nation-states institutionalize transnational processes with programs that advocate concrete financial and political ties between sending and receiving communities of migration (Glick-Schiller and Fouron, 1998; Mahler, 1998; Smith, 1998).

Transmigration is fostered by the compression of space and time in globalization (Harvey, 1989). In other words, the option of transmigration is promoted by the greater access of migrants to advanced forms of communication. Yet why do migrants turn to transnational institutions? Migrants usually do so to negotiate their stunted integration in settlement. They create transnational institutions (such as transnational families and hometown associations) because they have not been fully incorporated into the host society (Glick-Schiller et al., 1995; Ong, 1999). By situating themselves in "transnational social fields," migrants counteract their marginal status in the host society (Appadarai, 1996; Basch et al., 1994; Goldring, 1998). For example, they benefit from their higher social status in the sending community as well as from the higher purchasing power of their wages (Basch et al., 1994; Goldring, 1998).

In the introduction to their collection of essays *Transnationalism from Below*, Guarnizo and Smith (1998) propose the use of a "mesostructural," or intermediate, level of analysis to the study of transnational processes.[3] From research on transnationalism, we have learned about the formation of transnational institutions in which migrants function, whether they are families (Laguerre, 1994; Basch et al., 1994), networks (Rouse, 1991, 1992), community organizations such as hometown associations (Smith, 1998), political groups (Glick-Schiller and Fouron, 1998), or business enterprises (Ong, 1999). At the same time, we have learned that it is important to look within these institutional formations of migration and account for the "everyday practices of ordinary people" that take place in transnational institutions (Guarnizo and Smith, 1998). Indeed, transnational institutions, while determined by structural constraints, are created by the everyday practices of migrants. This indicates that the intermediate and subject levels of analyses are intimately related analytic approaches that are differentiated mostly by a question of emphasis between social process and subjection.

GENDER

By considering the constitution of social relations in institutions, feminist scholars of migration have significantly advanced the intermediate level of analysis. For one, they have rightly shown that institutions are sites of patriarchal ideologies (Pessar, 1999).

An analysis of social relations illuminates social patterns in institutional processes. Feminist scholars of migration have shown, for example, that the social relation of gender organizes, shapes, and distinguishes the immigration patterns and experiences of men and women (Hondagneu-Sotelo, 1994; Pedraza, 1991). They have brought to the foreground the different labor market concentration and incorporation of male and female migrants (Hondagneu-Sotelo, 1994; Mahler, 1995); the different social spaces and networks men and women create and inhabit in the migrant community (Hagan, 1994; Hondagneu-Sotelo, 1994); and the different experiences of men and women in the migrant family (Friedman-Kasaba, 1996; Grasmuck and Pessar, 1991; Hondagneu-Sotelo, 1994; Kibria, 1993). Accounting for social relations in institutions underscores the divergences caused by gender, class, and/or generation in migration and shows that these divergences come not without social conflicts (Hondagneu-Sotelo, 1994, 1999; Kibria, 1993).

Literature on female migration has also illustrated the reconstitution of gender within migratory processes. In particular, studies have concluded that migration, which involves the movement "from one system of gender stratification to another" (Zlotnick, 1990), reconstitutes the position of women in the labor market and household (Glenn, 1986; Grasmuck and Pessar, 1991; Hondagneu-Sotelo, 1994). In the receiving country, migrant women experi-

ence a certain degree of gender liberation because of their greater contribution to household income and participation in public life (Hondagneu-Sotelo,
1994; Kibria, 1993). However, studies are careful to point out that even with
these advances, patriarchy is not eliminated but is somehow retained in migration (Pessar, 1999).

Researchers have also included gender in discussions of the causes of migration. In a study of Central American refugees in Washington, D.C., Repak (1995) establishes that gender is a determinant of migration by showing
that the greater demand for low-wage female workers in this particular receiving community initiated the primary migration of women. Yet for the
most part, women remain secondary migrants (Donato, 1992). That is, they
migrate to create or reunify a family. Even so, this does not necessarily mean
that women play a secondary role in migration (Hondagneu-Sotelo, 1994).
As Toro-Morn (1995) argues using the case of Puerto Rican migrants, the
secondary migration of women is part of a family strategy for survival.

Scholars of gendered migration generally warn against ghettoizing gender as applicable only to women (Pessar, 1999; Tyner, 1999). As a solution,
they recommend comparative studies of male and female gendered experiences. Though I recognize this need in migration research, I nonetheless opted
to focus solely on migrant women. The absence of men in my study does not
represent a digression from viewing gender as a central analytical principle
in the study of migration. A sole focus on the experiences of women in
various institutional settings can still advance gendered migration research.
Such studies can continue the new direction in migration research that accounts for the intersections of race, class, gender, and foreign status in the
lives of male and female migrants (Pessar, 1999; Espiritu, 1997). One way of
doing so is through the lens of migration as a process of subject formation.
Thus, the next section focuses on the constitution of the subject and their dislocations, which are shaped by multiple forms of oppression. This accounts
for the intersections of race, class, gender, and citizenship in the lives of migrant Filipina domestic workers.

Subject Level of Analysis

The subject level of analysis diverges from the intermediate level by not cen-
tering its analysis on social processes and the social relations constituted
within these processes. This approach does not seek to document the formation of social processes. Instead, social processes are considered settings for

the process of subjection. This mode of analysis moves beneath the structural and institutional bases of social processes to deconstruct their minute effects on the subject. It does so to identify the subject-positions constituted within social processes.

In this view, social processes generate boundaries of "existence" and "exercise." Taking place in institutional agencies—which, according to Foucault, maintain "regimes of truth and power" (Ong, 1999)—social processes produce discourses. In its broadest sense, discourse refers to a particular system of meanings communicated by language and practices (Weedon, 1997).[4] Discourses are emitted through institutional agencies, which in turn are given meaning by these "regimes of truth and power." From the discourse produced in institutional regimes arise subject-positions, which are "a contradictory mix of confirming and contending 'identities'" (O'Sullivan et al., 1994: 310).[5]

As subject-positions are generated by discourses that maintain institutional agencies, I examine social processes not only to document the institutional transformations engendered in migration (for example, community formation, constitution of migration flow, labor market incorporation, and transformation of household) but also to establish social processes and their corresponding institutions as the contexts in which a migrant subject exists and acts, the contexts from which emerge particular subject-positions. By defining the subjectivity of migrant Filipina domestic workers, I seek to identify their multiple subject-positions, or what I prefer to call "dislocations" or "narratives of displacement" to emphasize the subordinate conditions of their migration.

Dislocations are the challenges that Filipina domestic workers encounter as they navigate through social processes of migration. They are the segmentations embodying their daily practices in migration and settlement. As such, they are the stumbling blocks and sources of pain engendered within social processes of migration. Dislocations define the experience of migration from the perspective of the migrant subject. They are "the conscious and unconscious thoughts and emotions of the individual, her sense of self, and her ways of understanding her relations to the world" (Weedon, 1997: 32).

Dislocations stem specifically from the structural location inhabited by the migrant. In the case of migrant Filipina domestic workers, they emerge from their structural location as racialized women, low-wage workers, highly educated women from the Philippines, and members of the secondary tier of the transnational workforce in global restructuring.

By examining the subject-positions of migrant Filipina domestic workers,

I follow the trajectory established by women of color feminist theorists on ways to account for the multiple intersections of race, class, gender, sexuality, and nation (Alarcón, 1990; Grewal and Kaplan, 1994; Lorde, 1984; Mohanty, 1991; Trinh, 1989). First, this approach avoids universalisms and instead follows the analytic trajectory established in women of color feminism to emphasize specificities in location (Lorde, 1984; Mohanty, 1991). At the same time it stresses the specific position of subjects in sets of relationships. Women of color feminist theorists tend to account for the specific contexts of experiences in order to avoid the exclusivity unavoidably rendered by universal notions of race, class, and/or gender (Grewal, 1994). Thus, they insist that subjects are constituted only in their situatedness in multiple and intersecting axes of domination (Alarcón, 1990; Sandoval, 1991).

Second, this approach builds from Trinh Minh-ha's conception of the self as composed of "infinite layers" instead of a "unified subject, a fixed identity" (Trinh, 1989: 94). By placing in the foreground the dislocations that constitute the conjuncture-based identity of migrant Filipina domestic workers, I underscore their marginal location in multiple discursive spaces of race, gender, nation, and class. I highlight how these intersecting axes of domination leave them "decentered" and "fragmented" subjects (Grewal and Kaplan, 1994; Grewal, 1994). By focusing my analysis on dislocations, I avoid the highly criticized projection of a whole unitary subject and instead promote the feminist project advocated by theorists such as Norma Alarcón, Stuart Hall, and Gayatri Spivak to view identity as an incomplete and ongoing process. With this in mind, my study provides only a partial picture of the complicated positioning of migrant Filipina domestic workers in "webs of power relations" (Foucault, 1983).

Why do I insist on viewing migration as a process of subjectivization? Only by documenting the subjectivity of migrant Filipina domestic workers can I account for their experience of migration. Dislocations are the defining characteristics of experience. As such, my study interrogates the meanings of these dislocations to explain the experience of migration. As Joan Scott says, "Experience is, in this approach, not the origin of our explanation, but that which we want to explain" (1992: 38). In this case, the experience that I want to explain is the constitution of parallel lives among migrant Filipina domestic workers in different locations.

A subject level approach is not at all foreign in the social sciences. In her groundbreaking study of transnational practices in the Chinese diaspora, *Flexible Citizenship* (1999), Aihwa Ong is one of the first scholars to apply a subject level of analysis to the study of migration and transnationalism. Following the Foucauldian notion of "governmentality," Ong sees institutions as "regimes of truth and power" that regulate and discipline the actions of the migrant subject. While looking at institutions as settings of subject making, Ong examines transnationalism through an analysis of the everyday practices of Chinese transnational subjects and the institutional and structural contexts that condition these practices in order to illuminate the "cultural logic" of these conditioned practices. In the process, she shows that analyzing everyday practices is a viable approach to understanding global and institutional processes of migration. In other studies of migration, the subject level of analysis comes closest in the consideration of the "politics of location," which recognizes that relationships and experiences are determined by one's structural location in multiple axes of domination (Mohanty, 1991). Yen Le Espiritu (1999), for instance, considers "social structural locations" as a starting point of analysis in the study of Asian immigrant families. A few scholars have also delved into the theoretical conception of a subject to better understand how the transnational activities of migrants are situated and conditioned by localized contexts (Guarnizo and Smith, 1998; Sorensen, 1998).

My analysis of migration as a process of subject formation does not end with a documentation of dislocations. It includes an equal consideration of the actions undertaken by migrant Filipina domestic workers to ease and resist their dislocations. Judith Butler contends, "The analysis of subjection is always double, tracing the conditions of subject formation and tracing the turn against these conditions for the subject—and its perspective—to emerge" (1997: 29). In the formulation of migration as a process of subject formation, migrants resist larger structural forces by responding to the dislocations that these forces have generated in their lives. In making this point, I want to emphasize that the average migrant Filipina domestic worker does not come to realize her world through the understanding of larger systems such as patriarchy and global capitalism. She instead does so through the particular dislocations that these systems have generated in her everyday experience of migration (see Foucault, 1983: 212).

Foucault refers to such resistances to power as "immediate struggles" (Foucault, 1978, 1983). The notion of immediate struggle is precisely what Butler describes as the "turn" taken by subjects against the conditions of their formation. Because immediate struggles are always present in relations of power, functioning within their circuits, they do not necessarily have to directly confront larger structures in society to be effective tools for change.[6] For their strength, immediate struggles rely on their multiplicity, irregular forms, and constant presence within the operation of power.

Even though the forms of resistance that migrant Filipina domestic workers deploy against dislocations do not involve the direct diminishment of structural or institutional power, their acts of resistance must be credited with possible interventions against the ways that structural inequalities operate in shaping their everyday lives. Understanding such a claim requires a brief introduction to the Foucauldian subject. Although subjects are constituted by external forces, the consequences of their actions are not always reducible to the macrostructural forces that shape them. Actions bear an affective quality in relation to structures because power operates as "an action upon an action" (Foucault, 1983: 220). Foucault writes that "power exists only when it is put into action, even if, of course, it is integrated into a disparate field of possibilities brought to bear upon permanent structures" (Foucault, 1983: 219). In other words, dislocations emerge from exercises of power imposed on migrant Filipina domestic workers by agents—a category that includes these women—of the state, labor market, family, and community. The macroprocesses that dislocate migrant Filipina domestic workers are deployed only in action. As such, dislocations are not ontologically rooted in institutions. Instead, they are constituted by the practices that create and maintain institutions. Consequently, they can be negotiated through the realignment of these constitutive practices.

Yet negotiation does not necessarily signify elimination. The means by which migrant Filipina domestic workers choose to ameliorate the dislocations they encounter in migration ironically involve conforming to these dislocations. In fact, the means by which migrant Filipina domestic workers resist their dislocations actually re-create structural inequalities. This is the "bind of agency" that Butler (1997) speaks of, the subject's simultaneous "recuperation" and "resistance" of power. Agency is at the same time "a resistance that is *really* a recuperation of power" and "a recuperation that is *really* a resistance" (Butler, 1997: 13). This occurs because a subject can never be completely removed from the process of its constitution. As I stated, agency is conditioned and therefore limited by the social processes from which it emerges and takes place. This means that resistance, as it recuperates power, does not necessarily bring positive change.

This contention actually raises a larger theoretical question regarding agency. If agency emerges within and not outside the process of subjection, how is agency possible? To answer this question, I rely on the explications of the Foucauldian subject provided by Butler (1997, 1995, 1992). Butler writes: "If in acting the subject retains the conditions of its emergence, this does not imply that all of its agency remains tethered to those conditions and that those conditions remain the same in every operation of agency" (1997: 13).

For the subject, the "conditions of its own subordination" is disabling and enabling, because the enactment of power involves a shift from power as externally "acting on" to constitutively "acted by" subjects (Butler, 1997: 12, 15). As power shifts from being an external force to a constitutive force enacted by the subject, "the subject eclipses the conditions of its own emergence " (Butler, 1997: 14). In the process, the subject does not escape the external forces "to which it is bound," but instead its actions exceed the forces of its constitution (Butler, 1997: 17). It is precisely through this conditioned agency that subjects intervene to shape the process and condition of their constitution.

Consequently, when acting against dislocations, migrants do not necessarily impose interventions against structural processes but may also intensify and re-create hierarchies among migrants and their families, migrants and their employers, and migrants and other migrants. As mothers, for example, migrant Filipina domestic workers cope with the pain of family separation by intensifying filial authority through the suppression of their own and their children's emotional needs. As domestic workers, they resist the downward mobility of migration by emphasizing and taking advantage of their higher social status compared to that of poorer women in the Philippines. For instance, they hire their own domestic workers. As a final example, domestics in Rome heighten the alienation that they experience in the migrant community by expediting the accumulation of savings through the commercialization of friendships in the community (for example, charging a fee for personal favors) when resisting the dislocation of nonbelonging.

In summary, my study maps the subject formation of migrant Filipina domestic workers through the illustration of how particular subject-positions or dislocations are constituted in migration. Following Butler, I frame my analysis of subjection around two questions: What are the particular dislocations that define the experience of migration for Filipina domestic workers in Rome and Los Angeles? How do they then turn against these dislocations?

Conclusion

In this book, I approach the study of migration from three levels of analysis. These approaches neither contradict nor override one another. Moreover, the subject level approach builds from the two other approaches so as to interrogate the constitution of the migrant as a subject regulated by various axes of domination. Following the process of this constitution requires an understanding of the contexts in which it takes place. Thus, it requires an understanding of globalization and its corresponding macrostructural trends as well as the institutional processes that function as the regimes in which the subject is regulated by structural forces in society.

CHAPTER 2

The Philippines and the Outflow of Labor

In this chapter I begin my examination of the dislocations of migration as I analyze the subject positioning of migrant Filipina domestic workers vis-à-vis the outflow of labor. Caught in the contradictions of nationalism in globalization, migrant Filipina domestic workers are denied full citizenship at both ends of the migration spectrum. Neither fully integrated in receiving nations nor completely protected by the Philippines, they are at most only partial citizens.

Partial citizenship emerges from the contradictory positioning of migrant Filipina domestic workers within the discourse of nationalism in globalization. In particular, the "opposite turns of nationalism," which as I have noted refers to the "denationalization of economies" and "renationalization of politics" (Sassen, 1996b), initiate domestic workers' subjection as unprotected nationals of globalization. Under the opposite turns of nationalism, the globalization of the market economy propels their labor migration as it simultaneously stunts their full incorporation into the receiving and sending nation-states.

To develop my conception of partial citizenship, I begin with a brief overview of the constitution of the Filipino labor diaspora, which is both gender and class stratified. I then describe the modes of migration into Italy and the United States in order to qualify my discussion of the outflow of labor. In the next two sections, I examine how globalization imposes the dislocation of partial citizenship on members of this stratified labor diaspora in relation to both sending and receiving countries of migration. In the final section, I analyze the turn that migrant Filipina domestic workers take against their experience of partial citizenship. Using the writings published in the multinational monthly magazine *Tinig Filipino*, I show that migrant Filipina domestic workers turn to the construction of the Philippines as "home" to regain citizenship as an identity.[1]

The Filipino Diaspora

As I have noted, gender distinguishes the labor migration patterns and experiences of men and women. This could not be truer in the case of the Philippines, where women and men are deployed to different regions of the globe. Women migrate to destinations with a greater demand for entertainment and service workers. In contrast, male migrants are usually channeled into heavy production and construction occupations (Tyner, 1994).[2] As a result, the outflow of labor from the Philippines consists of two distinct gendered flows.

In effect, the gender makeup of Filipino migrant populations in various nations is highly incongruent. While men compose the majority of Filipino migrants in the Middle East, women do in most other destinations. In 1991, Japan Immigration Association statistics indicate that 99,710, approximately 80 percent, of 125,329 Filipinos legally residing in Japan are women (Osteria, 1994: 54). A Philippine government survey shows that in 1996 women composed 83.3 percent of Filipino migrants in Hong Kong, 77.1 percent in Singapore, and 78.3 percent in Italy (Philippine National Statistical Coordination Board, 1999).

The regional disproportion of men and women in the diaspora indicates that women migrate independently of men. As such, they do not fit the classic mold of female migrants, as they are neither "dependent" nor "secondary" migrants (Morokvasik, 1984; Zlotnick, 1995). Instead, women in the United States and Italy are more likely to sponsor the migration of their family. In the United States, Filipino migration has been a female-dominated stream since 1960, because the shortage of medical personnel resulted in the direct recruitment of Filipina nurses (Espiritu, 1997). In Italy, the need for domestic workers initiated the primary migration of women just like it did in Washington, D.C., for Salvadoran women (Repak, 1995).

In the diaspora, the labor market distribution of Filipina migrant workers varies according to levels of immigrant integration and policies in nation-states. Professional women, due to their direct recruitment in the 1960s and 1970s and the Civil Rights movement in the 1960s, tend to be concentrated in the United States (Espiritu, 1995; Pido, 1986). Filipino migrant women in

most other destinations, such as Europe, Asia, and the Middle East, are segregated in low-wage service sectors (CIIR, 1987). The illegal trafficking of
Filipino women has also led to their concentration in sex industries, especially in Japan but also in the Middle East (Osteria, 1994; Sarmiento, 1991).[3]
A staggering number of Filipino women have also entered Australia and other
countries, including Germany, Finland, Norway, and the United States, as
mail-order brides (CIIR, 1987; Tolentino, 1996).[4]

In the late 1980s, official government figures indicated that there were
fewer than 300,000 migrant Filipina domestic workers worldwide (Heyzer
and Wee, 1994: 39).[5] However, government statistics cannot provide a reli-
able account of the number of Filipina domestic workers, because they ex-
clude undocumented workers who leave the country with temporary nonmigrant visas (for instance, tourist visas). There are many more of them
than the official records report. Because undocumented migrants from the
Philippines are concentrated in receiving countries with a larger proportion
of women than men (for example, Italy, Spain, and Japan), the actual number of domestic workers more than likely exceeds official government statistics. Among a select few countries and regions, a conservative estimate of
at least 600,000 can be drawn from figures given by nongovernmental organizations: there are approximately 130,000 –150,000 domestic workers in
Hong Kong; 200,000 in Italy; 50,000 in Spain; 36,000 in Singapore; and
200,000 in the Middle East (Constable, 1997; Tolentino, 1996: 58).

Modes of Outmigration to Italy and the United States

Despite the knowledge in the Philippines of the lack of protection for migrant workers, one out of every ten Filipinos still wants to seek employment
outside the country (Tolentino, 1996). The prevalence of outmigration has
instilled in the public psyche the view described by Sarah Mahler of the
youth in traditional sending communities in El Salvador: "To keep up with
the Joneses, they knew that they had to migrate" (1998: 714). But among the
large number of workers who aspire to labor migration only a select few
meet their goal because outmigration is made a much more difficult process
by the renationalization of politics. The enforcement of strict border control
in various destinations of the diaspora coupled with restrictive conditions of
settlement increase the resources required of potential migrants.

Mobility is not equally accessible to prospective migrants (Mahler, 1998).

The question then is what resources enable only a select group of Filipino workers to migrate? According to literature on international migration, the selectivity and persistence of migration flows depend on social networks and "migrant institutions" (Goss and Lindquist, 1995).[6] In the case of the Philippines, financial resources also determine the likelihood and destination of migration.

While recruitment agencies and social networks do direct, maintain, and over time increase migration flows from the Philippines, migration to Rome and Los Angeles for domestic workers is also directed by other forces. Specifically, economic resources possibly achieved by the earlier migration of other family members enable individuals to afford the option of migration to either of these two cities. The fees charged by recruitment agencies vary according to the destination of the migrant. Cost is not only determined by the distance between the receiving country and the Philippines but also by the prospective wages of workers in the receiving country.

In the diaspora, what one can afford determines one's destination. Recruitment agencies charge approximately U.S.$600 in fees for a job placement in Hong Kong, where in 1993 the monthly salary of domestic workers, as stipulated by labor contracts, was H.K.$3200 (approximately U.S.$410) (Constable, 1997). In Singapore, which is another low-cost destination, the average salary of foreign domestic workers is even less, amounting to only U.S.$200 per month (Yeoh et al., 1999). In contrast, the average salary of domestic workers in Italy is much higher, as are the fees charged by recruitment agencies, which in the early 1990s were not less than U.S.$5000. The cost of migration to Italy is also higher, because greater risks are involved in this enterprise. Unlike those specializing in the recruitment of workers to Hong Kong, agencies catering to prospective migrants to Italy are not state-sanctioned but illegal enterprises that assist with undocumented migration.

Also requiring economic resources, migration to the United States has long been an elusive goal for most Filipinos. Stringent requirements for those not qualified for permanent migrant visas have forced many prospective migrants to enter the United States with a temporary nonmigrant visa, which is often granted only to those with economic security, as it requires proof of property, investments, and savings in the Philippines.

The higher fees for migration to Italy and the stringent requirements for entry into the United States indicate that class is another factor influencing the direction of labor migration from the Philippines. While the option of migration for poorer migrants to these two countries is made possible by the assistance of earlier migrants, the greater economic security of the middle class does increase the likelihood of migration for the latter group. The large number of highly educated women in my sample supports this observation.

What are the modes of migration used by the women in my study? With the exception of one woman who crossed the border clandestinely from Canada, all of the women in Los Angeles entered the country with valid legal documents (see Table 7). Among my sample, sixteen women entered with temporary nonmigrant visas, four women qualified for entry through family reunification (that is, through the sponsorship of parents or fiancé), and five women entered with temporary work permits as companions of business investors from the Philippines. In contrast to domestic workers in Rome, research participants in Los Angeles did not use recruitment agencies. Instead, most relied on social networks to gain knowledge of the opportunities for and process of migration to the United States. For example, all of the women in my study had friends, family, or acquaintances willing to host their "visit." While family reunification migrants and those accompanying Filipino professionals did not need to have substantial financial resources, the temporary migrants, the "tourists," who constitute the majority of my sample, clearly did.[7] Meeting the tourist visa requirements does not guarantee entry, however, as the number of applicants often exceeds the quotas established by the United States government. In general, the women in my study found entry to the United States to be a difficult and time-consuming process that required a strategic plan of presentation to officials. It entailed the solicitation of advice and letters of invitation from earlier migrants and the preparation of proof of property. Having anticipated the difficulty of migration to the United States, most interviewees had expressed their surprise over the approval of their applications.[8]

Just as Dominicans who lack networks to enter New York seek employment in Europe, migrant Filipinos who cannot enter the United States go elsewhere, including Italy (Sorensen, 1998). Interviews in Rome confirm the difficulty of entry to the United States, as many members of the community had applied for visas unsuccessfully, even with the presence of relatives in the country. Moreover, many women expressed plans of eventually migrating, if not to the United States then to Canada, and hoped that their tenure in Rome would assist them in this process.

Most research participants in Rome entered Italy clandestinely, meaning they crossed the Italian border illegally. Many women first stepped foot on the European continent in an eastern country and then proceeded to travel

to Italy with the prearranged assistance of coyotes who work with recruitment agencies solicited by prospective migrants in the Philippines.[9] Of forty-
six female interviewees in Italy, thirty entered illegally with the assistance
of recruitment agencies, or "travel agencies" as they are referred to in the
community. Other research participants crossed the border with valid visas
for entry: eleven with temporary nonmigrant visas, two with temporary
worker visas, and three with family reunification visas.

Patterns of outmigration to Italy can be distinguished temporally. The
eight research participants who migrated before 1983 all came as tourists.
Not one of them solicited the assistance of recruitment agencies. Instead,
they relied on information shared by friends. An official visa was not required of Philippine citizens until 1981, and until 1983 a tourist visa to Italy
could be obtained from any country in Europe.[10] Since then, only three of
the women were able to enter the country with tourist visas. When the number of foreign workers visibly increased during the early 1980s, Italy imposed more stringent requirements for temporary nonmigrants and forced
prospective migrants to enter clandestinely. This created the demand for the
services of illegal "travel agencies" in the Philippines. Thus, after 1983, these
migrant institutions became the dominant mode of migration to Italy from
the Philippines.

As it is surprising that a large migrant community of Filipinos has formed
in Italy, migrants explain that they had sought labor market opportunities in
Italy after hearing of the high wages that domestic workers received. Earlier
migrants, some of whom entered as direct hires and some of whom literally
stumbled upon the labor market opportunities in Italy while visiting as genuine tourists, had shared this information with them. Direct hires are labor
migrants recruited from the Philippines to work in Italy as domestic workers by prospective employers. They enter the country with valid work permits. The arrangements are informally negotiated by the individual domestic worker and prospective employer but, beginning in 1987, have required
the consent of both receiving and sending states.[11] One can speculate that the
concrete ties enabling Italian employers to hire domestic workers from the
Philippines can be traced back to the strong presence of the Roman Catholic
Church in most regions of the Philippines. For example, one of the two
women in my sample who entered as direct hires was approached by her
community's parish priest about working in Italy as a domestic worker. Since
the enactment of the 1989–90 Martelli Law, family reunification became another strategy for legal entry into Italy. Yet among my sample, only three

women utilized this option. Most women do not enter as direct hires as well, even though this prearranged contract is a more economical option, perhaps because Italian employers are unwilling to cover the cost of travel for prospective domestic workers when so many are already available locally.

As I stated, most Filipinos migrating after 1983 enter Italy via the assistance of recruitment agencies. The fees charged by these agencies have increased steadily over time, along with Italy's reputation as a receiving country offering high wages and minimal risks of deportation for undocumented migrants. The family of Michelle Fonte witnessed this steady increase. The cost of migration that had amounted to only 65,000 pesos (U.S.$3250) for her sister in 1986 jumped to 85,000 pesos (U.S.$4250) for Michelle in 1989 and catapulted to the exorbitant amount of 300,000 pesos (U.S.$12,000) in 1994 for another sister. This amount is actually fairly high in relation to the other migrants whom I interviewed in Rome. In my study, women who left the Philippines in 1990 and 1991 paid "travel agencies" approximately 110,000 to 120,000 pesos (U.S.$4400 to $4800) and an additional U.S.$2000 to a coyote. By 1993, the cost of migration had increased to no less than 200,000 pesos (U.S.$8000).[12]

The experiences of women migrating illegally can be divided into two distinct flows: before and after the late 1980s and early 1990s. Until the late 1980s, the enforcement of border control by Italian authorities had been fairly lax, making the journey into Italy not a very difficult process. Migrants often had a valid visa for entry to a Western European country bordering Italy (for example, Switzerland or Germany). From there, they simply rode a train or bus across the border without stopping and eluded inspectors by feigning sleep or conveniently disappearing into the restroom.

By the early 1990s, the character of the typical journey into Italy changed drastically with the tightening of border control throughout Western Europe and even Italy, which had always had a reputation for "being 'flooded' by an uncontrollable 'wave' of migrants" (Santel, 1995: 76). Participation in the 1990 Schengen Agreement, which instituted an open-border policy within the European Union, forced the Italian state to give in to pressures imposed by other European countries to implement a stricter border regime (Foot, 1995; Santel, 1995; Zolberg, 1993). The fall of Communism in Albania in 1990 also precipitated greater border control on the eastern shores of Italy. For Filipina migrants, the tightening of border control transformed their journey into a more harrowing experience, one that now entailed the risking of lives. Hence, ironically, while the Martelli Law granted social rights to

Italy's temporary migrants, it also led to the creation of physically inhumane conditions of migration.

Since 1990, the journey of Filipina domestic workers into Italy has actually begun to resemble that of Mexican migrants into the United States. While it has been said that the danger of migration to the United States from Mexico deters families from having women migrate prior to men, Filipino women lead the migration across the dangerous borders of Italy. Incarnacion Molina's journey exemplifies the experience of the 1990s migrants, many of whom hid in cargo ships without ventilation, storage areas of tour buses, or the dust-filled ceiling of trains or walked across the mountainous terrain of Europe to reach Italy. I quote her story extensively to illustrate the struggles undergone by women to reach the destination of Italy.

> Coming here was horrendous. I did not think that I was going to survive. My plane landed in Turkey. From Turkey, we took a tourist bus and went to many different countries, even those with a war . . . ; then we went to Yugoslavia. . . . We had a visa for Turkey and Yugoslavia. We were really tourists. . . .
>
> In Yugoslavia, we even checked in a hotel [covered by the $2500 they had additionally paid the "guide" arranged by the agency] . . . , and after three days, Yugoslavians picked us up in taxis. There were thirty-one of us, and we were divided into two groups of fifteen and sixteen. I was in the first batch. We were put in taxis—three per taxi.
>
> We rode the taxi around 5:30 in the evening and just drove. Then, all of a sudden, the taxi stopped. I guess the taxi stopped because they saw the police coming. The driver made us get off and run to the side of the road, onto the fields and hide like soldiers. Then after the police passed us, the taxi called us back. It was dark and there were many trees. We were asked to get off, and, there, three people met us. They took us to the side of the sea, where there was a speedboat waiting for us.
>
> We rode the speedboat . . . covered by a heavy tarp. . . . We were so frightened because the waves were so strong. We thought that we were going to die out there. When the boat stopped, we thought that we finally made it. But actually, we stopped because there was a spotlight going back and forth on the water, watching for boats coming.
>
> Then, the speedboat moved again and . . . we made it. It was around five in the morning. We were told that we made it and to get off. It was muddy where we had to go through and we had to run for cover in these bushes. . . . We waited and, finally, someone came to get us. . . .

Then, that person took us through this rough area that was rocky and muddy. I kept on falling on the ground. We did not walk for long, maybe fifteen minutes, but it was difficult. Then, we had to climb up this tall wall. . . . The guide carried us over, and I fell jumping down. . . . Fortunately, I was not injured.

[By that time], it was bright already, and I think our guide got worried because the police could see us more easily. So, we were abandoned there. It was daylight. We were left in the middle of nowhere. We did not know where we were and where we were going to go. . . . It was hot and we were just standing around there. . . . The people with me were very frightened. . . . They were very nervous about any sounds . . . ; [then] a Doberman came running to us. . . . It was barking and barking. It left and came back with the police in five minutes. They took us to the police station. . . .

We did not answer any questions. We pretended not to speak English. They asked for our passports, and they saw that we had visas for Yugoslavia. Afterwards, they made us clean ourselves because we were very muddy. Then, they fed us. Someone asked us how we got there, and someone responded that we got lost.

Then, they took us to the headquarters of the police, and there we were interviewed again. They were very nice to us, though. . . . They were feeding us throughout the day. At midnight, they told us we could return to Yugoslavia. . . .

[Returning to Yugoslavia by train the next day], we were standing around the middle of this plaza and a Filipina came up to us and asked us if we were Filipinos. We really did not know where we were. We didn't say anything, but we did hear explosions [because of the ongoing war in the former Yugoslavia]. . . . We explained to her how we were deported back from Italy and she told us that she was going to help us. So, she took us to the hotel.

We did not have any of our things that we left with our original tour guides. If we had our return tickets, we would have preferred to go back to the Philippines.

After two days, we tried again. Taxis picked us up again. Mama mia! This time around we were just walking and walking. We walked from 5:30 in the evening to 4:30 in the morning nonstop through the mountains. A street I can walk on, but there, it was rugged and uneven. [Laughs.] Jump, you jump, get down, you get down. We were like soldiers. [Laughs.] We were walking and walking. I was so tired. I don't think anyone could be prepared to go through what we had to go through.

There were grapes there and the guides would pull the grapes and feed me so that I could walk. . . . I was always falling. I was bruised all over my body.

Then, when it was 4:30 in the afternoon, I remember passing through this area with water. I remember drinking water there. [One guide] led us through a cornfield. Then, that guide suddenly screamed. That was a warning for us to run back, because there were guards and border patrol ahead. She was seen by the soldier and that was why she screamed. The guard was chasing her. So, we were also seen because we were right behind her. So, we all ran back through the cornfield and tried to hide.

[Then we got deported once again. . . .] They took us back to the train and together, once again, we went back to Yugoslavia. There, we went back to the hotel where the Filipina woman who arranged this for us was waiting for us. She had told us that she was going to stay, in case something happened to us.

Two days, we stayed there. Then, we were taken out again. Taxis, once again, picked us up. We were so tired. We were no longer excited. We said that if we were caught again, we would ask to be deported to the Philippines. We were so tired, but we walked again. We walked again from early evening to the early morning.

This time, we walked through a flat surface, not a mountain. We went through a different area, but it was flat. The only thing we had to do was when a car went by, we had to run and hide for cover by the bushes on the side of the road. We kept on walking and walking. The last place we had to walk through was very thorny. It was unpaved. By the early morning, we had made it. We saw our guide and we felt sorry for him. He was bruised and scarred all over, because he led the way and cleared our path. We had a little bit of scratches, but we were not bloody. We had jackets that we used to cover our faces as we walked.

When we got through, we were taken to these cornfields and there, taxis waited for us. The taxis took us to the train station where we caught a train to Rome. We walked from 5:30 in the evening to seven in the morning. It was daylight when the taxi picked us up. The taxi driver bought our tickets for us. We had to give him the money. . . .

When I got to Rome, my sister was there. I was in contact with her. Whenever I was about to leave Yugoslavia, I called her. . . . She rushed me out of the station. She took me to her apartment. I did not work for one month. I just rested. My body was bruised all over. My right foot was inflamed. My toenails fell off from falling and falling in the mountain. Mama mia! I had to go to the doctor because my feet were very inflamed. I could not leave the house for one month.

Incarnacion Molina is not alone in vividly remembering her harrowing and physically excruciating journey. In the community, the difficulty of migration is a frequent topic of conversation. One's journey is a shared experience that strengthens one's feelings of allegiance to other migrants who survived what they often describe as an experience they would never again willingly undertake.

Though her experience generally speaks of the struggles encountered by the 1990s migrants, Incarnacion faced more fortunate circumstances than others did. Many who were caught at the border were deported to the Philippines and not to an Eastern European country and therefore had to pay for the exorbitant fees charged by "travel agencies" once again. While Incarnacion anticipated the difficulty of crossing the border, most women had been ill prepared for the physical challenges of their trip, for example, not having brought appropriate clothing or shoes. Moreover, many women recall having met destitute Filipinas stranded in cities as far away from Italy as Moscow, migrants left there with neither their return ticket to the Philippines nor sufficient funds to pay for the services of yet another coyote. The successful migrants whom I interviewed in Rome often had to cross the border more than once and had brought with them additional funds to cover unanticipated costs. When recalling their experiences, Filipina migrants often express their amazement over their survival, as they are aware of the fact that not all of those who tried to enter Italy since 1990 have done so successfully. They have also heard of stories of migrants who had perished along the way due to hunger and cold. Yet a striking observation that they always make points to the courage of Filipino women, as they have noticed that they rarely encountered women of other nationalities but only ran across male migrants during their journey to Italy.

In summary, the discussion of the modes of migration to Rome and Los Angeles shows that economic resources also determine the flow of migration into these two cities. While women in Rome could cover the high costs of migration by incurring informal loans in the sending community, to do so they must have secure collateral, such as ownership of property. Thus, women from poorer backgrounds constitute a minority in my study. Of the poorer women in my sample, most came to Italy before 1983, when the costs of migration were still relatively low. In the United States, poorer women usually relied on the sponsorship and assistance of employers.

The Partial Citizenship of Migrant Filipina Domestic Workers in Globalization

The globalization of the market economy has created a high demand for Filipina domestic workers to provide low-wage labor in more-developed nations. Not surprising then is the great financial investments that many of my interviewees had made to secure their option of migration. However, globalization also stunts the political, civil, and social incorporation of these female labor migrants as it increases the demand for their low-wage labor.

The opposite turns of nationalism place poor nations with export-based development strategies in a quandary. On the one hand, the denationalization of economies compels these nations to respond to the demand for low-wage labor and extend their range of exports to include their able-bodied workers. On the other hand, they cannot enforce the protection of their exported nationals due to the renationalization of politics. In the same vein, the recipients of these (secondary-tier) migrant workers do not accord them the same rights as their own nationals. Hence, migrant Filipina domestic workers are rendered nationless by the contradictions of nationalism in globalization. Even so, the labor diaspora has come to be a particular effect of globalization in the Philippines that the state promotes regardless of the growing threat to its unprotected citizens.

The paradox that defines the incorporation of migrant Filipina domestic workers in the state regime is also observed by Bakan and Stasiulis, who comment: "For the Third World non-citizen in search of First World citizenship, gaining access to social rights—particularly 'the right to a modicum of economic welfare and security'—commonly supersedes entry to civil and political rights" (1997a: 45). For the most part, economic gains achieved in migration entail the loss of civil and political rights, first from the nation of citizenship, which loses juridical-legislation rights, and second from the host nation-state, which relegates unequal rights to migrants along the lines of race, class, and gender (Lowe, 1996). Globalization consequently imposes upon migrant Filipina domestic workers social and political barriers that limit their ability to develop a sense of full membership in their host societies.

By insisting that the opposite turns of nationalism result in the partial citizenship of migrant Filipina domestic workers the world over, I do not mean to disregard the nuances engendered by the different contexts of reception in the diaspora. I only mean to emphasize the reality of globalization and the similarities engendered by the workers' similar role in various local economies.

Migrant Filipina domestic workers do indeed share the experience of partial citizenship. In various destinations of the diaspora, they are not protected by labor laws and as such are vulnerable to the exploitation of employers, including sexual harassment and abuse, excessive work hours with no overtime pay, and substandard living conditions. For example, women who have been confined in the home of their employers are commonly found in shelters for abused migrant Filipina domestic workers in various countries in the Middle East and Asia (Alcid, 1994; Migrante, 1996). As unwanted citizens, they are also relegated to the status of temporary settlers whose stay is limited to the duration of their labor contracts. Usually, contracts bind them to stay with their sponsoring employer regardless of working conditions. In Hong Kong, for instance, domestic workers who flee abusive employers automatically face deportation proceedings due to the stringent legislation imposed against foreign domestic workers in 1987 (Constable, 1997). Further sending the message that only the production and not the reproduction of their labor is desired, nations such as Singapore prohibit migrant Filipina domestic workers from marrying or cohabiting with native citizens (Bakan and Stasiulis, 1997b). Pregnancy is furthermore prohibited for migrant Filipina domestic workers in the Middle East and Asia (Alcid, 1994; Chin, 1998; Lan, 1999). Finally, state policies in various destinations of the diaspora, for example, Taiwan, deny entry to the spouse and children of the migrant domestic worker (Lan, 1999).

Taking into account the nuances engendered by differences in domestic policies among the receiving nations of migrant Filipina domestic workers, partial citizenship comes in different degrees and levels of exclusion. More inclusive than receiving nations in Asia and the Middle East, Italy allows guest workers to stay for as long as seven years, as opposed to the short-term contracts of two years in jurisdictions such as Hong Kong. Moreover, permits to stay in Italy do not restrict Filipina migrants to the sponsoring employer but do however limit them to domestic work (Campani, 1993a, 1993b). Finally, in Italy temporary residents have been eligible for family reunification since 1990. Regardless, migrant Filipina domestic workers are still restricted to the status of guest workers in Italy. Moreover, second-generation Filipinos— children of guest workers born in Italy—are not granted Italian citizenship automatically. Still, migrants are welcomed into Italy by more inclusive poli-

cies than in most other destinations in the diaspora. This is one of the reasons why Italy is a more coveted destination among prospective Filipina migrants and consequently a much more expensive destination.

Eligibility for full citizenship is available in a few receiving nations in the
diaspora, including Spain, Canada, the United States, and Australia. In Spain
and Canada, migrant Filipina domestic workers are eligible for full citizenship after two years of legal settlement. Despite the seemingly more liberal
and inclusive policies in these nations, political and social inequalities, as Bakan and Stasiulis (1997a) have astutely pointed out using the case of Canada,
still mar the incorporation of migrant Filipina domestic workers. In Canada,
the Live-in Caregivers Program requires an initial two years of live-in service of foreign domestic workers before they can become eligible for landed
immigrant status. During this time, they are restricted to the status of temporary visitors, are denied a family life, and are more prone to face abusive
working conditions, including long hours and inadequate pay. Without the
protection of labor laws granted to Canadian workers, migrant domestic
workers in Canada—the majority of whom are Filipinos—have fewer rights
than full citizens.

Partial citizenship is also imposed on migrants in the United States. While
the United States accords full membership to its legal migrants (they can
eventually gain citizenship and the right to participate in the host polity,
which is not the case in most other destinations in the diaspora), the global
trend of the renationalization of politics has in fact threatened the integration of migrants into this country. For example, the United States has enforced strict regulations, such as ineligibility for Social Security to elderly
migrants and the denial of public services to undocumented migrants in California. For the most part, the belief that the presence of migrants burdens
the economy and drains government services has raised public resentment
against migrants (Martin, 1995).

Moreover, citizenship in the democratic body of the United States is
marred by race, gender, and class inequalities that emerge, in this case, in the
segmentation of a particular group of skilled Filipina migrants in domestic
work. This segmentation must be seen as part of the larger relegation of
women of color into low-wage sectors of the economy (Lowe, 1996). The construction of Asian immigrants as foreigners is another factor stunting their
integration. The successful use of cultural defense in criminal cases involving Asian Americans, for instance, is based on the judiciary system's static
construction of Asian culture as "foreign" and "different" (Koptiuch, 1996).
Migrant Filipina domestic workers, along with other migrants, also contend

with the criminalization of illegal migrants in the renationalization of politics. In addition to the deportation of illegal migrants, this criminalization is reflected in the denial of social services. Feeling the exclusion brought by the rise of nativism, migrant Filipina domestic workers—even those with legal status—consequently cannot easily perceive of the United States as a permanent home, and most interviewees in Los Angeles consider themselves temporary migrants.

The Philippines and Its Unprotected Migrant Citizenry

With the denationalization of economies, labor migration has sprouted in exceedingly large numbers. The United Nations in 1980 estimated that around 78 million people resided in a country other than where they were born (Zlotnick, 1995).[13] In the late 1990s, the estimated number of people residing outside of the country in which they were born had grown to 120 million individuals, a figure that likely excludes undocumented migrants (Sassen, 1996b).

Designated export-based nations in the global labor market such as the Philippines, Bangladesh, and Sri Lanka do not simply seek investments of transnational corporations and export products or goods that they manufacture in free-trade zones. They also export the bodies of their citizens to induce foreign currency into their economies (Lycklama á Nijeholt, 1994). The Philippines does so to a growing extent as the number of bodies annually exported has increased steadily since the 1970s. While fewer than 50,000 in the early to mid-1970s, the number of overseas contract workers annually deployed jumped to 266,243 in 1981 and escalated to more than 700,000 in 1994 (Martin, 1993a).

The Philippine economy relies on the deployment of workers to ease high unemployment and underemployment rates, provide workers with additional skills training, and generate foreign currency from the remittances of foreign-employed workers (Abella, 1992; Center for Women's Resources, 1995). Emigration, however, has only patched over the structural problems of the Philippine economy. First, deployed workers include professional and skilled workers.[14] Considering the small percentage of the skilled workforce in the Philippines, migration results in the shortage of certain skilled labor in the economy (Asis, 1992).[15] Moreover, many migrants are plagued by nontransferable skills and relegated to low- or semiskilled employment. Consequently, they do not gain valuable skills in migration. In addition, remittances have not stimulated economic growth (Abella, 1992). The foreign debt of the Philippines, which has "ballooned to $35 billion," depletes the economic gains of migration (Rosca, 1995: 526). Without the achievement of sustainable development, the full integration of the Philippines into the global economy retains the nation's dependence on exported labor. Thus, it seems that the Philippines cannot end its cycle of economic dependency on emigration in the foreseeable future. In 1991, economic growth in the Philippines did not lead to lower rates of emigration; contrary to the predictions of government officials, the country actually witnessed a considerable increase in its labor migration outflow (Battistella, 1992).

Though migration, in particular to the United States, is a legacy of colonialism and, as such, a long-standing tradition in the modern history of the nation, the contemporary outflow of labor from the Philippines is of a much wider and larger scale than earlier. This is a distinct effect of globalization, which has expanded the traditional sending communities of migration to include every region of the nation. In contrast, earlier migration flows were primarily from the northernmost region of the Philippines. Contemporary migration is a central component of the export-led development strategy implemented in the Philippines through the intervention of the International Monetary Fund and World Bank.[16]

In 1974, the Ferdinand Marcos regime implemented the "manpower exchange programme" in the Philippines. Its goals were the development, promotion, and regulation of overseas employment (Basch et al., 1994). Government ministers and President Marcos himself canvassed for the importation of Filipino workers into the Middle East, other Asian countries, Europe, the United States, and Canada. By the time Marcos was deposed in 1986, export-led development was so well in place in the economic infrastructure of the Philippines that his successors have continued to depend on the exportation of labor to sustain the economy.

With the relegation of the Philippines to an export-based economy, the globalization of the market economy requires the Philippines to depend on outmigration. Remittances from deployed workers sustain the Philippine economy with the smooth flow of foreign currency. Moreover, the Philippines does gain economic benefits from the exportation and commodification of the bodies of its workers. Without labor outmigration, the rate of unemployment would increase by 40 percent (Castles and Miller, 1998). As one of the largest labor exporters in the world, the Philippines also reaps remittances amounting to its second largest source of foreign currency, next to electronics manufacturing. In the first eleven months of 1994, labor migrants sent

$2.6 billion to the Philippines through the banking systems (Karp, 1995). According to economists, if funds sent through private finance companies, letters, and return migrants are considered, the total cash infusion could be as much as $6 billion a year (Karp, 1995).

As a result of these gains, the government has created the iconic representation of its mostly female overseas workers as the nation's "modern-day heroes"; this facilitates the nation-building project of the Philippines to enter the global market economy as an export-oriented economy. The construction of the positive imagery of migrant workers as "heroes" moreover promotes the process of emigration, as such an iconic figure stabilizes the dependence of the Philippine economy on female outmigration.

The gains motivating the iconic representation of the mostly female overseas migrant workers come not without their costs. First, the exportation of workers magnifies the overturning of state governments by the global labor market. Moreover, the sovereignty of the Philippines diminishes with its inability to protect its overseas nationals. For example, the failure of President Ramos to convince Singapore's prime minister, Goh Chok Tong, to reopen the investigation of the case of Flor Contemplacion, who was convicted of murdering another Filipina domestic worker, Delia Maga, and her young ward, was more than a cause of national embarrassment. It also brought to the forefront inequalities underlying the relationship of sending and receiving nations in globalization: the lesser economic power of sending nations vis-à-vis receiving nations means a lesser political power for sending nations. Without political power, sending nations of secondary-tier workers cannot protect their overseas nationals.

The Philippine government is caught in a deleterious situation: they deploy workers around the world to generate foreign currency as they simultaneously lack the economic prowess to protect their citizens working in more economically endowed countries. Though international human rights codes may declare the rights of transnational citizens, the fate of migrant Filipina domestic workers is for the most part dependent on the host society.

Since outmigration is a state-sanctioned flow, the Philippine government does attempt to offer protection to the overseas contract workers whose placement they monitor through official contracts with receiving states throughout Europe, Asia, the Middle East, and the Americas. The Department of Labor and Employment (DOLE) maintains jurisdiction over overseas contract workers through the Philippine Overseas Employment Administration (POEA), which monitors the exit of workers, and the Overseas Workers Welfare Administration (OWWA), which provides services to migrants in receiving nations. OWWA aids migrants in various countries by providing free legal assistance and counseling, assistance with repatriation, insurance coverage, and loan programs for housing and microbusiness enterprises (Stasiulis and Bakan, 1997). However, the assistance that OWWA can offer its constituents is limited by its lack of power to override the laws and jurisdiction of receiving nations. For instance, a Philippine government–sponsored welfare center in Saudi Arabia was closed down "because the Saudi government thought that providing shelter to runaway maids constituted foreign intervention in their internal affairs" (Alcid, 1994: 176). Moreover, the labor conditions established by POEA, such as salary rates and days off, similarly lose bearing with the loss of jurisdiction upon migration. In Malaysia, for example, the "state is not legally bound to recognize contracts that are signed overseas" (Chin, 1998: 198). Consequently, migrant Filipina domestic workers receive lower salaries and fewer rest days than those stipulated by the POEA as fair standards of employment.

The greatest cost of exportation is the vulnerability of bodies in migration. This is shown by the highly publicized return to the Philippines of the corpses of abused workers, including the entertainment service worker Maricris Siosin of Japan and the domestic worker Delia Maga of Singapore. The vulnerability of overseas workers is without doubt a tremendous threat to the maintenance of a steady outflow of exported bodies for the Philippines. It calls into question the reduction of humans to exported products. The emergence of a national consciousness about the vulnerability of overseas workers is a threat that the Philippine government attempts to contain. Government officials downplay the brutalities faced by their "modern-day heroes" as "rare incidents" and usually treat these incidents on a case-by-case basis instead of systematically (Gatmaytan, 1997). In doing so, the state consciously downplays the human side of migration and renders the experiences of its overseas contract workers as having lesser importance than their roles as generators of foreign currency.

Hence, the state advocates the construction of its nationals—the heroines of the Philippine economy—as objects of globalization. Overseas contract workers are manufactured products of the Philippines, placed in the same category as electronic goods. As a source of foreign currency, the commodified body of overseas workers is a central component of the gross national product of the Philippines. As unprotected nationals, migrant Filipina domestic workers experience a de-subjection in globalization. They are commodities of the state whose production generates surplus value for both sending and receiving nations at the cost of their abject vulnerability as nationless citizens (Daenzer, 1997). In globalization, the distinctions between the flows of labor and goods are consequently diminished in the hands of capital.

The Construction of the Philippines as "Home"

> "Saang dako ka man ng mundo, Hong Kong, Australia, Singapore o Saudi, babalik at babalik ka rin . . . " (In whatever corner of the world you are in, Hong Kong, Australia, Singapore, or Saudi Arabia, you are eventually going to return . . .) so a song goes. And just like species of birds who migrate from their place of origin during the winter season to another place, so they won't feel the pangs of coldness, we, too, migrant workers are bound to go home for good after our stint abroad. No matter how long it has been, what achievements we have accomplished and what factors have driven us to be home at last. At long, long last. (Pelegrin, 1994: 7)

Filipina labor migrants consider the Philippines to be the "place where they really belong" (Pelegrin, 1994: 8). "Home" is the Philippines. It is the place where they are liberated from the physical confines of domestic work. It is the place where they are protected from the harsh conditions of domestic service and racism in receiving societies. For them, "returning home" signifies the end to their reification in globalization. By "going home," they will no longer be commodities sold by the Philippine government to guarantee a smooth flow of foreign currency into its economy. "Home" is the place from which they are displaced and to which they must return to end their dislocation of partial citizenship.

Migrant Filipina domestic workers reclaim a sense of citizenship by emphasizing their legal membership in the nation-state of the Philippines. As such, writers in *Tinig Filipino* frequently refer to themselves as "heroes" to emphasize their important role in the nation-building project of economic development in the Philippines. In *Tinig Filipino*, the word "home" has become synonymous with the Philippines. In fact, *Tinig Filipino* frequently promotes the eventual return migration of its writers and readers and often features stories of successful return-migrants in the Philippines. The Philippine government and the various nations that receive Filipinos as migrant workers most likely applaud the promotion of return migration in *Tinig Filipino*. For the Philippine government, the construction of the Philippines as home guarantees the smooth flow of foreign currency into the economy. For receiving nations, it supports the anti-immigrant sentiments brought on by the renationalization of politics. Moreover, it diverts migrant Filipina domestic workers from claiming their right to civil, social, and political membership in receiving states.

Although the Philippines is referred to as "home" or the "homeland," new ties to the receiving country undeniably form in migration. A mother who after four years in Hong Kong wants to go "home for good" to her husband and children in the Philippines still asks, "But why . . . is it hard now to leave this land of milk and honey? Am I one of those who fear to go back to our country for good?" (Villaruz, 1995: 62). Another domestic worker, Betty Atiwa, agrees when she says: "For me, going back home for good is both pleasant and depressing. Pleasant in the sense that I could see and live in my beloved country and be with my family again. Depressing because I will see poverty again" (1995: 42). The fear of returning "home" to the Philippines is engendered by the fear of returning to the situation they had hoped to escape.

It is not surprising that migrant Filipina domestic workers do not go "home" even though they articulate the desire to do so. Research on various groups of migrant women indicates that women are less pressed to return home than are their male counterparts whose status declines upon migration. Constable makes a similar observation of migrant Filipina domestic workers in Hong Kong. They tend to renew their overseas contracts so as not to risk losing the freedom and independence that they have gained in migration (Constable, 1999). Rather than going "home," many migrant Filipina domestic workers in Italy, for example, would rather migrate to the United States or Canada, where they can gain permanent residency and have more opportunities for labor market advancement. Ironically, migrant Filipina domestic workers in the United States do not necessarily feel at "home" despite the more inclusive conditions of settlement in this country.

The hardships that Filipina domestic workers encounter in their process of emigration also deter them from "going home." The struggles of crossing the border—from the difficulty of obtaining legal documents to the United States to the high costs and physical strain of the journey into Italy—convince Filipina domestic workers in both countries to prolong their stay and maximize their financial gains.

With the view of the Philippines as their rightful "home," discussions among Filipino migrant workers in *Tinig Filipino* about the political economy of their labor solely concern their economic contributions to the Philippine economy and, with very few exceptions, do not in any way regard their labor market participation as having provided economic benefits to the receiving nation. In their writings, they never critique exclusionary policies of receiving countries directly, nor do they demand the extension of their legal status from temporary to permanent settlers in light of the economic benefits that their low-wage labor provide receiving countries. Ironically, receiving countries are usually seen as benevolent nations that have provided opportunities not available in the Philippines and for which they believe they should be grateful. In contrast, critiques of the Philippine government and its economy abound in *Tinig Filipino*, and the recurring discourse regarding "home" concerns the contradictory relationship that they have with the Philippine economy as migrant laborers who are displaced from the same economy that flourishes from their displacement.

The cynicism of Filipino migrants especially shows in their critiques of their representation as the "modern-day heroes" of the Philippine economy. Articles in *Tinig Filipino* indicate that Filipina domestic workers are aware that they are displaced from an economy that labels them as heroes, yet they know they are not rewarded for their heroism, because as heroes the country pushes them to leave with the knowledge that they cannot be protected as heroic citizens.

> We are called the living heroes or the new heroes. Yet why are we called "heroes" when we are slaves in other countries. Oh, OCWs (overseas contract workers)—the heroes without monuments. Yes, we earn a little bit more yet the pain of our bodies, minds and most of all feelings are equal to none. Why does the government, instead of supporting our college graduates and youth and pushing them to strive in our country, actually allow them to leave the country yet without any sufficient protection as citizens? . . . . When can you finally provide us with a peaceful and simple life? (Plandano, 1995: 60, translated from Tagalog to English)

The cynicism of migrant workers is also manifested in their pessimism about the state of the Philippine economy. They consider labor migration to be a self-perpetuating cycle that only patches up the economy. As a result, they do not foresee an end to their outflow because they argue that migration hurts the economy with the loss of its many skilled laborers.

> In the latest survey, almost 6.5 million Filipinos are working in rich countries like Saudi Arabia, USA, Japan, Hong Kong, etc. And some of us [overseas contract workers] are proud of it because we contribute a big amount of dollars in our national treasury every year. However, in my humble opinion, it is quite unfair because we spread our talent,

knowledge, and expertise to other countries instead of using them in our homeland. Perhaps it is one of the reasons why our country's economy is still way down below. The best brains and other professionals who are supposed to serve and work in our country are utilized in other countries. On the contrary, we cannot blame those who decide to be migrant workers because our government cannot provide them with jobs to satisfy their financial necessities. (Gutierrez, 1995: 31)

In *Tinig Filipino*, discussions of the economic crisis in the Philippines generally reflect the view of Gutierrez, as they neither reach the level of the interstate system nor consider structural inequalities between developing and advanced capitalist countries. Instead of situating the economic problems of the Philippines in their global context, writers in *Tinig Filipino* blame the nation-state.

Consequently, the solutions posed by domestic workers are limited to the nation-state. For example, Gutierrez calls for a "clean-up" of the Philippine government: "I think the solution for cutting out the root of poverty is a strong-willed government who will work for a standardization of our educational system and who will impose punishment to all corrupt leaders and hoodlums in uniform" (1995: 31). They also acknowledge the need for the government to invest their remittances in the development of the economy's infrastructure. However, the authors of these articles have yet to acknowledge the fact that a large portion of their remittances covers the $1.8 billion of annual interest on loans accumulated from debts to the World Bank and the International Monetary Fund (Rosca, 1995).

Analyzing the discourse on "home" is significant in understanding the settlement of Filipina domestic workers as transnational laborers. The turn that they have taken toward the construction of the Philippines as "home" ironically retains their dislocation of partial citizenship. This construction supports the renationalization of politics in globalization. Moreover, it inhibits migrant Filipina domestic workers from claiming their rights of full citizenship in the various receiving nations of the diaspora. By turning to the construction of the Philippines as "home," they avoid contesting that their full incorporation is denied by the escalating resentment against migrant workers in receiving countries, the low wages that prevent migrant workers from raising their families in receiving communities, and their status as guest workers in most receiving countries other than the United States, Australia, and Canada. However, as globalization continues to demand their labor, they in turn are unlikely to return "home."

Under global restructuring and the transnational capitalist economy, Filipina domestic workers, along with other workers from developing countries, are needed more than ever to fill the demand for low-wage migrant labor in advanced capitalist countries. As the economic need for low-wage workers persists (and grows) and as the dependence of the Philippines on their remittances continues, Filipina domestic workers extend their duration of settlement. Without doubt, the denationalization of economies keeps them exiled away from "home." As a result, they are unlikely to achieve the legal status of full citizenship in the Philippines, reap the benefits of the responsibilities bestowed on them as the "heroes" of the nation, and receive the rights and protections that they have earned from the fulfillment of these responsibilities.

Conclusion

Filipino labor migrants are located in a multitude of industrialized countries around the world. As such, they have come to represent a diaspora, a contemporary labor diaspora that is gender and class stratified. This diaspora should be considered a labor diaspora because its formation is situated in the globalization of the market economy and the designation of the Philippines as an export-based economy. The Philippines exports not only goods but also workers. Second, this labor diaspora is in fact gendered, as men and women maintain two distinct labor migration flows. As such, it should be emphasized that this diaspora is composed primarily of independent labor migrants. Finally, this gendered labor diaspora is also class stratified, and there is a hierarchy of destinations.

This hierarchy partially emerges from the "opposite turns of nationalism" in globalization. While migration is promoted by the "denationalization of economies," the "renationalization of politics" and the stricter enforcement of border control make it a difficult process. Emigration consequently demands a large investment in social and material resources. This demand results in a hierarchy in the diaspora, with Italy, the United States, and Canada belonging in its upper tier. These destinations tend to be more legally inaccessible and consequently more expensive to reach than are countries in Asia or the Middle East.

This hierarchy is also somehow reflected in migrant Filipina domestic workers' experience of partial citizenship. The more inclusive the country, the more of a coveted destination it is in the diaspora. Still, partial citizenship is a shared dislocation for migrant Filipina domestic workers that is produced by macroprocesses of globalization. In the context of the opposite turns of nationalism, this subject positioning develops from their construction as "modern-day heroes" of the Philippine economy and status as guest workers in most receiving states. Both promote their citizenship in the Philippines at the expense of their partial citizenship in receiving states. In the case of the United States, partial citizenship is promoted by the abject construction of Asians as foreigners (Lowe, 1996).

In this chapter, I have shown that the contradictory trends of nationalism in globalization foster the stunted incorporation of migrant Filipina domestic workers vis-à-vis the nation-state. While the renationalization of politics limits their integration into host societies, the denationalization of economies demands their low-wage labor and consequently encourages their migration to nations witnessing the renationalization of their local societies. This subordinate status promotes feelings among Filipino migrant workers that the Philippines is the only nation that they can rightfully refer to as "home." They have in turn used the construction of the Philippines as "home" to negotiate their dislocation of partial citizenship. In the process, this redirects them away from rightfully claiming their full membership in receiving states.

CHAPTER 3

The International Division of Reproductive Labor

The previous chapter established that Filipino men and women usually migrate independently of each other. My query into the lives of migrant Filipina domestic workers now moves to the causes of their independent migration. Significantly, numerous responses of interviewees to the question "Why did you migrate?" concern issues of gender inequality in the Philippines. They include domestic violence, labor market segmentation, and the unequal division of labor in the family. Traditional discussions of the causes of either male or female migration, which usually are based solely on economics, cannot fully explain such responses. However, while these responses do not question the applicability of the political economy of globalization to the causes of migration for Filipina domestic workers, they do suggest that gender distinguishes the structural causes of independent migration for men and women.

To account for the gendered political economy of migration, I extend discussions of the "international division of labor" in globalization from a sole consideration of productive labor to include analyses of reproductive labor. Reproductive labor refers to the labor needed to sustain the productive labor force. Such work includes household chores; the care of elders, adults, and youth; the socialization of children; and the maintenance of social ties in the family (Brenner and Laslett, 1991; Glenn, 1992). By focusing on reproductive labor, I emphasize that gender is a controlling factor of the outflow of labor in globalization and show another dimension by which gender shapes the economic divisions of labor in migration.

Relegated to women more so than men, reproductive labor has long been a commodity purchased by class-privileged women. As Evelyn Nakano Glenn (1992) has observed, white class-privileged women in the United States have

61

historically freed themselves of reproductive labor by purchasing the low-
wage services of women of color. In doing so, they maintain a "racial division of reproductive labor" (Glenn 1992), which establishes a two-tier hierarchy among women.

My analysis of reproductive labor extends the important formulation of
Glenn to an international terrain so as to consider issues of globalization and
the feminization of wage labor. The globalization of the market economy has
extended the politics of reproductive labor into an international level. The
migration and entrance into domestic work of Filipino women constitute an
international division of reproductive labor. This division of labor, which I
call the international transfer of caretaking, refers to the three-tier transfer
of reproductive labor among women in sending and receiving countries of
migration. While class-privileged women purchase the low-wage services of
migrant Filipina domestic workers, migrant Filipina domestic workers simultaneously purchase the even lower wage services of poorer women left behind
in the Philippines. In light of this transnational transfer of gender constraints
that occurs in globalization, the independent migration of Filipina domestic
workers could be read as a process of rejecting gender constraints for different groups of women in a transnational economy.

The international transfer of caretaking links two important but separate
discourses on the status of women—Glenn's (1992) discussion of the "racial
division of reproductive labor" and Sassen's (1984) discussion of the "international division of labor." It demonstrates that these important formulations need to be expanded to take into account transnational issues of reproduction. To develop my argument, I first analyze the situation of migrant
Filipina domestic workers in the Philippines and the receiving nations of the
United States and Italy. My discussion establishes the subordinate position
of women in the labor market and family at both ends of the migration spectrum. I then build on this by adding the migration links that illustrate the international transfer of caretaking. By presenting this division of labor, I establish that global capitalism and patriarchy are macrostructural forces that
jointly determine the subject-positions of migrant Filipina domestic workers
in globalization.[1]

The Hidden Causes of Migration

Economic and political processes without doubt determine the migration of
Filipina domestic workers. In response to one of the first questions that I asked

in the interview—"Why did you migrate?"—I expected answers that fit classic theoretical formulations of the causes of migration. Hoping to show that women are also economically motivated migrants and not just passive dependents of male migrants, I anticipated answers that could be explained by economic disparities between developing countries like the Philippines and industrialized countries like the United States and Italy. As expected, all of my respondents had been partially driven by economic motives. For example, Michelle Fonte, a single woman who in 1989 followed her sister to Rome, states:

> My sister was the first one here. The truth is that our family had a lot of debts in the Philippines. Our land was just about to be confiscated by the bank. My sister couldn't afford to pay for the debt on her own. So what she did was she took me over here. When I got here, we helped each other out and we were able to pay for the debt on time.

Many responses mirrored Michelle's. Some respondents even looked at me strangely, seeming to wonder why I would ask such an obvious question before they proceeded to tell me about the economic insecurities of the middle class in the Philippines. In the Philippines, where at least 70 percent of families live in poverty, a middle-class status does not constitute a comfortable and secure lifestyle (Israel-Sobritchea, 1990). The middle class in the Philippines especially took a sharp downturn in the mid-1980s with the further devaluation of the peso by the International Monetary Fund. As Basch et al. state, "By the 1980s, even a schoolteacher could not afford to buy more than two chickens a month and could only purchase low quality rice" (1994: 232).

Filipino men and women share the economic displacements that spur labor migration in global restructuring. However, the different meanings of "economic" migration for men and women should be elucidated, considering that gender shapes the family and local economy of the Philippines. With this in mind, I now look at the position of women in the family.

In the Philippines, women confront the traditional gender ideology of the patriarchal nuclear family: men are expected to sustain the family and women reproduce family life. Consequently, gender distinguishes the meaning of independent labor migration for men and women. For women, labor migration in itself questions gender prescriptions in society. As ideological constructs of feminine identity are molded from "mothering and caring roles in the domestic arena," the independent migration of women constitutes a direct liberation from traditional duties and roles (Israel-Sobritchea, 1990).

In Rome and Los Angeles, most respondents migrate to help sustain the family, which is an obligation that stems for the most part from the extremely strong bond of family allegiance and filial piety in the Philippines (Chant and McIlwaine, 1995; Paz Cruz and Paganoni, 1989). Yet the meaning of migration as a strategy of family maintenance is very different for men and women. By migrating to sustain the household, women reconstitute the traditional gender division of labor in the family as they take on the role of income provider. Because independent migration frees working women of household constraints, migration is not just a family strategy but a covert strategy to relieve women of burdens in the family. As Filipina feminist scholar Carolyn Israel-Sobritchea observes, "Despite the growth of female labor force participation, there has not been a commensurate decrease in their child care and household responsibilities" (1990: 35). Most Filipino women do not have the means to relieve themselves of the double day, or the "second shift."

If we consider the gender stratification imposed on women in the family, we can then see that migration as a strategy of family maintenance entails a negotiation of how to perform (gendered) family duties. In the traditional Filipino household, daughters—more so than sons—are expected to care for their parents in old age. As the only daughter in her family, Lorna Fernandez of Rome, for instance, felt a great sense of responsibility for her family but simultaneously felt suffocated by the duties she was expected to perform.

> I am the only girl and the oldest in my family. I have all brothers. There were many reasons why I came here. I had a good job. [She finished in the top ten of the national board exam for midwifery.] I was employed in a private office for seven years. I was making decent money. But I wanted to leave because even if you have a decent salary in our country, it does not allow you to save any money. And then, I kept on thinking that my parents are not going to see their situation improve very much. . . . So one of the reasons I came here was for my family. . . . I came here also for the change. I was very tired. I was sick of the routine I was in. Every month, I received my salary and divided it up to my parents, brothers and then hardly any would be left for me. . . . The first thirty-seven years of my life was given to my family, and I feel this is just when I am starting out for myself.

While the family is considered a central site of support and assistance, some single women simultaneously desire to be liberated from the demands and responsibilities of familism.

Examining the position of women in the Philippine labor market also differentiates the meaning of economic migration for men and women. Although the lack of opportunities in the Philippine economy affects both men and women, the sex segmentation in the Philippine labor market further aggravates the already limited opportunities of women. In the Philippines, the ideology of women as caretakers constrains their productive labor activities in many ways, including their segregation in jobs resembling "wife-and-mother roles" such as household work on plantations and professional work in nursing and teaching (Chant and McIlwaine, 1995; Eviota, 1992). Because women are only expected to subsidize the primary income of men, female jobs are often less valued and far less lucrative than comparable men's work.[2] For example, field work on plantations pays more than household work (Eviota, 1992). In addition, women have fewer chances for promotion than do men (Eviota, 1992; Lopez-Rodriguez, 1990).

Despite these constraints, women do participate in the productive labor force. In 1992, the female share of total employment in the Philippines reached 37.7 percent (Chant, 1997). Like migrant women from the Dominican Republic, most migrant Filipina domestic workers have premigration paid work experience (Grasmuck and Pessar, 1991). Since they have greater means than other women to migrate, educated women in the Philippines may turn to employment opportunities outside the Philippines as a method of negotiating their low wages. Many of the research participants in Rome and Los Angeles formerly employed in "female professions" (for example, teachers and administrative assistants) sought the higher wages that they could earn outside the Philippines, even if only as domestic workers.

Examining the positions of Filipino women and men in the family and labor market demonstrates that they are not equally displaced in the overarching structure of the world-system. In the case of the Philippines, women have to contend with a gender-stratified economy, a fact that may have stimulated female outmigration. This assertion possibly contradicts the common assumption that the increased number of manufacturing jobs in free-trade zones in Third World countries, because it creates greater labor market opportunities for women, displaces male workers and, as a result, indirectly causes the emigration of men. It is important to point out that the female labor force in the Philippines is not subsumed under manufacturing. Multinational firms only guarantee a few jobs, significantly less than agriculture, for example. Though only a very small number of women in my study held manufacturing jobs in the Philippines, the constant turnover of the manufacturing workforce may also promote the migration of female manufacturing workers (Eviota, 1992). After factory employment, women face dim prospects in the Philippine labor market and, as a result, may turn to migration.

Corroborating the deduction that independent female migration can hypothetically be seen as a process of escaping gender constraints are the intense responses of women to the simple and seemingly obvious question "Why did you migrate?" In Rome, fourteen of the twenty female respondents who were legally married when they had migrated wanted to leave an abusive or unfaithful husband or had irresponsible partners and could no longer afford to raise dependents as single mothers. For example, some migrated because they could no longer tolerate the infidelity of their husbands.

> You know why I came here? I had to leave the Philippines. If I didn't, I would have ended up killing someone. I had caught my husband with another woman. (Trinidad Borromeo)

> My husband used to beat me up and have affairs. Then he left me for another woman. . . . I went to Kuwait after my husband and I separated. See, I tried to commit suicide two times. The first time I swallowed poison and the second time I slashed my wrists many times. At the hospital, my mother was able to talk to me, and she told me that if I can't take the actions of my husband, I should just go abroad. I was still very young, and I already had my children. (Clarita Sungkay)

In other cases, women had to escape domestic violence.

> I came to Italy in 1983 to look for a job and also a change of environment. . . . You have to understand that my problems were very heavy before I left the Philippines. My husband was abusive. I couldn't even think about my children. The only thing I could think about was the opportunity to escape my situation. If my husband was not going to kill me, I was probably going to kill him. . . . My problems with him were so heavy. He was abusive. He always beat me up, and my parents wanted me to leave him for a long time. My children, I left with my sister. I asked my husband for permission to leave the country, and I told him that I was only going to be gone for two years. . . . I was just telling him that so I could leave the country peacefully. . . . In the plane. . . I felt like a bird whose cage that had been locked for many years had just recently been opened. Nine years he abused me. He was very strict, and he tried to control every situation. Often, I could not leave the house.

When I was able to escape, I felt free and felt so loose. Deep inside, I felt homesick for my children, but I also felt free for being able to escape the most dire problem that was slowly killing me. (Ruby Mercado)

These disturbing testimonies suggest a pattern of abusive male behavior that pushes women to leave the Philippines. They turn to migration to escape debilitating situations in the household.

According to British sociologists Sylvia Chant and Cathy McIlwaine, institutionalized practices of "male superiority within the Filipino household include the practice of wife-beating. Domestic violence is viewed as 'ordinary' and 'normal' within the context of marriage and stems from the polarized socialization of men as aggressive and assertive and women as passive and submissive" (1995:13). The rampancy of domestic violence in the Philippines truly shows the contradictory process of patriarchy. Patriarchy persists despite the benefits gained by Filipino women from their society's matrilineal and matrilocal culture such as their comparable level of educational attainment and high rate of formal labor market participation (Eviota, 1992).

Women, at least those with resources (such as networks and funds) emigrate instead of facing ostracism in the community against divorce or separation, for which they as women are more often blamed than men (Israel-Sobritchea, 1990).[3] Divorce is not a legal option for couples in the Philippines even though legal separation can now be granted on the basis of physical violence and incest. Moreover, legally separated individuals do not have the option of remarriage. Legal restrictions and the burden of cultural expectations (for example, the tremendous value on family cohesion for the benefit of children and the immense influence of Catholicism) constrain the option of women to leave abusive spouses permanently. Chant and McIlwaine add, "It should also be noted that grounds for separation on the basis of sexual infidelity are strongly weighted in favour of men, in that a wife only has to have sexual intercourse with another man for this to be granted, whereas a charge of adultery against a husband has to involve concubinage" (1995: 14–15). Not surprising then is the fact that some women believe that they can only escape their marriage by taking advantage of the migrant networks and agencies that are well in place in a traditional sending country such as the Philippines.

Other interviewees decided to emigrate after their husbands abandoned them and they were left to raise their children on their own. Jennifer Jeremillo, for example, sought the higher wages of domestic work in Italy because she could no longer support her children with the wages she earned as a public school teacher.

> After three years of marriage, my husband left me for another woman. . . . My husband supported us for just a little over a year. Then, the support was stopped, everything was stopped, the letters stopped. I have not seen him since. . . . I think of my children's future. There I would be the only one working, without a husband and supporting my children on my own. I knew that my salary was not enough for their future, for their schooling and everything. So I decided to come here even though I had to borrow a lot of money. It cost me 200,000 pesos [U.S.$8000] to come here. Just to pay for the agency was 150,000 pesos [U.S.$6000].

While, on the surface, women who are abandoned by their husbands seem to be motivated solely by the economic benefits of migration, their economic motive cannot be situated solely in the overarching world-system of global capitalism. It must also be placed in the context of gender inequalities that have shaped their experiences and positions as single mothers. Since women are more likely to be abandoned by their husbands than vice versa, it is important to emphasize how this is caused by double standards in male and female sexual practices in the Philippines.[4] Thus, it is this gender inequality that places these women in a position of economic need for migration.

The case of married women in Rome is actually not reflected in my Los Angeles sample, which only includes two women who had cited similar reasons for migration. However, the absence of domestic violence or other marital problems as motivating factors for migration to Los Angeles is not caused by social differences between the two groups, because they belong in the same class. Instead of social differences, this discrepancy can likely be attributed to the more difficult process of migration to the United States. More stringent requirements for prospective migrants delay the migration of women wanting to leave the Philippines quickly.

My finding in Rome is actually supported by the observations of the editor of *Tinig Filipino*.

> In my casual talks with lots of my fellow women overseas contract workers especially the married ones, I found out that there seems to be a certain common factor that binds them—that leaving their families for overseas gave them temporary relief from the sacrifices that go with their marriage. Others are blunt enough to share that their main reason for coming abroad is not merely to earn money but to escape from their

bitter relationships with their husbands. Very rightly so. For no mother could ever afford to leave her young children and her home if the situation at home is normal. (Layosa, 1995b: 7)

As my findings in Rome seem to reflect the situation of Filipina domestic workers in some of the other countries of the labor diaspora, theoretical discussions of the causes of migration have to consider the system of gender inequality in the Philippines, which, in the case of these women, manifests itself in the limited options they have for divorce and the double standards in male and female sexual activities. For Filipinos, these inequalities are aggravated by the burden to uphold the traditional norm of nuclear families.

Highlighting the gender relations and divisions in the Philippines complicates discussions of migration. Patriarchy, which operates as a discrete system within the sending country of the Philippines, is a hidden cause of migration for women. Thus, this system must be included in any formulation of the macrostructural determination of female migration, although, not without an equal consideration of the system of gender inequality in receiving countries.

The Racial Division of Reproductive Labor

Migrant Filipina domestic workers depart from a system of gender stratification in the Philippines only to enter another one in the advanced capitalist and industrialized countries of the United States and Italy. In both sending and receiving nations, they confront societies with similar gender ideologies; that is, reproductive labor is relegated primarily to women. Yet racial, class, and citizenship inequalities aggravate their position in receiving nations. This is demonstrated by their labor market incorporation, which is their official entryway into another system of gender inequality. Migration initiates their entrance into the "racial division of reproductive labor" (Glenn, 1992). They are incorporated into the labor market not only to serve the needs of the highly specialized professionals in "global cities" but also to relieve women of their household work.

In the industrialized countries of Asia, the Americas, and Europe, the number of gainfully employed women has climbed dramatically in the last forty years (Licuanan, 1994; O'Connor, 1996; Reskin and Padavic, 1994). In the United States, women represented 46.5 percent of gainfully employed workers in 1992, a considerable increase over 32.1 percent in 1960 (Reskin and Padavic, 1994: 24–25). In Italy, the downward trend in the labor force participation of women from 1959 to 1972 has since taken a reverse direction (Meyer, 1987). In fact, Italy has witnessed an increasing number of married women in the labor force but surprisingly a decline in the number of younger single women engaged in paid work (Goddard, 1996). In the case of Italy, it has been argued that women are turning away from reproducing families and concentrating on their advancement in the labor market (Specter, 1998). Italy, though known to be "the traditional 'bambini' country," has the lowest birth rate in the world at only 9.6 per 1000 inhabitants (Beck and Beck-Gernsheim, 1995: 102).

While the share of female participation in the labor market has risen in industrialized countries, women remain responsible for the reproductive labor in households. According to Hochschild (1989), in these times of a "stalled revolution," at least in the United States, the vast majority of men do less housework than their gainfully employed partners. A significantly larger number of women have to cope with the double day because women still perform a disproportionate amount of housework, childcare, and social relations with kin and community. Similarly in Italy, *doppio lavoro* (literally meaning double work) has been a recurring theme in the Italian feminist movement since the early 1970s (Birnbaum, 1986). While Italian feminists demanded "wages for housework" beginning in 1975 (Birnbaum, 1986: 135), it can be said that Italian women have since taken a new tactic. Refusing to reproduce the family altogether is a unique response to the double day and a means by which many Italian women minimize their reproductive labor directly.

In both Italy and the United States, elderly care should also be included in the long list of women's household responsibilities. Due to advances in medicine and nutrition, the elderly make up a rapidly growing population, but especially so in communities of "middle- and upper-class whites" in the United States (Abel, 1990: 73). In Italy, the elderly likewise make up an increasing proportion of the population, due primarily to the country's zero-population growth (Beck and Beck-Gernsheim, 1995; Specter, 1998).

In her study of the household division of labor in two-income families, Hochschild (1989) found that men who earned less than their wives were those who were less likely to share housework. An economic logic concerning household division of labor is thus too simplistic. It does not consider the backlash caused by what men perceive as the threat of women's labor market participation (Reskin and Padavic, 1994: 21). In the case of men who earn less than their female partners, women's higher gainful earnings destroy the (socialized) identities accorded to them by patriarchy. Avoiding housework is thus the most tangible means by which they can still maintain their place in the patriarchal order. In a patriarchal society such as the United States, the increasing number of working women are left with the choice of purchasing the services of other, meaning less-privileged, women or working a double day.

While a higher joint income does not guarantee a more egalitarian distribution of housework between the sexes, it does give families the flexibility to afford the services of other women. To ease the double day, many overwhelmed working women have turned to day-care centers and family day-care providers, nursing homes, after-school baby-sitters, and also privately hired domestic workers (Glazer, 1993; Glenn, 1986; Hochschild, 1989; Nelson, 1990; Reskin and Padavic, 1994; Rothman, 1989a, 1989b). As Joy Manlapit, a provider of elderly care in Los Angeles, observes:

> Domestics here are able to make a living from the elderly that families abandon. When they are older, the families do not want to take care of them. Some put them in convalescent homes, some put them in retirement homes, and some hire private domestic workers.

The labor market incorporation of migrant Filipina domestic workers fits into Glenn's schema of the racial division of reproduction of labor. In Italy and the United States, they join the ranks of other groups of working-class women who have historically performed the reproductive labor of more privileged women.[5] In doing so, they free their employers to pursue more rewarding gainful employment. Reflecting the observations of Glenn, Jacqueline Andall finds a direct correlation between the entrance of migrant women into Italy and the entrance of native Italian women into the labor force:

> The migration of women into Italy began at the same time as a number of changes were taking place in the role and position of Italian women within society. When, in the 1970s, an increased number of Italian women began to assert themselves outside the domestic sphere, this had repercussions on the Italian family. This change in Italian women's activity became a pull factor in the migration of women from developing countries. (1992: 43)

Not surprisingly, 36.4 percent of illegal workers in Italy are doing domestic work (Calavita, 1994).

Glenn's formulation of the racial division of reproductive labor suggests that the economic demand for the low-wage labor of domestic workers arises not solely from the concentration of highly specialized professional service workers in "global cities" but also from persisting gender inequalities in the families of these professionals. To fully consider the politics of reproductive labor in migration, I now expand and reformulate the concept of the racial division of reproductive labor by placing it in a transnational setting. In doing so, I situate the increasing demand for paid reproductive labor in receiving nations in the context of the globalization of the market economy.

The International Division of Reproductive Labor

Globalization has triggered the formation of a singular market economy. As such, production activities in one area can no longer be understood solely from a unilocal perspective. Likewise, reproduction activities, especially as they have been increasingly commodified, have to be situated in the context of this singular market economy. In this sense, reproduction activities in one area have concrete ties to reproduction activities in another area. With the feminization of wage labor, global capitalism is forging the creation of links among distinct systems of gender inequality. Moreover, the migration of women connects systems of gender inequality in both sending and receiving nations to global capitalism. All of these processes occur in the formation of the international division of reproductive labor.

This division of labor places Glenn's (1992) concept of the racial division of reproductive labor in an international context under the auspices of Sassen's (1984) discussion of the incorporation of women from developing countries in the global economy. It is a transnational division of labor that is shaped simultaneously by global capitalism and systems of gender inequality in both sending and receiving countries of migration. This division of labor determines the migration and entrance into domestic service of women from the Philippines.

The international transfer of caretaking is a distinct form of international division of labor in which Filipina domestic workers perform the reproductive labor of class-privileged women in industrialized countries as they leave their own to other women in the Philippines to perform. This international division of labor refers to a three-tier transfer of reproductive labor among women in two nation-states. These groups of women are (1) middle- and upper-class women in receiving countries, (2) migrant Filipina domestic workers, and (3) Filipina domestic workers in the Philippines who are too poor to migrate.

In the article "Economy Menders," Linda Layosa, the editor of *Tinig Fili-pino*, gives a partial description of the international transfer of caretaking.

> Indeed, our women have partially been liberated from the anguish of their day-to-day existence with their families and from economic prob-lems, only to be enslaved again in the confines of another home, most of the time trampling their rights as human beings . . . . We have to face the reality that many of our women will be compelled to leave the confines of their own tidy bedrooms and their spotless kitchens only to clean an-other household, to mend others' torn clothes at the same time mend our tattered economy. (1995a: 7)

In her description, she falls short of mentioning who takes up the household work that migrant Filipina domestic workers abandon upon migration. Most likely, they are other female relatives but also, less-privileged Filipina women, women unable to afford the high costs of seeking employment outside of the Philippines. Thus, migrant Filipina domestic workers are in the middle of the three-tier hierarchy of the international transfer of caretaking.

Under the international transfer of caretaking, women's migration from the Philippines is embedded in the process of global capitalism. At the same time, gender is also a central factor of their migration: the process of migra-tion for women involves escaping their gender roles in the Philippines, easing the gender constraints of women who employ them in industrialized coun-tries, and finally relegating their gender roles to women left in the Philippines.

The international transfer of caretaking refers to a social, political, and eco-nomic relationship between women in the global labor market. This division of labor is a structural relationship of inequality based on class, race, gender and (nation-based) citizenship. In this division of labor, there is a gradational decline in worth of reproductive labor. As Rothman (1989a: 43) poignantly describes, "When performed by mothers, we call this mothering . . . ; when performed by hired hands, we call it unskilled." Commodified reproductive labor is not only low-paid work but declines in market value as it gets passed down the international transfer of caretaking. As care is made into a com-modity, women with greater resources in the global economy can afford the best-quality care for their family. Conversely, the care given to those with fewer resources is usually worth less.

Consequently, the quality of family life progressively declines as care is passed down the international transfer of caretaking. Freed of household con-straints, those on top can earn more and consequently afford better-quality care than can the domestic workers whom they hire. With their wages relatively low, these domestic workers cannot afford to provide the same kind of care for their family. They in turn leave them behind in the Philippines to be cared for by even lesser-paid domestic workers. Relegated to the bottom of the three-tier hierarchy of reproductive labor, domestic workers left in the Third World have far fewer material resources to ensure the reproduction of their own family.

In the international transfer of caretaking, Filipina domestic workers do not just ease the entrance of other women into the paid labor force but also assist in the economic growth of receiving countries. Patricia Licuanan, in reference to households in Hong Kong and Singapore, explains:

> Households are said to have benefited greatly by the import of domestic workers. Family income has increased because the wife and other women members of working age are freed from domestic chores and are able to join the labour force. This higher income would normally result in the enlargement of the consumer market and greater demand on production and consequently a growth in the economy. (1994: 109)

By spurring economic development, the international transfer of caretaking retains the inequalities of the global market economy. The low wages of migrant domestic workers increase the production activities of the receiving nation, but the economic growth of the Philippine economy is for the most part limited and dependent on the foreign currency provided by their low wages.

A similar observation can be made of the employing families in the international transfer of caretaking. Freed of reproductive labor, the family employing the migrant domestic worker can increase the productive labor generated in their household. The mobility of the Filipina migrant domestic worker and her family is for the most part dependent on the greater mobility of the employing family. The same relationship goes for domestic workers in the Philippines and the migrant domestics who employ them.

The case of Carmen Ronquillo provides a good illustration of the international transfer of caretaking. Carmen is simultaneously a domestic worker for a professional woman in Rome and an employer of a domestic worker in the Philippines. Carmen describes her relationship to each of these two women:

> When coming here, I mentally surrendered myself and forced my pride away from me to prepare myself. But I lost a lot of weight. I was not used to the work. You see, I had maids in the Philippines. I have a maid

in the Philippines that has worked for me since my daughter was born twenty-four years ago. She is still with me. I paid her three hundred pesos before, and now I pay her 1000 pesos [U.S.$40].

I am a little bit luckier than others because I run the entire household. My employer is a divorced woman who is an architect. She does not have time to run her household so I do all the shopping. I am the one budgeting. I am the one cooking. [Laughs.] And I am the one cleaning too. She has a twenty-four and twenty-six year old. The older one graduated already and is an electrical engineer. The other one is taking up philosophy. They still live with her. . . . She has been my only employer. I stayed with her because I feel at home with her. She never commands. She never orders me to do this and to do that.

The hierarchical and interdependent relationship between Carmen, her employer in Italy, and her domestic worker in the Philippines forms from the unequal development of industrialized and developing countries in transnational capitalism, class differences in the Philippines, and the relegation of reproductive labor to women. The case of Carmen Ronquillo clearly exemplifies how three distinct groups of women participate in the international transfer of caretaking. While Carmen frees her employer (the architect) of domestic responsibilities, a lower-paid domestic worker does the household work for Carmen and her family.

Wage differences of domestic workers illuminate the economic disparity among nations in transnational capitalism. A domestic worker in Italy such as Carmen could receive U.S.$1000 a month for her labor.

I earn 1,500,000 lira [U.S.$1000] and she pays for my benefits [for example, medical coverage]. On Sundays, I have a part-time; I clean her office in the morning and she pays me 300,000 lira [U.S.$200]. I am very fortunate because she always gives me my holiday pay [August] and my thirteenth month pay in December. Plus, she gives me my liquidation pay at the end of the year. Employers here are required to give you a liquidation pay—equivalent to your monthly salary for every year you worked for them, but they usually give it to you when you leave; but she insists on paying me at the end of the year. So, [in] December, I always receive 5,400,000 lira [U.S.$3600].

Carmen's wages easily enable her to hire a domestic worker in the Philippines, who, on average, only earns the below poverty wage of U.S.$40 per month. Moreover, the female domestic worker in the Philippines, in exchange for her labor, does not receive the additional work benefits Carmen receives for the same labor, for example, medical coverage. Not surprisingly, migrant Filipina domestic workers, as shown by their high level of educational attainment, tend to have more resources and belong in a more comfortable class strata than do domestic workers in the Philippines. Such resources often enable Carmen and other migrant Filipina women to afford the option of working outside of the country.

The Overlooked Participants: Children and Women in the Philippines

> The private world remains devalued, as poor people become the wives and mothers of the world, cleaning the toilets and raising the children. The devaluing of certain work, of nurturance, of private "domestic" work, remains: rearing children is roughly on a par—certainly in terms of salary—with cleaning the toilet (Rothman, 1989a: 252).

While the devaluation of "rearing children" could be lamented as a tragedy for children, the experiences of the different groups of children (and elderly) in the international transfer of caretaking should be distinguished between those who remain cared for and those who are not and those who regularly see their parents/children and those who cannot. The fact that "rearing children is roughly on a par . . . with cleaning the toilet" means that migrant Filipina domestic workers usually cannot afford the higher costs of maintaining a family in industrialized countries due to their meager wages. In the United States, where women of color have traditionally been caregivers and domestic workers for white families, mothering is diverted away from families of people of color. Sau-ling Wong defines "diverted mothering" to be the process in which the "time and energy available for mothering are diverted from those who, by kinship or communal ties, are their more rightful recipients" (1994: 69). Historically, a married black domestic worker in the United States "typically saw her children once every two weeks, leaving them in the care of the husband or older siblings, while remaining on call around the clock for the employer's children" (Wong, 1994: 71). Although now in an international context, the same pattern of "diverted mothering" could be described for Filipina, Latina, and Caribbean domestic workers, as many are forced to leave their children behind in the country of origin (Colen, 1995; Hondagneu-Sotelo and Avila, 1997). The question then is, who cares for these "other" children?

In the Philippines, it is unusual for fathers to nurture and care for their children, but since not all migrant Filipina domestic workers hire domestic workers, some men are forced to give in to the renegotiations of household division of labor led by the migration of their wives. Usually, however, other female relatives take over the household work of migrant Filipinas.[6] In these cases, nonegalitarian relations among family members should be acknowledged, considering that for female family members left in the Philippines, "the mobility they might achieve through migration is severely curtailed" (Basch et al., 1994: 241). However, hired domestic workers—a live-in housekeeper or *labandera* (laundry woman who hand washes clothes)—also free migrant Filipina domestics of their household labor. Almost all of my interviewees hire domestic workers in the Philippines. This should not be surprising considering that the average wage of domestics in the Philippines is considerably less than the average wage of migrant domestics.

In discussions of the international division of (productive) labor, the women who cannot afford to work as domestic workers in other countries are equated with those who do so. For example, migrant Filipina domestic workers and female low-wage workers in the Philippines are considered to be equally displaced in global capitalism. Maya Areza, who dreams of retiring in the Philippines after a few more years in Los Angeles, reminds us of the structural inequalities characterizing relations among women in developing countries when she states:

> When I retire I plan to go home for good. I plan to stay at my parents' house. . . . I would just lounge and smoke. I will get a domestic helper who I can ask to get my cigarettes for me. . . . My children and my cousins all have domestic workers. You can hire one if you have money. It's cheap, only 1000 pesos [U.S.$40]. Here, you earn $1000 doing the same kind of work you would do for one thousand pesos there! I won't have a problem with hiring one.

Because migrant Filipina domestic workers are usually in the middle of the hierarchical chain of caretaking, they maintain unequal relations with less-privileged women in the Philippines. Under the international transfer of caretaking, the unequal economic standing of nation-states and discrepancies in monetary currencies are prominent factors that distinguish the position of female low-wage workers in advanced capitalist and developing countries. They differentiate, for example, the position of domestic workers in the United States and Italy from domestic workers in the Philippines. Migrant Filipina domestic workers surely take advantage of these differences in wages and maintain a direct hierarchical relationship with the domestic workers whom they hire in the Philippines. In the international transfer of care-taking, domestic workers hired by families of domestic workers abroad are the truly subaltern women.

Conclusion

As gender differentiates the causes of migration for men and women, it is very problematic to simply apply women's experiences to traditional male models of migration. To move away from additive approaches in the treatment of women, it is important to consider how gender stratification interlocks with other systems of inequality to determine the causes of women's migration. Migration is a movement from one distinct patriarchal system to another, bound by race and class, in transnational capitalism. Therefore, it should be analyzed from a gendered perspective of the political economy.

The hierarchy of womanhood—involving race, class, and nation, as well as gender—establishes a work transfer system of reproductive labor among women, the international transfer of caretaking. It is a distinct form of transnational division of labor that links women in an interdependent relationship. Filipina domestic workers perform the reproductive labor of more privileged women in industrialized countries as they relegate their reproductive labor to poorer women left in the Philippines. This demonstrates that production is not the only means by which international divisions of labor operate in the global economy. Local economies are not solely linked by the manufacturing production of goods. Under globalization, the transfer of reproductive labor moves beyond territorial borders to connect separate nation-states.

The formulation of the international division of reproductive labor treats gender as a central analytical framework for understanding the migration of Filipina domestic workers. It shows that the movement of Filipina domestic workers is embedded in a gendered system of transnational capitalism. While forces of global capitalism spur the labor migration of Filipina domestic workers, the demand for their labor also results from gender inequalities in receiving nations, for example, the relegation of reproductive labor to women. This transfer of labor strongly suggests that despite their increasing rate of labor market participation, women continue to remain responsible for reproductive labor in both sending and receiving countries. At both ends of the migratory stream, they have not been able to negotiate directly with male counterparts for a fairer division of household work but instead have had to rely on their race and/or class privilege by participating in the transnational transfer of gender constraints to less-privileged women.

A central contradiction in the maintenance of gender inequalities is that they hinder as much as they facilitate the migration of women. In the Philippines, gender stratification spurs the migration of women in resistance to male abuse, the double day, labor market segmentation, and single motherhood. Escaping gender stratification is a hidden cause of migration. For example, migration alleviates the household reproductive labor of married women, while single women escape gender-defined duties in the family. But as they are relegated to domestic work in the labor market, they enter another patriarchal society. Ironically, women in industrialized (Western) countries are often assumed to be more liberated than women are in developing countries. Yet many women are able to pursue careers as their male counterparts do because disadvantaged migrant women and other women of color are stepping into their old shoes and doing their household work for them. As women transfer their reproductive labor to less and less privileged women, the traditional division of labor in the patriarchal nuclear household has not been significantly renegotiated in various countries in the world. This is one of the central reasons why there is a need for Filipina domestic workers in more than a hundred countries today.

Though the underlying theme of dislocations was not the focus of analysis in this chapter, my discussion of the international transfer of caretaking as a division of labor has touched upon some of the dislocations that migrant Filipina domestic workers encounter in migration. First, being in the middle entails the maintenance of a transnational household structure and consequently involves experiencing the pain of family separation. Second, being in the middle also means being part of the middle class of the Philippines. This alludes to the dislocation of contradictory class mobility and the partial citizenship granted to them by receiving nations that fail to acknowledge their educational training prior to migration. Returning to my analysis of dislocations, the next two chapters address the dislocation of the pain of family separation.

CHAPTER 4

The Transnational Family: A Postindustrial
Household Structure with Preindustrial Values

Anth 330 (handwritten annotation)

In this chapter I trace the structural and cultural factors that propel the re-configuration of contemporary migrant households from nuclear to trans-national structures. By transnational families or households, I refer to fami-lies whose core members are located in at least two nation-states.[1] Most of the domestic workers in my study are income producers of transnational families. In fact, 77 percent (twenty of twenty-six) of research participants in Los An-geles and 89 percent (forty-one of forty-six) in Rome maintain such house-holds. While working in Italy or the United States, their families—spouses, children, and/or parents—remain in the Philippines. Considering that they usually migrate alone, we can safely assume that most of them have main-tained transnational households since the time of migration. While some single women who migrated have formed new families, most have not, and many who bore children in Rome opted to send them back to the Philip-pines. As I noted, women with children living in the Philippines constitute a greater portion of my sample in both Rome and Los Angeles: twenty-five of forty-six in Rome and fourteen of twenty-six in Los Angeles.[2]

The formation of transnational households is not exclusive to Filipino la-bor migrants. Various studies have documented their formation among con-temporary migrants from the traditional sending countries of Haiti and Mex-ico (Basch et al., 1994; Chavez, 1992; Curry, 1988; Hondagneu-Sotelo, 1994; Laguerre, 1994; Massey et al., 1987). From some of these studies we have learned that macroprocesses of globalization prompt the formation of trans-national households. Migrants create transnational households to maximize resources and opportunities in the global economy. They mediate unequal levels of economic development between sending and receiving nations, le-gal barriers that restrict their full incorporation into the host society and

80

polity, and the rise of anti-immigrant sentiments (Basch et al., 1994; Glick-Schiller et al., 1995; Laguerre, 1994).

These constitutive features are not particular to global capitalism. Instead, they are old practices—long-standing realities—which are only being redeployed with greater speed and force with the advent of globalization. As such, transnational families are not particular to present-day migrants. They have historically been a common form of household maintenance for temporary labor migrants in various regions of the world. The earliest Chinese migrant workers in the United States, guest workers in Western Europe, and Mexican braceros in the southwestern United States, to name a few examples, adopted split-households because of, similar to current conditions, disparate levels of economic development between sending and receiving countries and legal barriers against the integration of migrants (Glenn, 1983). Yet differences do exist between transnational households in the past and present. While split-households in earlier migrant communities were homogeneous and composed primarily of a male income-producer living apart from female and young dependents in the sending country, contemporary split-households, for example, those from the Philippines and the Caribbean, include income-producing women migrants (Basch et al., 1994).

Contemporary transnational households also involve a different temporal and spatial experience. They inhabit postmodern spaces as relationships in these families function through the process of "time-space compression . . . , the speed-up in the pace of life, while so overcoming spatial barriers that the world sometimes seems to collapse inwards upon us" (Harvey, 1989: 240). Although transnational family members perform daily activities across vast geographical distances, they overcome spatial barriers through the rapid flow of money and information. Due to advancements in technology, information about family members can be received instantaneously, and money can be transferred to urban centers of Third World countries within twenty-four hours.

Transnational households form not merely in response to structural forces of globalization. As Nancy Foner states, "the family [needs to be] seen as a place where there is a dynamic interplay between structure, culture and agency—where creative culture-building takes place in the context of external social and economic forces as well as immigrants' premigration cultural frameworks" (1997: 961). From this observation, we can infer that migrants are only able to form transnational households because of cultural resources that instill collectivism in the family. Linda Basch and her colleagues agree. Viewing transnational family networks as "the underbelly of the global penetration of capitalism," they explain that migrant parents rely on extended family networks for the care of the children whom they send back or leave behind in Haiti, the Philippines, or St. Vincent (1994: 170). The maintenance of transnational households ensures the maximization of income and the accumulation of savings and property and, through the transfer of childcare, promotes and strengthens extended kin ties.

While research on the transnational family reveals that its formation results from both structural and cultural factors, we can still gain more knowledge of the emotional stresses generated by its formation. Though studies have acknowledged the emotional stress incurred from prolonged separation (Chavez, 1992; Curry, 1988) and the higher risk of permanent separation in these families (Hondagneu-Sotelo, 1994), they at most have only given the emotional tensions in transnational households a cursory glance. As I indicated, one of the central dislocations that defines the subjectivity of migrant Filipina domestic workers emerges from the formation of transnational households. Transnational households impose the pain of family separation. My discussion of this dislocation, which is divided into two chapters, delves more deeply into this emotional stress. In this chapter, I establish the constitution of this dislocation. In the next chapter, I examine the effects of this dislocation and the means by which migrant Filipina domestic workers negotiate these in their everyday lives.

In this chapter, my discussion is divided into three main sections. First, I describe the Filipino transnational family by providing vignettes of each of the three types of transnational households found in the Filipino labor diaspora: households with one parent abroad, two parents abroad, and adult child(ren) abroad. Second, I document the structural forces that propel the formation of transnational households. Third, I enumerate the cultural resources enabling the formation of such households.

A Typology and Profile of Migrant Families in the Filipino Diaspora

Although beginning with the household as a central unit of analysis could dangerously promote the assumption that the family represents a singular collective interest and may conveniently mask social inequalities within the family, I find that the household provides a useful point of departure for analyzing the complexities of migration (Thorne, 1992). By giving a typology of migrant households, I document the reconstitution of households and family relations in migration.[3] In my discussion, the family is not considered a collective unit but is instead presented as a contentious site that involves conflicting interests among its members.

There are generally two types of households in Filipino migrant communities—nuclear and transnational (see Table 8). Nuclear households are those whose family members live in close geographical proximity. For the most part, migrant families that fall under this category can be divided into two subgroups—traditional and nontraditional. Family members in traditional nuclear households share a common residence. In Rome, only two of forty-six women maintain this household structure. Notably, they are two of five lesbian women in my sample and are placed in the category of traditional nuclear households because they have shared a residence with their respective domestic partners for at least ten years. In Los Angeles, three of twenty-six women belong in traditional nuclear households. They had all migrated to Los Angeles as single women, married American men, and in turn formed new families.

Family members of nontraditional nuclear households also live in close proximity to each other but, unlike traditional nuclear families, retain separate residences. In nontraditional nuclear households, domestic workers live with employers and visit their families only during nonworking days, usually weekends. These families resemble those of African American domestic workers in the South during the last century (Katzman, 1978; Wong, 1994). Only two domestic workers in Rome and two in Los Angeles maintain such households.

Nuclear households—traditional or nontraditional—are a rarity and constitute a small portion of my sample. Only five of thirty married individuals in Rome and five of twenty married individuals in Los Angeles maintain such households. In both cities, migrants in nuclear households usually have no more than one dependent. In Rome, nuclear households tend to form in temporal stages of migration, with one parent migrating before other members of the family and the rest individually following in different stages.[4]

In Rome and Los Angeles, the transnational household is a more dominant strategy of household maintenance for Filipina domestic workers. Transnational households can be further divided into three subcategories: one parent abroad, two parents abroad, and adult child(ren) abroad households. One parent abroad transnational households are those with one parent—a mother or a father—producing income abroad while other family members carry out the functions of reproduction, socialization, and the rest of consumption in the Philippines. In two parents abroad transnational households, both parents work abroad and the children usually reside together in the Philippines under the care of other relatives. Finally, adult child(ren) abroad transnational households are those with adult children whose earnings as migrant laborers provide necessary or additional financial support to relatives in the Philippines.

Twenty domestic workers in Rome and twelve in Los Angeles are part of one parent abroad households. Not all of them have children. Of the three without children, one woman in Los Angeles left her husband behind in the Philippines, and two are daughters who followed mothers to Rome but left siblings behind in the Philippines.

In my sample, seven individuals in Rome and three in Los Angeles maintain two parents abroad transnational households. Clearly, a much smaller percentage of domestic workers run this type of household. One single woman falls under this household category because she followed her parents to Rome but left brothers and sisters behind in the Philippines. The rest of them are married women with children. In these households, children tend to stay together with other relatives, usually grandparents, but in some cases families have chosen to divide their children between the Philippines and Rome or Los Angeles. In these cases, there is quite an imbalance in intergenerational relations, as parents maintain closer ties to children living with them than with those living in the Philippines. The different experiences of children in these families incite jealousy among siblings and most likely aggravate the emotional strains and tensions wrought in transnational families.

The last type of household found in my study is the adult child(ren) abroad transnational household, which consists of families with migrant adult children supporting immediate family members in the Philippines. Situating adult single migrants without children in a household category presented quite a dilemma in the construction of a household typology. While I could have placed single migrants in the category of "independent household," I found that strong family ties between single migrants and relatives in the Philippines would be nullified by classifying them as single householders. With the formulation of the category adult child(ren) abroad transnational households, I link single migrants to dependent relatives in the Philippines and emphasize the interdependent transnational ties that they sustain in migration. In Rome, fourteen of twenty single individual migrants fall under this household category, while five of six single migrants, none of whom have children, do in Los Angeles. In my entire sample, only one single woman in Los Angeles does not send remittances to her family in the Philippines, because her parents and all of her siblings also live in Los Angeles. She thus falls under the category of single householder.

To illustrate the complex family relations in the various household forms in my study, I now present a series of vignettes of each type of transnational household found in the diaspora. I place the migrant family under a microscope to interrogate its transformations, household dynamics, and the meanings and consequences of migration to family relations. Recognizing and examining the various ways and means by which migrants maintain their families illustrate the social process of transnational household formation. Hence, analyzing migrant households reveals the structures that control migrant life and the resources that migrants utilize to perform essential household tasks.

ONE PARENT ABROAD TRANSNATIONAL HOUSEHOLDS

In my study, the most common form of household maintenance found among domestic workers is the one parent abroad transnational household, a unit with one migrant parent—usually a mother—working outside of the Philippines for a prolonged period of separation from her or his family. Children in transnational households are usually of student-age, which is not surprising considering the high expenses incurred during this stage of the family life-cycle (Massey et al., 1987). The predominance of one parent abroad transnational households in my sample not only indicates the growing number of independent women migrants from the Philippines but also suggests the reconfiguration of the gender division of labor in families.

The question then is whether husbands and fathers left behind in the Philippines nurture the children under their care. Of thirty-two female interviewees in this household structure, my sample includes four widowed women, ten separated women, three single mothers, and two children who later followed their mothers to Rome.[5] Prior to the migration of mothers, many children in one parent abroad transnational households were already growing up without fathers. In a few cases fathers had passed away, but for the most part the father had formed a second family with another woman in the Philippines. Of the spouses of ten separated women in my sample, six had children with other women prior to the migration of their "first" wives and two had other children after migration. Among them, only one father retains close ties to his children. Thus, similar to two parents abroad transnational households, at least half of the families in one parent abroad transnational households are those of children left behind in the Philippines with neither their father nor mother. This section presents two vignettes, one of a woman in Los Angeles and another in Rome. The first is of a family with a father present in his children's lives, and the other is one with a father who has two sets of children in the Philippines. Both vignettes illustrate the struggles undergone by transnational mothers in balancing the emotional and material needs of the children whom they have left behind in the Philippines.

VICKY DIAZ

In 1988, Vicky Diaz—a thirty-four-year-old mother of five children between the ages of two and ten years old—left the Philippines for Taiwan. Lured by the financial rewards of employment outside the Philippines, Vicky had been neither content with her salary as a public school teacher in the Philippines nor comfortable with the insecurities of running a travel agency in Manila. Although made more lucrative by the greater demand for employment outside of the Philippines in the last ten years, the business of travel agencies had not been as profitable in the late 1980s. Vicky decided to move to Taiwan, because there the wages of a domestic worker would give her a more secure income.

In Taiwan, Vicky worked as a housekeeper, a factory worker, but mostly as a janitor, for which she earned a salary of approximately U.S.$1000 a month. Vicky, who speaks English very well, also subsidized her earnings by teaching English part-time at nights. Although satisfied with her earnings in Taiwan, Vicky found the situation of illegal workers such as herself made more tenuous by the greater enforcement of restrictive polices against migrants in the early 1990s. In 1992, Vicky decided to leave Taiwan and return to the Philippines.

Yet her return to the Philippines after five years in Taiwan turned out to be just a stopover before migrating to the United States.

> From Taiwan, I only stayed in the Philippines for three months. I used this time to fix my papers to come here. After Taiwan, my real target was the States. It was because I knew that America is the land of promises and the land of opportunities. I had several friends who went to America and never went back to the Philippines. I figured it was because life was wonderful in the United States. . . . So, why not give myself the same opportunity?

Although geographically distanced from her children for at least five years, Vicky did not seem at all interested in spending "quality" time with them. The prolonged distance from her family seemed to have fostered feelings of emotional distance in Vicky. Only a few months after her return to the Philippines, Vicky used her savings from Taiwan to pay a "travel agency" U.S.$8000 for the use of another woman's passport to enter the United States. As Vicky states, "You know, in the Philippines, nothing is impossible if you have the money."

Considering her middle-class status after running a travel agency in the Philippines and ability to raise such a huge sum of money for her trip to the United States, one can easily wonder why Vicky risks such a prolonged separation from her family. In the last nine years, Vicky has spent a total of only three months with her husband and children in the Philippines. Clearly an absentee mother for most of her children's adolescence, Vicky explains that it is for her family's benefit that she works outside the country:

> They were saddened by my departure. Even until now my children are trying to convince me to go home. . . . The children were not angry when I left because they were still very young when I left them. My husband could not get angry either because he knew that was the only way I could seriously help him raise our children, so that our children could be sent to school.

Vicky insists that her family needs her higher earnings outside of the Philippines. Although aware of her children's persistent requests for her to return to the Philippines, Vicky is not convinced that her family can sustain its middle-class status without her earnings.

In Los Angeles, Vicky was initially employed as a domestic worker, primarily caring for a two-year-old boy for a wealthy family in Beverly Hills. As the mother "would just be sitting around, smoking and making a mess," Vicky cleaned, cooked, and cared for the boy for $400 a week, clearly a sharp contrast to the $40 she pays her own family's live-in domestic worker in the Philippines. Vicky did not like being a housekeeper for two main reasons, the physically demanding load and the excruciating loneliness heightened by the contradiction of caring for someone else's children while not caring for her own.

> Even though it paid well, you are sinking in the amount of your work. Even while you are ironing the clothes, they can still call you to the kitchen to wash the plates. It was also very depressing. The only thing you can do is give all your love to the child. In my absence from my children, the most I could do with my situation is give all my love to that child.

Not completely indifferent about the separation that her family has endured for almost ten years, Vicky does entertain feelings of regret over missing the formative years of her children's adolescence.

> What saddens me the most about my situation is that during the forma-
> tive years of their childhood, I was not there for them. That is the time
> when children really need their mother, and I was not there for them.

Yet for Vicky, the economic rewards of separation soften its emotional costs.

> In my one year in the U.S., I was able to invest on a jeepney. I wanted
> to do that so that no matter what happens with me, my husband does
> not have a hard time financially. . . . *Of course, I have neglected them,*
> *and the least I could do to make up for this is to make their lives a little*
> *bit easier. I could ease their lives for them materially.* That's how I
> console myself. . . . Besides the jeepney, there's the washing machine
> and TV. In the Philippines, it is hard to get to buy these things, right?
> At least they are not desolate and are at least provided for well. (my
> emphasis)

To overcome the emotional gaps in her family, Vicky relies on commodify-ing her love and compensates for her absence with material goods. While Vicky claims that she works outside of the Philippines so that her family does not become destitute, it is actually more accurate to say that Vicky works in Los Angeles to sustain a comfortable middle-class life for her family in the Philippines.

Vicky hopes that her family will eventually reunite in Los Angeles, be-cause she is convinced that there are dismal opportunities available for her family in the Philippines. Without legal documents, however, she is unable to sponsor the migration of her family. Obtaining legal status continues to be the biggest challenge for Vicky and has been the main obstacle blocking the reunification of her family. Yet while Vicky aspires to the relocation of her entire family to the United States, her children prefer to witness the re-unification of their family much sooner and would rather have Vicky return to the Philippines.

JUDY REYES

Judy Reyes migrated to Rome in 1991, leaving behind her three daughters and one son between the ages of two months and nine years old under the care of her husband in the Philippines. Economics had not been the primary motivation for Judy's migration. In the Philippines, she had a rewarding career, a job she loved, and a salary that along with her husband's afforded her family a comfortable middle-class life in Manila. Migration had actually been Judy's way of escaping a horrible marriage.[6] Although it had been her ambition to go to the United States or Canada, Judy had to settle for Italy, a more viable destination, for she had two sisters who had been working in Rome since the early 1980s. Costing her U.S.$6400, the two-week trip to Italy depleted her savings, and she incurred a large debt to one of her sisters in Rome.

Life in Rome has been far from comfortable or enjoyable for Judy. Reflecting on her experiences, Judy mentions undergoing three major traumas. The first was the harrowing voyage to Rome through a war-torn country in Eastern Europe. The second has been her downward mobility from her position as a registered nurse in the Philippines. The third concerns the pain she feels over family separation, most especially from the four-year-old son she had left when he was a two-month-old infant.

While able to reconcile the downward mobility in her labor market status, Judy still copes with the distress of family separation.

> The first two years I felt like I was going crazy. You have to believe me when I say that it was like I was having intense psychological problems. I would catch myself gazing at nothing thinking about my child. Every moment, every second of the day, I felt like I was thinking about my baby. My youngest, you have to understand, I left when he was only two months old. . . .

Judy carries a tremendous amount of emotional strain—guilt over her absence, especially missing her son's formative years; the burden and anguish over lost time with her children; and sadness over the unfamiliarity developing in her family, such as not knowing who prepares her children's breakfast every morning.

In any given month, Judy sends her children U.S.$300 to $500. Even so, they have been forced to live apart in the Philippines due to the continued irresponsibility of their father. Judy's children are divided among different relatives—two live with their father in Manila, another in the province with her maternal grandmother, and the youngest also in Manila but with her sister-in-law.

> My children are studying. The oldest is in first year high school. The second is in the sixth grade. The third is nine years old and is in the

third grade. My mom in the province has recently taken her to the province because their caretaker has not been able to really watch this one. Then the four-year-old is now in kindergarten and is being taken care of by my sister-in-law.

The money that she sends to subsidize her husband's income for the care of her children is not enough to keep them together, as the husband continues to spend money on "women" and "going out with friends."

In light of her persisting problems with her husband, it is not surprising that Judy is anticipating their permanent separation.

I have a joint account with my child. It is my secret account so I am prepared no matter what happens to the two of us. I experienced what it was like to take care of my children on my own—financially supporting them with my salary without any help from him. It was hard.

Nonetheless, she also holds on to the possibility that her husband will somehow change for the better, hoping that her time in Rome will serve as a lesson that will make him realize his past errors.

He finally realized that he needs me now that we are apart. [She cries.] . . . I have not shown him any ill feelings. I have been very diplomatic in how I tell him what I did not like in our relationship. People have told me that I am such a martyr. But I tell them that I have four children, and it is important to me that my four children have a relationship with their father.

Once my children can think for themselves, maybe we can separate. But if I cannot bear our relationship anymore, that is when I am going to decide. I need to raise my children first and let them know that they have a father. . . .

He keeps on saying that he wants it to work, but he is with his other family all of the time. I ask him why he even maintains a relationship with us because he hardly gives us any time. I told him that it probably would be better if he packed his clothes and moved to his other family. But he is embarrassed because the other woman is not educated and is a gambler. . . .

His brothers and sisters tell me to have a little bit more patience. They tell me that they know that their brother is wrong, and he will probably change. They have cried to me, asking me to come back, and I told them I will only come back once their brother has changed. . . .

Though her in-laws are trying to convince her to stay in a bad marriage, Judy has this sinking feeling that her husband will never change. To avoid socially and culturally influenced pressures from family and community to keep her marriage intact—even with an unfaithful husband—Judy hopes to find a way to settle in the United States or Canada, countries where there will be more opportunities for her children than in the Philippines and where, in contrast to Italy, they will not be limited to domestic work.

TWO PARENTS ABROAD TRANSNATIONAL HOUSEHOLDS

Although there are far fewer two parents abroad transnational households than one parent abroad transnational households in my study, this is still a common strategy of household maintenance in Filipino migrant communities. In this section, I illustrate the dynamics and relations in two parents abroad transnational households using the stories of two families in Rome, the difference being that in one family all of the children reside in the Philippines, while in the other the children are divided between Rome and the Philippines. From these vignettes, we learn of two parental attitudes regarding separation: one set of parents consciously tries to ease the emotional tensions in transnational families; the other is less willing to confront them. Although I have chosen not to profile any of the families in Los Angeles, intergenerational relations in these families reflect those that I feature. Only the circumstances forcing the formation of split-households are different, as the undocumented status of parents in Los Angeles has primarily prevented them from petitioning for the migration of their now adult children.

LOLITA AND ANTONIO MAGSINO

With the help of her sisters-in-law, Lolita Magsino migrated to Rome in 1984. Her husband, Antonio, followed ten months later. In leaving the Philippines, he left four young children between the ages of two and seven years old under the care of Lolita's mother.

> I have been here for eleven years. . . . It is ingrained in my head when I came here because it reminds me of how many years I have been struggling. . . . I followed my sisters-in-law who have been here since 1981. Within ten days, I had a job. I knew that it was going to be domestic work because that was the job of my in-laws. . . . I came from a very poor family. I am used to working. It is nothing to me. I lack knowledge so any job is good enough for me. As long as you are hard working

here, you have money. . . . I came and my husband followed me after
ten months.

In the Philippines, Lolita and Antonio lived in a nipa hut with their four children, barely making ends meet with the money that they earned farming
and selling vegetables.[7] Not surprisingly, they took advantage of the opportunity to go to Italy to secure a more stable future for their children.

Lolita and her husband only worked as domestic workers for five years.
Since 1990, she has worked as a full-time vendor of Filipino food in Rome.
Lolita sells her food near a central bus transfer point where Filipinos and a
few Peruvian women stop by between one job and the next to take their
lunch break before they have to run to their afternoon cleaning jobs. Very
business minded, she and her husband both run informal businesses in the
underground economy servicing the growing migrant community in Rome.
While she works as a vendor, he fixes cars for a living. Profits from their underground businesses enable Lolita and her husband to provide a comfortable life for their children. As they are legal migrants in Italy, their lives have
definitely improved from their modest beginnings.

Lolita and Antonio and three of their children currently live in an apartment near the bus stop where she works. But none of these children are
among the four she left in the Philippines more than a decade ago. Since migrating to Rome, she has given birth to three more children, all of whom she
decided to raise in Italy. The difference in her relationship with her two sets
of children is very stark—Lolita has visited her children in the Philippines
only once. While she could have attached them to her permit to stay as early
as 1990, she has not done so. In fact, her older children in the Philippines
have never met their younger brothers born in Rome.

Do you have children in the Philippines?
Four. We left them with our mother.
Do you miss them?
Yes. We are here sacrificing for them, so that they are able to be edu-
cated. That is why we can bear leaving them in the Philippines. We
sacrifice for the happiness of our children. We had no resources in the
Philippines. If we stayed in the Philippines, we would not have been able
to send our children to school. That is how it was.
I've noticed your children here, so some have been able to follow you?
No, I left four in the Philippines, and three, I gave birth to in Rome. I
have seven children.

Can you talk about your children?
My oldest is seventeen years old. He is a boy. Then there is a fifteen, thirteen, and twelve year old. Here, they are six, three and one and a half years old. [Pauses.]

I was working in houses until 1989, and since then, selling cooked food has been my livelihood.

Stumbling upon her "two sets" arrangement had been a surprise I sought to further probe but in the process repeatedly found myself facing a wall. When I first inquired about her children, Lolita only described them according to age, pausing for quite a long time, as she seemed to contemplate whether she should continue talking about them. In the end, she opted to redirect the interview toward her work experiences, leaving me to conclude that she herself cannot face the contradiction of raising two sets of children. Although she claims to work and struggle, using her own words, "for the happiness of her children," her discomfort and inability to earnestly discuss her relationship with them alluded to feelings of guilt and wrongdoing.

Throughout the interview, I persisted in inquiring about her children, and throughout my questioning she remained cold and mechanical.

Have your children met?
No. But my children in the Philippines have seen my children here in videos that I have sent home. I talk to my children in the Philippines once or twice a month.
Do you miss them?
Yes.
What does it feel like being apart from them?
After being apart for a long time, you stop being lonely. It is because you have to remember that you are here to sacrifice for them. It is important not to think negatively.

Completely avoiding discussions about the emotional strains in her family, Lolita argues that focusing on the "negative aspects of their relationship" would not do them any good and would only be self-defeating. Physical distance seems to foster detachment and emotional distance in the family, a reality that clearly stands out in her statement, "After being apart for a long time, you stop being lonely." Lolita's cold response is quite disturbing, especially if one considers what her children in the Philippines would feel knowing that their mother no longer felt lonely without them.

Although I had inquired about her feelings concerning her children in the Philippines, Lolita redirected the discussion to the material benefits she has been able to provide them, becoming much more comfortable and informative.

> From coming here, I have been able to have a house built in the Philippines. It is fairly small with nine bedrooms, and four bedrooms we rent out to students. It is close to the private school in our town. . . . We use the money paid by the boarders to pay for the utilities and the food. But we also send our children money every month. We send them 400,000 to 500,000 [U.S.$250–333] at the end of the month for their schooling, and during Christmas, we send them 1,000,000 [U.S.$667]. We send them 1,500,000 [U.S.$1000] at the beginning of the school year, when they have to buy school supplies. They need it to buy things.

Through the years, ties with her children in the Philippines have been commodified, based mostly on the monthly remittances she is obligated to send. Moreover, the intimacy between them has been reduced to regular phone calls. The clear lack of intimacy in her family is projected by her conscious containment of discussions about her children to the financial benefits that they have reaped from her earnings in Rome. Even though Lolita continues to financially support them, one can say that in relation to the children in Rome, they have been abandoned in the Philippines.

Lolita seems to lack any knowledge of her children's day-to-day activities, ironically because her responsibilities to her children in Rome prevent her from visiting their siblings left in the Philippines more frequently or even occasionally.

Have you visited them?
Once. It's just once because I have many children here.

When asked about why her children in Rome are not sent to the Philippines—as clearly the option of raising seven children in Rome would be much more difficult and would prevent them from accumulating savings for retirement—Lolita says that she wants them to have the educational opportunities available in Italy, which contrasts quite sharply with all of the other domestic workers I interviewed, for they are all resigned to the segregation of Filipinos in domestic service.

The hope of seeing more opportunities open for her children in Italy is her main reason for deciding to raise some in Rome and others in the Philippines. The possibility for these opportunities to arise, however, is quite slim, while her hopes for them cause great strains in her family. Moreover, if all of her children were raised in the Philippines, she and her husband would probably have visited them more frequently, rather than only once in eleven years. Not surprisingly, Lolita never compares her drastically different ties to her two sets of children.

> I am unable to go home frequently because I have so many children. I have to save every cent I earn for their future. What is important for me is being able to give each one of them land so that when they do get married, they will have a place to have for themselves. So, I don't know when I am going to go home. I plan to stay here as long as my knees are strong.

While Lolita plans to give each of her four children in the Philippines a parcel of land, she plans to send her three children in Italy to college. It seems that all of her children in the Philippines will always remain in the Philippines, while her children in Rome will stay in Rome.

Long after the interview, during one of my many visits to the bus stop, Lolita surprised me when she mentioned her children in the Philippines on her own accord for the very first (and actually only) time.

> My youngest in the Philippines recently told me: "Your children over there in Italy are those you love, they are your real children." It hurts but you know that you are sacrificing here for them. Everyone struggles here.

It saddened me to think that even when directly confronted by her children with their emotional difficulties and pain, she still downplays these tensions and comforts herself with the material benefits she has given them.

LUISA AND LUCIANO BALILA

Following her cousin to Rome, Luisa—the only college graduate in her family—migrated as a single woman in 1981 to assist her parents with the education of her younger siblings. In 1987, she married Luciano, a Filipino domestic worker whom she had met in Rome. During the first few years of their marriage, both Luisa and Luciano worked as live-in domestic workers and maintained a nontraditional nuclear household, seeing each other only on Thursdays and Sundays.

After giving birth to her first son in 1987, Luisa continued to live apart from Luciano and without his assistance struggled to care for their baby while

still having to work as a live-in domestic worker. Juggling two full-time responsibilities had actually been an impossible feat that left her on the verge
of a nervous breakdown.

> After I gave birth to my first son, I had some sort of nervous breakdown
> because the child did not sleep at night. . . . The child would go to sleep
> at four in the morning, and I would have to get up at 6:30 to prepare
> myself because at 7:30, the breakfast of my employer and the children
> had to be prepared. During the day, the baby was still crying and crying.
>
> Towards the end, I myself was so depressed. When the baby started
> crying, I would start crying. Everything I held fell. There came a time
> that even though I was very, very, very hungry, I could not eat because
> even as I held a spoon, my whole body would start shaking. I was very
> exhausted.
>
> My husband, Luciano, lived with his employer, and I lived with mine.
> And his employer was terrible; he wasn't allowed to sleep outside, not
> even once was he allowed to come over and help me. I had to look after
> that kid on my own for twenty-four hours a day, seven days a week, for
> months. When the baby was almost four months old, I went to see a
> doctor because I had lost eight kilos in one month. I looked like a corpse.
> I felt like I was going crazy. When I dropped a glass, I would start cry-
> ing. When Luciano called and I heard his voice, I would start crying. I
> felt hopeless. . . . I was just working and working. I did not have time to
> rest, and I was not eating well.

The demands of domestic work left Luisa physically unable to care for her
child. As a family, they had very limited options, first not being able to live
with each other and second needing the income of Luisa, because both of them
still had financial responsibilities to relatives in the Philippines. Luisa and Luciano did not have relatives on whom they could rely for childcare or financial assistance in Rome.

Literally on the brink of physical collapse, Luisa had no other choice but
to stop working. To finally give her body its much-needed rest and her baby
its proper care, Luisa returned to the Philippines for five months.

> So, I decided to go back to the Philippines. I told Luciano that whether
> he liked it or not, we were going to go home. So, I went to the Philip-
> pines and stayed in the Philippines for five months. I rested. Then I came
> back here and left my baby in the Philippines. Then before the baby was
> two years old, I took him back here.

Luisa realized that in order for Luciano and her to work, they would have to leave their child in the Philippines, where at least her mother and other relatives could provide him with care. But unable to bear the separation from their young child, Luisa and Luciano decided to bring him to Rome within less than a year.

Although with difficulty, Luisa managed to care for their son while keeping a full workload of various "part-time" cleaning jobs to which she took their young son along with her. They were finally able to rent a room in an apartment with other Filipinos and, as Luisa was left doubly tired by having their son with her the whole day, Luciano was often in charge of preparing dinner and other housecleaning chores. However, the birth of their second son after a year ended this manageable arrangement of family work. Now with two children in Rome, Luisa and Luciano found themselves shouldered not only with greater childcare responsibilities but also with more expenses. Hence, they decided it was best to send their infant son back to the Philippines. They could not afford to live solely off the wages of Luciano and, after Luisa's previous experience with their oldest son in Rome, knew that it was impossible for her to work and care for an infant at the same time.

After two years of maintaining a transnational household with two sets of children, Luciano and Luisa decided it would be best if they left both of their children in the Philippines, instead of having the younger one join them in Rome. Their decision was based in part on their past experiences. Both of them would have to work full-time to afford their higher costs of living, but only one of them would be able to do so because of childcare demands. Moreover, the higher living expenses in Rome would only prolong the time that they needed to accumulate the savings required to return to the Philippines. In addition, leaving their children in the Philippines would enable them to provide financial assistance to their extended families. Raising two children in Rome, even if already of school age, was also made less of a viable option by the informal nature of domestic work. Luisa explains:

> What I also experienced was when one of my children got sick, I had to stay at home for twenty days. So, I did not work for twenty days, but before those twenty days were over, the other one got sick. So, I had to excuse myself for another twenty days. Forty days I was in the house without any salary. Our work here as a part-timer is "no work, no pay."

As domestic workers, they do not receive employee benefits that ease the costs of reproduction, such as subsidized day-care facilities, sick leave, or maternal leave. Family and friends in the community usually work full-time and are not able to assist parents with the care of young children. As a result, parents are compelled to leave their children in the Philippines or send them there, where at least they would have the support of a wide kin network.

While her mother takes care of their two young children in the Philippines, Luisa and Luciano work part-time for four and two families, respectively. They are conscious of the physical tolls of a full schedule on each other's bodies and have set up an egalitarian division of labor in which Luciano does more housework because of his lighter workload. Pooling their monthly income of more than 3,000,000 lira (U.S.$2000), Luisa and Luciano rent a room for 600,000 lira (U.S.$400) a month and pay no more than 400,000 lira (U.S.$267) for household expenses. They send 500,000 lira (U.S.$333) to their children in the Philippines, while the rest of their income goes to their savings and property investments in the Philippines.

Luisa and Luciano have modest goals. They hope to build an apartment complex with four units, three of which they would rent out as their source of fixed income once they return to the Philippines. Although still quite tentative, they plan to reunite as a family before their children reach their teenage years. However, they do not plan to wait that long until they see them again. They visit them regularly, especially during life-cycle events like birthdays. Family separation is emotionally difficult for both Luisa and Luciano. They are also aware of the difficulty of separation for their children. As such, they—unlike Lolita Magsino—had been conscious of the detrimental effects that raising two sets of children would have to the child in the Philippines.

> I preferred that both of my kids grow up in the Philippines. . . . To me it's worse for one to be here and one in the Philippines, because then one will have a reason to be jealous of the other. One will think that we care about the other more than we care for him. I don't want one to grow up resenting us.

Luisa is actually one of the very few parents in my sample who is making concrete plans to return to the Philippines in the near future, as she sees return migration as her only option for immediate family reunification.

Besides its material constraints, raising children in Rome is not a viable option due to the lack of mobility for her children.

> I don't want my children to come here. Through observation and in my fifteen years here, I have seen what we "strangers" experience.[8] It's nice to be with your children here, but it is so hard to raise your children

here. It is so hard. They have more opportunities in the Philippines than they do here. If they are here, you can't afford to send them to the university. Universities here are costly and heavy. Vocational courses here like tourism or linguistics or whatever it is, at the end your children come out as domestics after they take these courses. Girl or boy, it's all the same. White-collar job opportunities in Rome are so slim. Maybe it happens to 5 percent of us.

College educated, Luisa and Luciano want their children to aspire to white-collar jobs when they are older. They believe that otherwise the struggle of being domestic workers in Rome will have been for nothing.

Like most other Filipinos whose citizenship is limited to the status of temporary workers, Luisa perceives herself to be a "guest" in Italy—graciously allowed by the state the privilege of earning the greater income its economy can offer—and foresees an inevitable termination of her permit to stay once the state has to give priority to its native workers. Witnessing the heightened anti-immigrant sentiment often discussed in the media, Filipinos predict their sudden mass deportation, a sort of doomsday for temporary migrant workers for which Luisa is prepared.[9]

If they send all of us strangers away from Italy, even though my husband and I don't have much money, we have a house that we can go home to. . . . I want to be able to have a consistent income if we decide to go back to the Philippines. We can rent the apartments out.

Among Filipino migrants in Italy, this common outlook on settlement hinders desires to bring children to Italy.

ADULT CHILD(REN) ABROAD TRANSNATIONAL HOUSEHOLDS

The subcategory of adult child(ren) abroad transnational households is where I place most single domestic workers in Rome and Los Angeles.[10] In the Philippines, adult children carry the responsibility of caring for elderly dependents in the family, sharing and dividing the load with brothers and sisters but with the greater responsibility often falling to single adults without children, particularly women. The identification of this type of household for single adult migrants highlights the deeply instilled cultural value of familism in the Philippines.

Not one of my interviewees has failed to provide financial assistance to their families. While I expected to find strong ties between adult single migrants and parents in the Philippines, I was surprised by the extension of family interdependency to include the financial support of brothers and sisters and their respective families. Most single migrants regularly send remittances to elderly parents. This is reflected in the survey results. Of 105 single women surveyed, 55 send remittances once a month, 28 every two to three months, and 11 occasionally; only 11 do not remit any funds. Of the women who remit monthly, the average amount of remittances is 540,094 lira (U.S.$360). Women who remit every two to three months send on average 733,929 lira (U.S.$489). Moreover, women who remit occasionally send on average 1,000,000 lira (U.S.$667). Fewer of their male counterparts remit funds regularly, and those who do usually send less. Of thirty-two single men surveyed in Rome, only eleven remit funds every month and five every two to three months. Those who remit monthly on average send their families 377,270 lira (U.S.$252), which is significantly less than what women send.

Single women send more because of the greater cultural expectation of daughters to provide for their families. Qualifying these figures, almost all of the female domestic workers whom I interviewed took the responsibility of covering the costs of at least one younger relative's college education, but more often than not they supported at least two relatives through college. Although some send greater remittances than others do and while some limit remittances to life-cycle events or when requested, most send remittances to families in the Philippines regularly. By adopting the role of income-producer for extended families in the Philippines, single adult women such as Valentina Diamante and Maria Batung maintain transnational households in migration. Hence, like most of the single women in my study, they cannot be regarded as single householders.

VALENTINA DIAMANTE

Valentina Diamante is a single domestic worker in her mid-twenties who followed three aunts and three sisters to Rome in 1990. Her migration was made possible by the female migrant network sustained in her family, with one sister financially sponsoring the migration of a younger sister as she comes of age.

In the Philippines, Valentina had only attended a year of college, majoring in hotel management. Not having enjoyed school, she decided that she could better help her parents with the schooling of her younger siblings by following her sisters to Rome.

Valentina is a live-in worker for a divorced Italian mother with two children. She earns a monthly salary of 1,000,000 lira (U.S.$667). True to her intention of coming to Rome to help her family, Valentina sends almost all of what she earns back to the Philippines.

> I send money monthly. It's because the others don't so much because they have their own families. I don't care that I am sending more than them. I think about my family more often than I think about myself. Sometimes, actually most of the time, I send them 1,000,000 lira.

Not left with spending money in most months, Valentina claims that this does not bother her because, as a live-in domestic worker, she has no personal expenses; her employer provides her with food, toiletries, and even clothing. On her day off, she does not even have to pay for public transportation because one of her older sisters picks her up from her employer's house.

Yet it was still surprising to learn that she does not keep some of what she earns for herself.

> That's what my employer told me. She asked me why I don't open a bank account, and I told her that it really is not possible because my sisters and brother are still going to school. Maybe I will start thinking about saving money for myself after one of them graduates. Right now, I have a bank account, but I only have 2000 pesos [U.S.$80] in it. [Laughs.] It's so embarrassing. I didn't want to actually, but my friend forced me to open one. That's my first bank account. I just opened it this year.

While many adult single women do send half of their monthly earnings to the Philippines, Valentina is the extreme example of someone putting her own needs aside for her family.

> I actually spent quite a lot of time with Valentina. She sometimes spent the night at my apartment. One day, when I was visiting her at her employer's home, a letter arrived from the Philippines. Upon reading it, she suddenly became distressed and could not help but comment sarcastically that she always gets a headache when she receives a letter because almost always it is a request for money. I asked to read the letter and found out that her parents were asking for additional funds to pay for the graduation dress of her sister, the costs of her other sister's participation as a muse in a town fiesta, and the party her parents feel obliged to give because of their daughter's role in the fiesta. They wanted at least U.S.$200. Valentina had actually not been upset by having to send them money but was upset over not having the money to send them. As it was the middle of the month, she had already sent them her entire pay of 1,000,000 lira (U.S.$667) fifteen days earlier. I asked her why

she does not get angry since the pressure imposed by her parents seems unfair; the request was not a necessity but honestly seemed frivolous. She explained to me that it is her duty to help them. Besides not needing the money herself, her parents, she explained, had not been the ones to decide to have their daughter, who she tells me is very attractive, participate in the fiesta. They themselves were pressured by the community to join, and it would be an embarrassment for the whole family if they did not throw an elaborate party to celebrate the selection of their daughter to represent the town. The townsfolk, who assume they are rich because of their daughters in Italy, will think badly of what they would perceive as her family's selfishness.

I was stunned that she did not seem resentful and could not believe anyone could be so self-sacrificing. That night, as it was her day off, I jokingly gave her 2000 lira (U.S.$1.30) to bet in the game *jueting*, a small scale lottery run by men in the Filipino community, and told her that maybe she would win the money that she needed to send to her family. Every Thursday and Sunday, one can select two numbers from one to thirty-two and bet 2000 lira, for which one can win around 450,000 lira (U.S.$300). I got into the habit of betting regularly but never won. To my amazement, Valentina won that night. I figured it was due to her good karma for all the sacrifices she has made for her family that finally, while she was able to send her family the money they had requested, she also had some for herself to keep.

MARIA BATUNG

Maria Batung has been working for a Filipino family in the United States for more than twelve years and supports her family in the Philippines with her earnings. In the Philippines, Maria also worked as a domestic worker—a nanny—because without a college degree or appropriate networks she did not have access to other types of employment in Manila. Maria had actually been attending college prior to entering domestic work, but she had to give up her educational aspirations because her parents, whose sole income had been her father's sporadic earnings as a carpenter, could not afford to send her or any of her five brothers and sisters to school.

In Manila, she usually worked for foreigners, mostly diplomats and businessmen. In 1980, ten years after she started working as a domestic helper, Maria accepted the offer of a former employer to move to London with them. Although she could have continued working for the English family, Maria decided, after four years in London, to take up the offer of another former employer, but this time for a job in the United States. Her present employers were migrating to the United States to establish an import-export rattan furniture business in Southern California and, by investing capital in the United States, qualified to bring a small number of employees with them, including Maria. They covered all of her travel expenses and the costs of obtaining legal papers. With their sponsorship, Maria was able to obtain a green card to stay in the United States permanently.

Maria has been very satisfied with her work, earning far more than she ever did in London (U.S.$150 per month), always having a manageable workload, and not having to deal with demanding or strict employers.

> I earn enough so that I could help my family in the Philippines. I get more than $1000 a month and everything is free. They pay for my Social Security and they handled my papers. They pay for my ticket home every year. When I go, they also give me vacation pay for two months. That is why I don't have a problem here. Everything is free, and they also cover my insurance. . . . It is OK. Anytime I want to leave, I can. . . . That is why I lasted long with this family. If that were not the case, I would have probably returned to the Philippines a long time ago.

Of all the employment benefits she receives, the one Maria appreciates the most is her annual vacation—two months' vacation pay and a round-trip ticket to the Philippines—for it affords her time to spend with her father. Very satisfied with her job, Maria plans to work for her employers until she is old herself.

Without personal expenses to cover, Maria sends most of her earnings to her family in the Philippines. She has sent numerous relatives to college, because she wanted to make sure that no one else in her family would have to abandon their studies and "settle" for domestic work as she was forced to do almost thirty years ago.

> *Do you send your relatives money?*
> I send my father money, and my nieces and nephews I equally sent to school. For every single sibling of mine, I sent one of their children to school. So there is no jealousy. The rest they could send to school on their own, but each one of them I sent at least one of their children to school. . . .
>
> So, I am very happy. Although I was not able to finish school, these are the ones that I was able to ensure finished their education. It is hard when you don't finish. I told them that they would have a hard time if they did not have a degree and that it was necessary that they finish school. . . .

Because Maria sends most of her earnings to the Philippines, she has not been able to accumulate any savings, an issue that is not of concern to her. With her legal status, she is secure that she will qualify to receive government aid such as Social Security once she retires.

Maria's earnings do not just cover the college education of younger relatives but also assist her family with their day-to-day living expenses.

> The last time I sent money it was for $500. That is the lowest. It is mostly $1000 or $600 or $700. So I have no savings. My bank is with all those that I sent to school. I also had a house built in the Philippines where my father lives right now. I had that house remodeled and everything. My father was telling me that maybe when I get older I would regret what I did because they would no longer recognize me. But I told him that they can do what they want to do, but I am happy that I was able to help them.

The generosity of Maria is voluntary, and her most satisfying rewards have been the love of her family and their appreciation for her tremendous financial support. While very appreciative of the money and material goods Maria provides them, Maria's relatives also wish that she would soon return and settle down in the Philippines so that they would have the opportunity to transform their relationship to one that is more intimate than the monthly remittances she sends them. A single adult migrant in a transnational family, Maria Batung works in Los Angeles to sustain her family in the Philippines.

The Postindustrial Family: Structural Factors of Transnational Household Formation

Having presented the three types of transnational households found in the Filipino labor diaspora, I now turn to a discussion of the structural and cultural factors that engender their formation. Numerous scholars have challenged the monolithic construct of the family as a "firm, unchanging entity, always similar in shape and content," but instead they posit that the family is a social institution that adopts various strategies in response to external structural, cultural, and ideological forces in society (Thorne, 1992: 6).[11] While there are debates on what constitutes legitimate family forms—usually between conservative advocates of the traditional nuclear family with a breadwinner husband-father and a stay-at-home wife-mother and advocates of more diverse family arrangements, including gay marriages and single-motherhood—my discussion of the family avoids questions of legitimacy and morality.[12] Instead, it focuses on questions of malleability, particularly highlighting the external forces that mold the formation of families into transnational structures.

Shifts in economic arrangements have historically coincided with shifts in family organization. According to sociologist Judith Stacey (1991), the family can be traced historically from premodern to modern to postmodern structures and arrangements. In preindustrial societies, the essential functions of the family—production, reproduction, consumption, socialization—generally remained within its institutional boundaries. Typically encompassing wide kin networks, premodern families maintained economically self-sufficient and land-based agricultural units that produced their own food and clothing (Kessler Harris, 1981; Mintz and Kellog, 1988). The coming of the industrial era in the late eighteenth century transformed household arrangements, although slowly, to the modern family. In contrast to the premodern family, the modern family inhabited a private space—a "haven in a heartless world"; sustained a clear-cut division of labor between the (productive) income-generating father and the (reproductive) nurturing mother; and relied on love as its enduring bond and stronghold (Stacey, 1991; Skolnick, 1991). In further contrast to premodern families, modern households were typically enclosed and mobile nuclear units. In the late twentieth century, contemporary economic transformations, that is, in global restructuring, have led to another shift in household arrangement, this time from the modern to the postmodern family.

According to Stacey (1991), the decline of unionized manufacturing jobs in postindustrialism translates to the breakdown of the family wage system—the backbone of the modern family—and consequently results in the greater dependence of families on the wage earnings of women, the decline of the nuclear family, and the diversification of household forms. Households now encompass varied social arrangements and relations. They include dual wage-earning households, domestic partnerships, single-parent families, and divorced families. Unlike premodern and modern families, the postmodern family is not bound to a definitive model with set characteristics. Instead, the postmodern family is freed of a set standard and embraces the diversity of family forms.

Although yet to be acknowledged in discussions of postmodern families, transnational households are in fact one of the many family arrangements that have subverted modern family norms. Fitting the "two-tier workforce" in the global economy, transnational families include those of low-wage migrant workers and also those of professionals (Reich, 1991). The latter includes "astronaut families" with "parachute kids," for example, children from wealthy families in Asia who are educated in nations with universally recognized educational systems.[13] The ability of wealthy families to freely cross borders distinguishes their transnational families from those of low-wage migrant workers, whose visits with family members are more sporadic. Lack of funds or an undocumented status often times restrain these migrant workers' movements. Strict border regulations also limit the option for dependents to join labor migrants.

What are the structural factors that propel the formation of transnational households among secondary-tier migrant workers in the global economy? Migrants respond to various social and economic realities of globalization, the first of which is the unequal development of regions. While affording their families a comfortable middle-class lifestyle in the sending country, the meager wages of low-paid migrant workers cannot provide a comparable lifestyle in receiving countries. As shown by the decision of Luisa Balila to leave her children behind in the Philippines and the observations of Vicky Diaz on how much more she can purchase in the Philippines with her low wages, the migrant family transcends borders and the spatial boundaries of nation-states to take advantage of the lower costs of reproducing—feeding, housing, clothing, and educating—the family in the Third World. The lesser costs of reproduction in sending countries enable migrant laborers to provide children with greater material benefits, including more comfortable housing as opposed to cramped living quarters forced by high rents in the burgeoning economic centers of global cities. With the formation of transnational households, the migrant family can expedite its goals of accumulating capital. Its spatial organization is in direct response to the forces of global capitalism, as the geographical split of the family coincides with the uneven development of regions and the unequal relations of states in the global economy.

As shown by the concern of Luisa Balila and Judy Reyes over the lack of mobility available to their children in Italy, migrants also form transnational households in response to the fueling of nativism—"neoracism" and xenophobia—in receiving societies.[14] Nativist grassroots organizations (for example, *Lega*, Americans for Immigration Control, Stop the Out-of-Control Problems of Immigration Today) aimed at the further restriction and exclusion of immigration have sprouted throughout the United States and the northern region of Italy (Feagin, 1997).[15] With nativism brewing in the United States and the increasing intolerance of Italians against immigrant laborers, migrant parents may not want to expose their children to the racial tensions and anti-immigrant sentiments fostered by the social and cultural construction of low-wage migrants as undesirable citizens (Ong, 1996).

Finally, migrants turn to transnational households to negotiate over restrictive measures against their integration into the host society. In Italy, the status of Filipino migrants as "guest workers" encourages the maintenance of transnational households: it guarantees continued ties to the "home" country to which they are legally bound to return. In the United States, lawmakers are entertaining the promotion of temporary labor migration and the elimination of certain preference categories for family reunification, including the preference categories for adult children and parents of United States citizens and permanent residents—the trend being to continue the labor provided by migrants but to discontinue support for their reproduction (Chavez, 1997). Many of my interviewees in Los Angeles have actually been caught in the legal bind of either being undocumented, like Vicky Diaz, or obtaining their legal status only after their children had reached adult age, when children are no longer eligible for immediate family reunification. In other words, while they may have wanted to sponsor the migration of children, they have legally been unable to do so.

The formation of transnational households corresponds with the opposite turns of nationalism in globalization. Receiving societies most likely support the formation of transnational households because such households guarantee them the low-wage labor of migrants without the responsibility for their reproduction. By containing the costs of reproduction in sending countries, wages of migrant workers can be kept to a minimum. While receiving countries need the low-wage labor of migrants, they want neither the responsibilities nor costs of the reproduction of these workers. Thus, the formation of transnational households, though a strategy of resistance in globalization, maintains the inequalities of globalization. Receiving countries benefit from the minimized wage demands of a substantial proportion of their workforce. Such economic benefits translate to increased production activities, rendering growth and profits for the higher-tier workers of receiving countries.

Without doubt, the formation of transnational households reinforces the limited integration of low-wage migrant workers. The separation of the migrant family stunts the incorporation of the migrant into the host society with the absence of children whose greater ability to acculturate usually paves the way for integration in settlement (Portes and Rumbaut, 1996). The consideration of the workings of border politics in the transnational household also illustrates how its formation curbs integration. On the one hand, the operation of transnational households transcends territorial borders, with the family acting as a conduit between localized communities in separate nation-states. On the other hand, transcendence does not signify elimination of barriers (such as borders).

Transnational households should not be praised as a small-scale symbol of the migrant's agency against the larger forces of globalization, because their formation marks an enforcement of border control on migrant workers. Transnational households signify segregation. They form because of the segregation of the families of migrant workers in sending countries. Thus, they result from the successful implementation of border control, which makes families unable to reunite. Border control further aggravates the tensions of transnational family life with the difficulty of return migration for undocumented workers. Family separation is consequently prolonged and may even extend to a span of a life cycle. Among my interviewees, for example, the length of separation between mothers and their now adult children extends to as long as sixteen years.

The Preindustrial Value System: Cultural Factors in Transnational Household Formation

Transnational households would not be able to form without the cultural values of mutual obligation and collectivism in the extended family. Filipino transnational households are in fact similar to African American families who migrated from the southern to the northern United States. Their separation, according to Carol Stack and Linda Burton, rests upon the strength of extended family kinship:

> The timing and sequencing of reproduction and migration is such that young adults first have children and then migrate to the North to secure jobs and send money back home. Their young children are left behind in the South to be reared by grandparents or older aunts and uncles. After an extended period of time, the migrating adults return to the South, and, for some, their now young-adult children repeat the cycle—they bear children and migrate North. (1994: 37)

In African American migrant households, extended family interdependency keeps the family intact through the prolonged separation of migrant parents in the North and children in the South. The collectivism found in African American split-households is mirrored in Filipino transnational households.

Despite this fact, transnational households have still come to signify the decline and disintegration of family values and consequently "the destruction of the moral fabric" of Philippine society (Tadiar, 1997: 171). Because they fail to fulfill the ideological notion of a traditional Filipino family, transnational households are considered "broken homes."

Filipino families are traditionally nuclear in structure. Members carry a strong sense of solidarity and obligation to members of their nuclear family and, though to a lesser extent, to their larger kin group inclusive of consanguineal, affinal, and fictive kin (Medina, 1991). The kinship base on which Filipinos may rely is extended by the multilineal and bilateral descent system in the Philippines. Filipinos maintain an equal sense of allegiance to maternal and paternal kin. Moreover, they extend their kinship network by including in their families fictive kin, ones obtained spiritually (for example, *compadrazgo* system of godparenting) or by cross-generational and cousin ties.

Transnational households are considered "broken" for a number of reasons. First, the maintenance of this household diverges from traditional expectations of cohabitation among spouses and children. Second, they do not meet the traditional division of labor in the family, as transnational mothers do not maintain social expectations for women to perform domestic chores. Notably, this expectation still stands despite the high labor force participation of women in the Philippines (Medina, 1991). Third, they move away from traditional practices of socialization in the family. While socialization is expected to come from direct supervision and interaction with parents as well as other adults, the geographic distance in transnational households mars the ability of mothers to provide direct supervision to their children.

Yet, the formation of these households depends on the persisting cultural value of *pakikisama* (mutual cooperation or familism), that is, sentiments of collectivism and mutual obligation among kin. Transnational households would not be able to form and reproduce without the cultural value of *pakikisama* and the mechanisms strengthening such an allegiance, including mutual assistance, consanguineal responsibility, "generalized family exchange networks" (Peterson, 1993), and fosterage. As such, transnational households have come to reveal the resilience of the Filipino family with the advent of globalization.

The operation of transnational households rests upon the strength of mutual assistance among extended kin in the Philippines. In transnational households, the migrant shoulders the responsibility of providing for primary and extended kin by remitting funds regularly. As mentioned, not one of my interviewees has failed to provide financial assistance to their families.

Another mechanism on which transnational families rely is consanguineal responsibility, the extension of responsibility to include parents, siblings, and even nieces and nephews for those without children. The high level of interdependency in extended families of Filipina domestic workers is first illustrated by the tremendous sense of responsibility that they have for extended kin in the Philippines. Many single domestic workers, like Maria Batung, shoulder the financial costs of reproducing the extended family by investing in the education of younger generations. While married domestic workers with children usually only pay for the schooling of their own children, those who had migrated as single women support extended kin prior to marriage. Besides sending remittances to cover the day-to-day living expenses of their parents and other relatives, Pacita Domingo Areza and Letty Xavier, for example, covered the costs of the college education of at least four nieces and nephews before getting married in the United States.

> I sent my sisters to school. . . . One finished a degree in education and the other one in commerce. One only finished high school. . . . Until now, I still help my nieces and nephews. I am sending them to school. With one of my brothers, I am helping him send his two children to college. One just graduated last March, and one has two more years to go. With one of my sisters, she has two children, and she does not have a job, and she is separated from her husband. I help her out—I am helping by paying for their schooling. Once all my nieces and nephews are done with their schooling, I can go back to the Philippines. (Pacita Domingo Areza)

> From the start, when I started working in the Philippines, I have helped my family significantly. My nieces and nephews, I sent them to school. . . . One of the first nephews I sent to school is a civil engineer. . . . The second one is a midwife, and the third one is a teacher. The next two sisters are also in education, and they are all board passers. My dreams have come true through them. Right now, one is in nautical school, and he is going overseas soon. Right now, I have stopped supporting them. Those I sent to school, I want them to be the ones supporting their younger brothers and sisters. They are their responsibilities already. I think I have done my part. (Letty Xavier)

Of thirteen migrant workers who at one point had been single women in Los Angeles, five sent at least three or more nieces and nephews to college. Others have also provided valuable financial support to their families. Besides subsidizing the everyday living expenses of elderly parents, some purchased a house, where their parents and siblings, including those with children, now live, and sent at least one younger relative to college.

Of eighteen women without children in Rome, five had a house built for their families and still subsidize the day-to-day living expenses of their parents. Others send monthly remittances, anywhere between 100,000 and 500,000 lira (U.S.$67 to $333), with those who send less sharing the responsibility of providing for their families with siblings also working outside the Philippines. Finally, most of them have covered the educational costs of the younger generation in their families. Without doubt, these women provide tremendous support to their families. Gloria Diaz of Rome explains that if they do not, they would feel guilty: "When I don't send money, I feel guilty because my mother is alone and it is my obligation to help."

As a consequence of their financial contributions, many migrant Filipina domestic workers claim that they have not been able to accumulate a sizable amount of savings. Ruth Mercado, for example, supports her parents and the family of her brother in the Philippines with the remittances she sends every month.

> I have not been able to save any money at this point (after seven years in Rome). Even though I am the youngest (of four children), I am the breadwinner of my family. I send them 500,000 lira [U.S.$333] every month. Life is hard when you are single. My sisters are married, and so my parents do not expect as much from them. My brother lives with my parents, and he does not have a job but has a lot of children. . . . So, I support his family. . . . At least I am able to help my family. Let's say I continued my career as a policewoman [in the Philippines], my salary would have just been enough for myself. Even though my life is physically demanding and I am far apart from my family, it's OK because I am able to help them.

In acknowledgment of their extensive support, younger members of their extended family often consider them to be second mothers. Nieces and nephews refer to them as "Mama" or "Nanay" (Mom) as opposed to just the customary reference of "Tita" (Aunt). For domestic workers, their financial assistance to the family gives them the most tangible reward for their labor. At the same time, their generosity guarantees them a well-established kinship base if they choose to return to the Philippines. This is premised on the cultural value of *utang na loob*, literally meaning debt of the soul, in which favors are returned with lifelong debt.

The cooperation of sending younger members of the extended family to college also operates on the system of "generalized family exchange" among kin (Peterson, 1993). In such a system, the success of one member of the family translates to the success of the family as a collective unit. Peterson defines this family exchange system to entail an open reciprocal exchange: "Generalized exchanges are those in which A gives to B, B gives to C, C gives to a D, and D gives to an A" (1993: 572). By sending one or more persons to college, domestic workers assume that those they send to school will reciprocate by later supporting the education of their younger siblings and relatives. These younger relatives are then culturally expected to provide care and support for the domestic worker once she chooses to return and retire in the Philippines. For instance, the process of migration in the family of Valentina Diamante functions under the basis of this family exchange system. As the last one in her family to migrate to Rome, Valentina is expected to provide the most financial support to her family in the Philippines.

The high level of interdependency among extended families is also reflected in the reliance of migrant parents on grandparents, aunts, and other relatives for the care of dependents left in the Philippines. In the Philippines, it is not uncommon for families to take in extended family members whose own immediate families may not be able to provide as much material or emotional security. Fosterage of children is in fact a common practice among extended kin in the Philippines (Peterson, 1993). For example, Cecilia Impelido, a street vendor in Rome, was raised by her grandmother for fourteen years. The arrangement, she claims, strengthened kinship ties to her maternal grandmother in the province as it eased the financial costs of reproduction for her parents in Manila. As shown by the dispersal of Judy Reyes's children to various households, transnational families are embedded in the cultural practice of fosterage.

Parents outside of the Philippines rely on other relatives to act as "guardians" of their children. In exchange, remittances sent by parents to dependents in the Philippines benefit other members of the family. Jennifer Jeremillo's remittances to her children in the Philippines extend to benefit her elderly parents.

> Right now, I send 500,000 lira [U.S.$333]. I have to pay for the domestic helper, and then I have a regular allowance for my kids, and then the rest is for my mother. I always send that amount, and that's about 8000 pesos [U.S.$320]; 5000 [U.S.$200] is for my parents. My parents are using the money to renovate and expand the house.

Another example is the transnational family of Cecilia Xavier, who legally resides in the United States with a working visa, but one of whose sons returned to the Philippines because of his undocumented status. Cecilia has not been able to petition for her children because she does not have permanent residency status. Unlike Jennifer Jeremillo in Rome, the caretakers of Cecilia Xavier's son in the Philippines are not in need of her monthly remittances for their daily subsistence. However, the presence of Cecilia's son in their household does benefit them by guaranteeing them a secure source of greatly demanded American goods to sell in their store.

> One of my sons, the eldest [of four], is still in the Philippines. I can no longer petition him because he is over twenty-one years old, and so we decided that he should go back to the Philippines and go to college there. . . . I think he is OK in the Philippines. He really did not want to go back to the Philippines, but at the end, he felt like he had no choice because he really wanted to go to school. So now, he lives with my sister, and he studies biology. I send him money every month, from $100 to $150. That is enough for him because he does not have to pay board and lodging. In exchange, I send my sister things. I send her "American" goods that she can sell in her store. I send boxes of things in exchange for my son's board and lodging.

The reciprocal bond of interdependency between migrant parents and "guardians" keeps the family intact: migrant parents usually rely on female kin—grandmothers, aunts, and other relatives—to care for the children whom they have left behind in the Philippines, while caregiving relatives are more than likely ensured a secure flow of monthly remittances.

Inasmuch as its maintenance is aided by relations with extended kin, transnational households strengthen extended family kinship, with children (and also elderly parents) acting as the enduring bond of interdependency. Migrants rely on extended kin to care for their dependents, while extended kin raise their standard of living with the financial support provided by migrant workers. The extended family bolsters the option of migration for individuals otherwise bound by duties and responsibilities to dependents in the Philippines. Thus, transnational households rely on the resilience of extended family bonds. They form not solely from the limits imposed by the structures of globalization and the manipulation of these structures by migrants. The persisting cultural value of familism assists with the formation of transnational households as much as the structural forces of globalization propel it.

Conclusion

To rephrase the question posed by Basch et al. (1994), are transnational families an epiphenomenon of immigration or a transgenerational process? They respond that it is likely that transnationalism will "continue as an arena of social relations" and will remain an intergenerational process "as long as conditions in both (sending and receiving countries) remain insecure and the flow of migration to the U.S. is unimpeded" (1994: 242–43). In the Philippines, the burgeoning number of transnational families corresponds with the steady increase of emigration that the country has witnessed in the last twenty years. The government hopes to curtail this trend with the implementation of "Philippines 2000," an economic strategy of rapid economic growth patterned after the "newly industrialized countries" of Asia (for example, Korea and Taiwan), which have manufacturing-based economies that are dependent on the heavy penetration of foreign investment.

As seen with the case of Mexico, the heavy injection of capital into an economy does not guarantee a "less subservient position in the global economy," nor does it decrease the flow of migration (Burbach et al., 1997: 8). Due to the formation of social networks, migration flows usually continue even after the erosion of their initial causes. Networks maintain the continued flow of migration with the deployment of information and resources. Like social networks, transnational households act as conduits of information. Hence, as transnational households promote the continued outflow of workers, they subsequently promote their further constitution as a strategy of household maintenance. In other words, their formation is a self-perpetuating cycle, one that can only be broken with a drastic improvement in the Philippine economy.

Although most Filipino domestic workers hope that they have not initiated a transgenerational process of migration, in some cases second-generation transnational households have formed with the migration of the now adult children of transnational parents, sometimes to a different country altogether. Migration does not necessarily provide tremendous economic security to the family. Transnational families often cannot discontinue nor decrease their dependence on foreign earnings. Because migrant parents invest most of their earnings in the family's day-to-day expenses, they are unable to invest in income-generating resources (for example, small businesses). Without a sufficient means of productive labor in the Philippines, migrant parents prolong their tenure abroad. The cycle continues across generations, as the earnings of the now adult children with college degrees cannot cover the costs of reproducing their own families. With forces beyond the control of the individual migrant, the economic insecurities resulting from globalization in the Philippine economy produce transnational families.

The question then is, How long do families undergo the pain of transnationalism? In *Gendered Transitions*, Hondagneu-Sotelo (1994) notes that the duration of separation had been significantly longer for earlier Mexican migrants but has shortened to two years or less among families migrating since the 1980s. In contrast, the duration of separation among migrant Filipina domestic workers extends to more than two years for most families, usually encompassing the entire duration of settlement. In my sample, parents with legal documents return to the Philippines sporadically. Visits to children often occur every four years for a period of two months. Migrant Filipina domestic workers attribute the infrequency of their return to the high costs of airfare and to the fact that they cannot afford to take time off work because of the dependence of their families on their monthly income. In addition, the fear of losing their jobs prevents them from visiting their families for an extended period. As they are limited to short visits to the Philippines, traveling becomes an excessive expense of funds that could otherwise be used on meeting the costs of reproducing the family.

In summary, the vignettes that I have featured illustrate that transnational families are creative responses to and adaptive strategies against the economic displacement of workers in developing countries. These vignettes show that the family is a complex social institution, a malleable and flexible institution that variably responds to external and internal pressures. Household arrangements are determined by multiple factors, including material needs, ideological norms, cultural beliefs, and collective and individual interests.

Yet the various forms of transnational households that I have illustrated do not only reveal the agency and resistance of migrants against structural forces in society but also point to an emotional dislocation that they undergo in migration. Transnational families are agonizing for both parents and children. To some extent, geographical distance unavoidably engenders emotional distance and strains among members of transnational families. Separation instills emotional injuries with which family members must cope in their everyday lives. This is a particular dislocation that should be acknowledged as part and parcel of the migrant experience of Filipina domestic workers, one acknowledged by an analysis of migration from the level of the subject and one that I will address more systematically in the next chapter.

CHAPTER 5

Intergenerational and Gender Relations in Transnational Families

Changes in household structure have significant impacts on the personal lives of migrant workers as well as on the relatives whom they have left behind in the Philippines. In the previous chapter, I established the salience of transnational households in the diaspora. My discussion touched upon the dislocation of the pain of family separation. In this chapter, I address the effects of this dislocation on migrant Filipina domestic workers and their children.

Without doubt, mothering from a distance has painful emotional ramifications both for mothers who leave and children who are sent back or left behind. The pain of family separation creates various feelings, including helplessness, regret, and guilt for mothers, and loneliness, vulnerability, and insecurity for children. Though already illustrated in the vignettes featured in the previous chapter, these emotions still beg to be understood systematically. As Hochschild (1983) has shown, emotions do not exist in a vacuum. Instead, they operate within the context of social structures. "Emotion is a sense that tells about the self-relevance of reality. We infer from it what we must have wanted or expected or how we must have been perceiving the world. Emotion is one way to discover a buried perspective on matters" (Hochschild, 1983: 85). Regulated by "feeling rules," emotions are determined by ideologies, and in the Filipino family, like in many other families, the ideology of woman as nurturer is a central determinant of the emotional needs and expectations of its members (Medina, 1991). If so, how are the feelings of mothers and children regarding separation influenced by gender ideologies of mothering?

In this chapter, I systematically address the emotional difficulties confronted by mothers and children in transnational households and examine the means by which mothers negotiate the dislocation of the pain of family separation. In doing so, I analyze the social reproduction of families, emphasizing the different social roles of mothers and fathers as well as the different positions of children and parents in transnational households. As sociologist Barrie Thorne states, "the specifics of daily life . . . cannot be adequately understood without systematic attention to underlying structures of gender and age" (1992: 14). In my discussion, I establish that socialized gender norms aggravate the emotional strains of transnational family life.

Transnational Family Reproduction

In parenting, there are three main forms of care expected to ensure the reproduction of the family: (1) moral care, meaning the provision of discipline and socialization to ensure that dependents are raised to be "good" moral citizens of society; (2) emotional care, meaning the provision of emotional security through the expression of concern and feelings of warmth and affection; and (3) material care, meaning the provision of the physical needs of dependents, including food, clothing, and education or skills-training to guarantee that they become producers for the family. Expectations of moral, emotional, or material care vary considerably in different societies and cultures. Ideological norms, particularly gender ideology, and the location of families in the political economy undeniably determine the abilities and expectations of parents toward the family's social reproduction.

In the Philippines, the family provides the material, emotional, and moral needs of its members, with limited intervention from the state.[1] Moral expectations are greatly influenced by the values and virtues of Catholicism (for example, honesty, faith, purity) and a high regard for filial piety—the respect for parents and elders in the community. Relations in the family are based on the cultural construct of *utang na loob*, and because the gift of life is irreplaceable, children are born with an irreplaceable debt and burden of gratitude to their parents.

In transnational households, are parents able to provide all three basic forms of care? They may be able to with the support provided by extended kin. Extended kin may, for example, assure the provision of moral care in transnational households. In a study of the effects of parental absence on migrant workers' children, Victoria Paz Cruz of the Scalabrini Migrant Center—in a survey of 212 high school and college students with international migrant parents and 90 with internal migrant parents living elsewhere in the Philippines—found in supplementary data from their teachers that "the great majority of the students in the sample (92.4%) have no special problem which has come to the attention of the guidance counselor or other school official(s)" (1987: 22). In a survey of "solo-parents" and guardians, Paz Cruz also found that children tend to get along better with their siblings, still respect their parents and guardians, continue to practice their religion, and have not shown any health problems (for instance, drastic change in energy level, weight, and appetite). Without doubt, the continued respect for elders and religious devotion among children indicates that extended kin instill strong moral values and traditions in transnational households.

In contrast, one can easily imagine that the provision of basic emotional care in the family is somewhat inadequate, considering that the emotional support provided by other relatives may not completely replace that of parents. This is shown by the needs of the children of Ruby Mercado, who states:

> When I saw my children, I thought that "Oh, children do grow up even without their mother." I left my youngest when she was only five years old. She was already nine when I saw her again, but she still wanted for me to carry her. [Weeps.] That hurt me because it showed me that my children missed out [on] a lot. They did not get enough loving from their parents, the loving they needed as they were growing up.

This example suggests that while parenting can be transferred to other relatives (Stack and Burton, 1994), the emotional care they provide might not be completely interchangeable with that of a parent. However, the absence of health and psychological problems among children does suggest that emotional care is also subsidized by the tremendous resource of extended kin acting as fictive mothers and fathers. Finally, with the third form of care, the increased income of transnational laborers surely provides families a greater amount of material security.

In general, it is very difficult to imagine a family whose members reside in different time zones and across vast geographical distances. It is even more difficult to imagine the reproduction of families in which children grow up with absentee parents. Standard conceptions of the family bring forth ideas of physical, mental, and emotional intimacy. As Arlene Skolnick comments: "The family is a place of enduring bonds and fragile relationships, of the deepest love and the most intractable conflicts, of the most intense passions and the routine tedium of everyday life. It is a shelter from the workings of a harsh economy, and it is battered by forces beyond its control" (1991: xvi). This poignant description of the family very much applies to those in the

Philippines, where transnational households are considered "abnormal," perceived as "broken homes," and thereby viewed as a tragedy in migrant communities and Philippine society.

The question then is why is this the case considering that traditional family values, particularly the collectivism instilled by *pakikisama*, is a foundational backbone for the formation of such families. To address this question, I now turn to a discussion of the pain engendered in the transnational family, presenting the perspectives of both mothers and children and highlighting the underlying gender ideologies that determine and control their feelings and emotions. My discussion shows that the reconstitution of mothering that has been forged by migrant Filipina domestic workers upon migration is stalled and made difficult to accept by traditional ideologies of family life.

The Pain of Transnational Parenting

> When the girl that I take care of calls her mother "Mama," my heart jumps all the time because my children also call me "Mama." I feel the gap caused by our physical separation especially in the morning, when I pack (her) lunch, because that's what I used to do for my children. . . . I used to do that very same thing for them. I begin thinking that at this hour I should be taking care of my very own children and not someone else's, someone who is not related to me in any way, shape, or form. Don't we think about that often? Oh, you don't, but we—the Filipino women over here—feel that all the time. The work that I do here is done for my family, but the problem is they are not close to me but are far away in the Philippines. Sometimes, you feel the separation and you start to cry. Some days, I just start crying while I am sweeping the floor because I am thinking about my children in the Philippines. Sometimes, when I receive a letter from my children telling me that they are sick, I look up out the window and ask the Lord to look after them and make sure they get better even without me around to care after them. [Starts crying.] *If I had wings, I would fly home to my children. Just for a moment, to see my children and take care of their needs, help them, then fly back over here to continue my work.* (Rosemarie Samaniego, widow, Rome; my emphasis)

Migrant Filipina domestic workers such as Rosemarie Samaniego are overwhelmed by feelings of helplessness: they are trapped in the painful contradiction of feeling "the gap caused by physical separation" and having to give in to the family's dependence on the material rewards granted by this separation. While they may long to return to the Philippines to be with their children, they cannot because of their family's dependence on their earnings. Emotional strains of transnational parenting include feelings of anxiety, help-lessness, loss, guilt, and loneliness.

Domestic work, borrowing the words of historian Jacqueline Jones (1985), is both a "labor of love" and a "labor of sorrow." Often saying that their sole motivating force for seeking domestic work is their love for their children (while ironically being away from these same children), migrant mothers seek every opportunity to maximize their earnings in order to send more money to dependents in the Philippines. Describing her situation, Clarita Sungkay— who sends her children at least U.S.$500 every month—states:

> My husband has a new family of his own. He has two children, I think.
> I actually went to their house when I found out that he had sold our
> house. There I found my two daughters working for them as baby-
> sitters. He was basically abusing my children. I cried. I felt terrible, but
> what could I do? I wasn't going to try to kill myself again because if I
> did that then nothing would happen to my family. . . . Now my two
> daughters live in their own apartment, which I pay for every month.
> Seeing them made me decide that I could not stop. If I stopped, yes, we
> would be together, but we would have nothing. We wouldn't have a
> steady income, and life [would] be very hard. We could be together in
> the Philippines, but we would not have any money. At least they now
> have families of their own. The youngest is the only one not married,
> but if we were together, what could we live off? They tell me that they
> want us to finally be together, but it's hard.

Like many other Filipina domestic workers, Clarita has worked outside the Philippines for most of her children's adolescence. Therefore, domestic ser-vice can also be aptly described as a "labor of sorrow." It is a labor of grief that comes from having to knowingly repress the longing to reunite the family be-cause of economic instabilities in the Philippines.

Besides the pain of helplessness, transnational parenting also involves overwhelming feelings of loss. For missing the growing years of children, many mothers are remorseful and admit to lost intimacy in the transna-tional family. In general, a surreal timelessness is felt during family separa-tion, and many mothers are suddenly catapulted back to reality the moment they reunite with their children.

> When I came home, my daughters were teenagers already. [Starts cry-
> ing.] When I saw my family, I dropped my bag and asked who were my

daughters. I did not know who they were, but they just kept on screaming "Inay, Inay!" [Mom, Mom!] I asked them who was which, and they
said, "I'm Sally and I'm Sandra." We were crying. I did not know who
was which. Imagine! But they were so small when I left, and there they
were as teenagers. [Weeps.] They kept on saying "Inay, Inay!" (Ermie
Contado, widow, Rome)

Maintaining transnational households is quite agonizing for migrant parents.
For them, missing their children's adolescence is an insurmountable loss,
which sadly turns into a deep-seated regret over the emotional distance it has
caused the family. As Ana Vengco, a single mother working in Rome for almost three years, explains, the small pleasures and familiarities obtained by
watching children grow up are irreplaceable.

I really, really miss my daughter. I really regret not being able to see
my daughter grow up, learn her hang ups, how she learned to brush her
teeth, walk. . . . I left my daughter when she was not even one year old
and now she is already three years old.

In transnational households, the absence of daily interactions denies familiarity and becomes an irreparable gap defining parent-child relations.

Transnational parenting also entails loneliness over the denial of intimacy.
Migrant mothers often battle with the grief imposed by constant reminders
of their children and the emotional distance engendered by unfamiliarity.

Whenever I receive a letter and I hear that one of my children is sick, oh
but I can't function for a week, and it's like I am also the one who is sick.
That's how I feel whenever I hear news that my children are sick. My
employer even predicts when I receive a letter that by the next day I will
be sick. It's true, and my employer knows it. (Gelli Padit, married, Rome)

My kids are still very young so they still don't know about my life
here. . . . They often ask my husband where I am and wonder why they
have not seen me yet, especially the youngest child of mine, the one
who was born here. What I really want is to be able to get papers, because I really want to see my children. . . . I always think about my children. I always worry about not sending them enough money. . . . Sometimes when I look at the children that I care for, I feel like crying. I
always think about how if we did not need the money, we would all be
together, and I would be raising my children myself. . . . That's what is
really hard about life here, being away from one's own family. Without

your family, you are just so much more vulnerable. (Analin Mahusay, married, Rome)

Without doubt, family separation aggravates the hardships of migrant life, highlighting the helplessness brought by the material constraints that enforce the formation of transnational households.

The pain of family separation is further intensified by caregiving tasks in domestic work. Taking care of children is not just taking care of children when, in the process of doing so, one cannot take care of one's own family. This contradiction accentuates the pain of domestic work and consequently results in an aversion to this job. As Ruby Mercado states, "Domestic work is depressing . . . . You especially miss your children. I do not like taking care of other children when I could not take care of my own. It hurts too much." Yet others find themselves resolving this tension by "pouring (their) love" to their wards, including Trinidad Borromeo, who states, "When I take care of an elderly, I treat her like she is my own mother." In doing so, they are able to feel less guilty for leaving behind their families in the Philippines.

With feelings of loss and loneliness filling their day-to-day migrant experience, how do mothers strategically negotiate the pain of family separation? I found that they do so in three key ways: the commodification of love, the repression of emotional strains, and the rationalization of distance by either justifying that the material gains provided by transnational households far outweigh their emotional costs to the family or by reasoning that physical distance is a manageable challenge; that is, regular communication eases distance.[2] In general, individual women use all three coping mechanisms, although not always consciously. For the most part, mothers justify their decision to leave children in the Philippines by highlighting the markedly visible material gains of the family. For example, Vicky Diaz and Lolita Magsino repeatedly did so during the interview. Mothers also struggle to maintain a semblance of family life by rationalizing distance. Judy Reyes and Luisa Balila—mothers featured in the vignettes in the previous chapter—phone their children in the Philippines regularly. While a few women explicitly deny the emotional strains experienced by their children, most women do acknowledge the emotional difficulties that they themselves feel regarding transnational mothering. Still, many of them repress these emotional difficulties.

How is love shown and given across vast geographical distances? In the field, I often heard women say, "I buy everything that my children need" or "I give them everything they want." They knowingly or unknowingly have the urge to overcompensate their absence with material goods, including Ruby Mercado who states:

> All the things that my children needed I gave to them and even more, because I know that I have not fulfilled my motherly duties completely. Because we were apart [since 1983], there have been needs that I have not met. I try to hide that gap by giving them all the material things that they desire and want. I feel guilty because as a mother I have not been able to care for their daily needs. So, because I am lacking in giving them maternal love, I fill that gap with many material goods. I buy them clothes, shoes; when they say they want a computer, I tell them to go ahead and buy one. They don't demand too much but often just ask for things that they may need.

Unable to provide their children with daily acts of care, transnational mothers such as Ruby tend to rely on commodities to establish concrete ties of familial dependency.

Without doubt, transnational mothers have regrets over separation, but they are able to withstand this hardship with the financial gains that they have achieved in migration.

> I have been lonely here. I have thought about the Philippines while I am scrubbing and mopping that floor. You cannot help but ask yourself what are you doing here scrubbing and being apart from your family. Then, you think about the money and know that you have no choice but to be here. (Incarnacion Molina, separated, Rome)

Working abroad guarantees mothers such as Incarnacion the financial resources that they need to ensure that their children eat daily meals of meat and rice instead of "dried fish" or "fried stale bread with sugar," attend college, and reside in their own home as opposed to a relative's.

Though many migrant laborers outside the Philippines attained some years of postsecondary education, they had not been able to achieve a secure middle-class lifestyle in the Philippines. So why do they bother to invest in their children's college education? Why not just have them work outside the country? The education of children is a marker of material security for migrant parents. Clearly, education is a central motivating factor for migration. As one domestic worker states, *"The intelligence of my children would be wasted if they don't attain a college degree;* that's why I made up my mind and I prayed a lot *that I [might] have a chance to go abroad for the sake of my children's education"* (Acgaoili, 1995: 14; italicized words translated from

Tagalog to English). Parents believe that the more educated children there are in their family, the greater the family's resources and the lesser dependence of its members on each other, which means that there would be less of a need for one to seek the higher wages of domestic work outside the Philippines in order to support other members of the family.

By operating under this mind-set, parents can rationalize the need to sacrifice intimate familial bonds for the collective family's material well-being. However, parents do know that they owe children a great deal of emotional work. Yet instead of paying children for their emotional debt with more time together, they purchase love with American or Italian designer clothing and school supplies. They equate love with monthly remittances. Parents weigh the pros and cons of transnational parenting and systematically conclude that the material benefits of their earnings compensate for the emotional costs inflicted in separation.

> My children understand our situation. Before, they could not understand life, what was going on, but now they understand why I was here and there. They know it was for financial reasons. [Starts crying.] They were studying, but you know . . . the guidance of the mother is different from the guidance of the aunties. They missed out in a way not having parents around. I suffered, but to me it was more important that they did not suffer the way I did. I did not want them to do the work that I had to do because I only had a high school education. I don't want them to live not being able to have what they want because the financial situation is not enough. (Maya Areza, separated, Los Angeles)

> After I had four children, I was teaching. But the money that I made as [a] teacher was not enough. Number one, there the children need education, clothing, and food. My salary was really not enough. That is why I decided to come here. . . . I used to send my children $1000 a month, but I stopped sending money when they all graduated from college three years ago. Now I send them $500 once in a while, and they divide that amongst themselves. . . . You ask yourself why you left your children, and then you think about their future so that you can be strong [that is, to withstand the geographical distance]. So, I have regrets but no regrets. . . . You [ask yourself] why you left them, but then you think that if you did not leave them, they would not have a future. My only real regret is leaving the youngest when she was still young. (Joy Manlapit, widow, Los Angeles)

Besides highlighting the material gains that they have achieved in sacrifice of family intimacy, migrant mothers also cope with the pain of family separation by repressing their emotions and rationalizing distance.

Many women spoke in a detached manner when directly asked about their thoughts and feelings over family separation. They avoided having to confront their feelings, consciously underplayed the emotional gaps caused by prolonged separation, and through it all emphasized the material gains that the family now enjoys, plus their ability to communicate from a distance.

> It is just like shutting one part of yourself and going to another place in your life, which is just temporary anyway. [Pauses.] If you think about it, you have more to gain. You have much to lose but so much more to gain. . . . You are only here for a short time and at least you can communicate. There are letters, and I make long distance calls every week. (Mimi Baclayon, married, Los Angeles)

> *Do you miss your children?*
> Of course. (Pauses.) It is hard but when you think about how much you are earning, you forget the loneliness. You can also call them on the phone. (Mila Tizon, married, Los Angeles)

> I miss my children of course but I am tranquil because I know that I am doing what God has set out for me to do. So, I know that God is extending his love to them. I have the assurance that how God takes care of me, he takes even more care of my children. . . . We usually call my children monthly. Then, we call them on their birthdays. We also communicate by letter. They do the same. (Tessie Mandin, married, Rome)

Despite their tendency to downplay the emotional tensions of transnational family life, these migrant mothers cannot completely deny the intimacy that they lose in migration. Hence, they struggle to amend this loss by regularly keeping in contact with their children in the Philippines. Not one of my interviewees, however, claims that their family achieves intimacy from such efforts. Instead, they recognize the limits in such forms of communication.

Nonetheless, migrant mothers do still try to convey love, affection, and care from a distance. They create "bridges" that compress the space that plagues their family relationships. As a writer in *Tinig Filipino* states:

> If our relationship with our loved-ones is on the stage of collapse, let's try our best to save it. If it is still possible. Let's try to construct a bridge for others to reach us—a bridge which is not a structure made of steel

or concrete, but one whose foundation has its maximum strength where no storm or any other natural calamities nor human forces could destroy. (Balangatan, 1994: 10)

Viewing physical separation as just one of the many challenges of contemporary family life, parents compress time and space and alleviate the physical distance in the transnational family by phoning or writing letters (Hondagneu-Sotelo and Avila, 1997). In the process, they keep abreast of the activities of their children and at the same time achieve a certain level of familiarity in the family. As Patricia Baclayon of Los Angeles comments, "There is nothing wrong with our relationship. I pay a lot for the phone bill. Last month, I paid $170, and that's two days of wages. They write too. Last week, I received four letters."

Ironically, the rationalization of distance, while reassuring for parents, could be stifling for children in the Philippines. Reassured by the familiarity that they achieve in "time-space compression," parents are more likely to consider prolonging separation. However, as feminist geographer Doreen Massey has elucidated, the "power geometry" in the process of "time-space compression" creates distinct experiences in the rationalization of distance.

This point concerns not merely the issue of who moves and who doesn't, although that is an important element of it; it is also about power in relation to the flows and the movement. Different social groups [in this case parents and children] have distinct relationships to this anyway differentiated mobility: some people are more in charge of it than others; some initiate flows and movement, others don't; some are more on the receiving-end of it than others; some are effectively imprisoned by it. (1994: 149)

In transnational families, power clearly lies with the parent, in particular the migrant parent. The process of "time-space compression" is unidirectional, with children at the receiving end. Migrant parents initiate calls and children receive them. Migrant parents remit money to children physically immobilized in the Philippines. They are trapped as "time-space compression" convinces parents that they have maintained close-knit ties through separation and allows parents to leave children waiting even longer.

Regardless of whether they successfully rationalize the geographical distance that characterizes their family life, why do some mothers repress the feelings of pain invoked in separation? Why do some downplay the emotional distance in the transnational family? Considering that larger structural forces of globalization constrain their ability to reunite the family, they sometimes cannot afford to confront their feelings. For the most part, the structural constraints that limit their options for raising their children do not allow for the confrontation of the emotional distance that plagues their intergenerational relationships. As Dorothy Espiritu—a domestic worker in Los Angeles who left her now adult children at the ages of nine to eighteen— explains, lingering over the painful sacrifice of separation only intensifies the emotional hardships of transnational family life:

> *Has it been difficult not seeing your children for twelve years?*
> If you say it is hard, it is hard. You could easily be overwhelmed by the loneliness you feel as a mother, but then you have to have the foresight to overcome that. Without the foresight for the future of your children, then you have a harder time. If I had not had the foresight, my children would not be as secure as they are now. They would not have had a chance. [Pauses.] What I did was I put the loneliness aside. I put every-thing aside. I put the sacrifice aside. Everything. Now, I am happy that all of them have completed college.

Many parents are like Dorothy, as they can only tolerate their family's geo-graphical distance by consciously, but more often unconsciously, repressing its emotional costs.

Emphasizing one's own suffering also helps parents cope with transna-tional parenting. An example is the case of Joy Manlapit of Los Angeles.

> *Is it difficult not seeing your children for a long time [ten years]?*
> It is hard on my heart to be away from my family. At first I could never resolve being apart from my children, but my friend told me that they are older now. They have all finished college, so that's it. . . . They got married. They got married—the second and third got married before they finished college. That was another burden. You have to make them finish school, then you have to make their spouses finish. Yeah, you have grandchildren, and you have to support them too. Because you are here, they think that you have a lot of money. Because they think of how much you earn and calculate it in pesos. They do not realize that you eat, sleep, and do everything in dollars as well. That is where they are wrong. They write and ask for money. You are angry, but then you are also concerned. You get mad because when they write they don't say "Mama, thanks for everything." Instead, they say "Mom, this is what else I need." [Laughs sarcastically.] I need this, I need that. They don't

bother asking you how you are, how you make a living, what you have to do to send them that money. Nothing.

To justify—mainly to themselves—their decision to maintain transnational households, transnational mothers suppress any ill-feelings or fears that their absence possibly imposes on their children and convince themselves that such a household is the best option for raising children and is equally—if not more—oppressive for them as unappreciated parents.

I also observed this attitude in the field. While attending a standard Sunday mass in Rome, I had only been paying attention half-heartedly to the ceremony that I already knew by heart due to my Catholic upbringing. However, I was suddenly caught off guard during the Responsorial Psalms, the part in which churchgoers pray collectively with the response, "Lord hear our prayers," when the woman deacon stated, "So that our families we have left in the Philippines understand our hardships and that they learn to be frugal." What struck me about this blessing was not its confirmation of the presence of transnational households in the community but instead its illumination of the migrant worker's perspective on the issue of family separation: it clearly centers on material benefits and the hardships that they personally undergo. Instead of praying for the safety and emotional security of family members, especially young children far apart from them, migrant workers worry that their families in the Philippines are neither spending their hard-earned money wisely nor appreciative of the sacrifices that they have made for the sake of the family.

Although most of my interviewees do recognize the "trauma" of children and the need to consciously weigh it against the material gains of transnational family life, some completely deny the emotional costs of separation. Not surprisingly, it had primarily been parents whose children are located in both the Philippines and abroad who preferred not to discuss intergenerational relationships. For example, after providing rich and descriptive anecdotes about her experiences migrating to and working in Rome, Incarnacion Molina—who has a new-born son in Italy and twelve- and fifteen-year-old daughters in the Philippines—transformed completely, suddenly becoming evasive, when prodded about her relationship with the daughters she has not seen for more than five years.

> *Do they know that you have another child here?*
> In a letter, I told them that I was pregnant. [Pauses.]
> *Did they respond?*

Yes. They said that what is done is done, so what could they do about it.
[Pauses.]
Are they jealous?
Of course they are. They can't help but know that my devotion will be
divided. [Pauses.]
Are they upset?
Probably.
Do you want your children to come over here?
Maybe.

Incarnacion's short responses and long pauses emanate from her discomfort. Uncomfortable with the jealousy incited by the birth of her son, Incarnacion admits that she "cannot afford to think about it" when questioned
about her feelings concerning her two sets of children. Becoming very
guarded for the rest of the interview, Incarnacion could not confront the effects of separation on her daughters, an issue she would rather have discussed
within the limits of the U.S.$600 monthly remittance that financially ties
them together.

In a similar vein, Jovita Gacutan—a domestic worker in Los Angeles
with children in both the United States and the Philippines—would rather
have not discussed her relationship with the youngest child she left in the
Philippines.

How old was your youngest child when you left the Philippines?
Thirteen years old. It was very hard leaving him.
How is your relationship?
I have been back four times.
Do you think he has some resentment?
I don't think so.
Do you think it is hard for him?
Ummm. . . .
Do you talk about it?
That is why I want to go back home.
What does he tell you?
Nothing really. ,
Do you feel less close to him than your older children?
No, no! I have been home four times, and I would stay there for two to
three months.
Do you plan to petition him to the U.S.?

No, I cannot. He is too old. He has to be younger than eighteen. I have
not applied for citizenship yet.
What are your plans?
I have no plans right now. I really don't know.

Besides giving the vaguest responses, Jovita became agitated when probed
about her son. Moreover, she vehemently denies even the slight possibility
of an emotional rift developing in her family. Like Incarnacion Molina in
Rome, Jovita struggles to rationalize her relationship with her youngest son
in the Philippines, a relationship that cannot be placed outside the context of
its different dynamics than with those children residing with her. For Incarnacion and Jovita, the different relationships that they have developed and
maintained with their two sets of children are inexplicable, transforming
into a grief that they are unwilling or unable to confront.

While the majority of the mothers in my study have left young children
in the Philippines, three women in Los Angeles stand out for having chosen
not to migrate until their children were much older. As parents, they believe
that the emotional gaps caused by separation would have been too great a
risk to impose on the family. Libertad Sobredo of Los Angeles explains:

> In the early 80s, my sister had already invited me to join her in the
> United States. My children were still young then and I told my sister
> that I could not afford to leave them. I could not turn my back on my
> children. Money can be earned anywhere, but if your children grow up
> undisciplined and neglected, they might grow up to be good but they
> might also grow up to be bad. If that happens, then that would be your
> fault as a parent. *Taking care of children is primarily the mother's role.
> The father is the person who is supposed to leave and make a living. He
> only comes home at night, but mothers are needed to always be there
> for their children.* . . . It came time [when] my children were older. I
> figured my youngest was twenty years old. My small business could be
> managed by my children and husband on their own. I thought it was
> the right time for me to come here. (my emphasis)

Signficantly, it is the gender ideology of motherhood that had delayed the
migration of a small number of women in my study, which in turn underscores the fact that most women had not felt constrained by gender norms
in the Philippines. Instead, most women made a conscious decision to escape them.

From the commodification of love to the "technological" management of distance, mothers find reasons to justify family separation and obscure the emotional costs of transnational parenting. Because reuniting the family means compromising its material security, they cannot afford to confront the emotional strains that threaten family relations nor dwell on emotional tensions only to exacerbate them. Although they ease the spatial barriers imposed on intimacy with postmodern communication, most parents do admit that technology cannot replace the intimacy that only a great investment in time and daily interactions can provide the family. Even so, they believe that the material benefits provided by transnational households abate any deficiencies in emotional bonds. As a result, they are able to extend the duration of family separation.

The Pain of Growing Up in Transnational Families

Regardless of household structure, whether it is nuclear, single-parent, or transnational, intergenerational conflicts frequently arise in the family. As many feminist scholars have argued, the family is not a collective unit. Instead, the family represents an institution with conflicting interests, priorities, and concerns for its members (Thorne, 1992). In transnational households, intergenerational conflicts are engendered by the emotional strains of family life. In this section, I illustrate the emotional strains experienced by the children left behind in the Philippines.[3]

Separation is equally agonizing for transnational mothers and children. Children, I found, are racked with loneliness, insecurity, and vulnerability. They also crave greater intimacy with their migrant parents. For example, the children in Paz Cruz's (1987) survey offer several reasons for their desire to reunite with their migrant parents: "I want them to share with us in our daily life, and I want our family to be complete"; "So that they will be there when we need them"; "We can share our laughters and tears"; and "I miss him/her a lot" (43). Denied the intimacy of everyday interactions in the family, children struggle to understand the motives behind their mother's decision to raise them from a distance. However, they do not necessarily do so successfully.

Three central conflicts plague intergenerational relationships between migrant mothers and the children whom they have left behind in the Philippines. First, children disagree with their mothers that commodities are sufficient markers of love. Second, they do not believe that their mothers recognize the sacrifices that they as children have made toward the successful mainte-nance of their families. Finally, while they appreciate the efforts of migrant mothers to create "bridges" of affection and care, they still question the ex-tent of these efforts. They particularly question mothers about their sporadic visits to the Philippines. As I noted, most of the documented migrants whom I interviewed return to the Philippines infrequently, once every four years.

For the most part, children recognize the material gains provided by sep-aration. Paz Cruz's (1987) survey indicates that about 60 percent of the chil-dren do not wish for their parents to stop working abroad. However, in con-trast to their mothers, they are less convinced that the material security that their families have achieved has alleviated the emotional costs of separation.[4] Claribelle Ignacio, for example, insists that the "material stability" brought by her mother's migration could not possibly replace the intimacy that her family has lost.

> My mother went to the United States and worked as a domestic worker. . . . She went to the States for a long time, when I was still young. I was separated from her for a long time, but she did go home every year. She just wanted to go to the States to be able to provide a good future for us. . . . I can say that it is very different to be away from the mother. Even if you have everything, I can say your family is broken. Once the father, mother, and children no longer have communication, even if you are materially stable, it is better to be together. If a child wants material goods, they also want maternal love. That is still impor-tant. When I was a kid, I realized that it is better if we stayed together and my parents carried regular day jobs. . . . It is best if the family stays whole, as whole as it can be. . . . Here it is hard. . . . Filipinos are blinded by material goods. That is not good for me. It is better if they are to-gether, with the family whole, because even if you have money, you cannot replace the wrongdoing that it caused and did to your family. (Claribelle Ignacio, thirty-six-year-old single domestic worker, Rome)

For children left behind in the Philippines, "staying together" and "keeping the family whole" are worth much more than achieving material security. However, children can make such sweeping claims more easily, because the material security provided by migrant parents affords them the luxury of de-manding greater emotional security; it is highly unlikely that impoverished children would make similar demands.

In *Tinig Filipino*, writings of children usually convey their longing for their mothers to return "home" to the Philippines. This desire is usually placed in either/or terms: "money or family" (Aratan, 1994: 34). For example, a letter written by a son to his mother in Hong Kong reads, "Mom, come home. Even if it means that I will no longer receive new toys or chocolates. Even if it means that I won't get new clothes anymore, just being close to you will make me happy. Dad and I are so lonely here without you around" (Daguio, 1995: 40, translated from Tagalog to English). The binary construction of "money or family" suggests that children consider these two to be mutually exclusive choices for their mothers. Moreover, an underlying suggestion is the wrongful decision of mothers for having chosen money instead of family. This line of reasoning disregards the fact that mothers migrate to provide money to the family.

A letter written by Nina Rea Arevalo to her mother indicates that children recognize that mothers do sacrifice the intimacy of family life for the sake of their children's material security. Despite this fact, children like Nina still demand the return migration of their mothers. They reason that the emotional gratification brought by the intimacy of everyday life is worth more than material security.

My dear mother:

How are you over there? Us, we're here wishing you were with us. . . . Mom, I was still very young when you left me with Kuya [older brother], Ate [older sister] and Dad. I still did not know the meaning of sadness. . . .

Do you know that they would cry when they read your letters? Me, I would just look at them. I grew up actually believing that letters are supposed to be read while crying. . . .

Mom, I am older now and I know how to read and write. . . . I am getting older and I need someone guiding and supporting me and that is you. I don't want to be rich. Instead I want you with me, mom. Doesn't God say that a family should always be together through hardships and happiness? But why are you far away from us?

. . . Kuya and Ate read somewhere that Filipino workers in other shores are the heroes of our country. But mom, come back and you will be the queen that I will be with every day.

My wish is that you come home this coming Christmas.

Your youngest child, Nina Rea
(Arevalo, 1994: 28, translated from Tagalog to English)

The poignant letter expresses the disposition of children in transnational families: they hunger for emotional bonds with absentee parents and wish for the intimacies of everyday interactions.

Children want their mothers to return to the Philippines in order to amend the emotional distance wrought by separation. For many, such as Evelyn Binas, geographical distance has created an irreparable gap in intergenerational relations. After graduating from college with a degree in computer science in 1994, Evelyn joined her mother in Rome, where they live in a room in the home of her mother's employer the size of a walk-in closet. Left in the Philippines at the age of ten with her father, brother, and sister, Evelyn still holds a deep-seated resentment against her mother.

> *Are you close to your mother?*
> No. There is still a gap between us. We got used to not having a mother, even my brother and sister in the Philippines. . . . I was independent. I always felt that I didn't need someone guiding me. . . . Even though we are [now] living together, there is still this gap. . . . My mother came home when I was in my second and fourth year of high school and then fourth year of college. . . . When my mother was home, we felt that our house was too crowded. We never stayed—we always went out. Whenever she was there, we never stayed home.
> *Do you think that you will ever be close to your mom?*
> No, not really. I don't think that I will really know how to open up to her. . . . *She should have gone home more frequently.* In Christmas, I hated the fact that our family was not complete, and I would see other families together. I don't think that we needed to come here to survive as a family. I see the homeless surviving together in the Philippines, and if they are surviving, why did my mother have to come here? My classmates were so jealous of me because of all my designer things. They tell me that they envy me because my mom is abroad. I tell them, "Fine, she is abroad, but we are not complete." Since the fourth grade, this is the first time that I actually spent Christmas with my mother. (my emphasis)

In contrast to other children, Evelyn asserts that she never looked forward to seeing her mother yet believes that "she should have gone home more frequently." Hurt and still feeling somewhat abandoned, Evelyn resents her mother for what seems to be the relegation of their mother-daughter relationship to just a few infrequent visits. Although unable to fully explain her feelings, Evelyn often cites the presence of a "gap" that hinders her ability to communicate and relate to her mother. Bitter about her mother's prolonged absence from her life, Evelyn is sadly resolved with the permanence of the emotional distance between them.

While the emotional insecurities engendered by geographical distance can be eased by the efforts of mothers to communicate and visit their children regularly, they can also be tempered by the support provided by extended kin. Jane Sapin, for example, grew up with her grandmother from the age of six, when her mother, followed by her father after two years, began working in Italy. Not until she was almost eighteen did she follow her parents and sisters to Rome. Yet Jane describes her childhood as "not so bad" because of the support and security provided by her extended family in the Philippines.

> It was not hard growing up without my parents because I grew up with my grandmother. So it wasn't so bad. I'm sure there was a time when there were affairs that you should be accompanied by your parents. That's what I missed. . . . I wasn't angry with them. At that early age, I was mature. I used to tell my mother that it was fine that we were apart because we were eventually going to be reunited. . . . I see my mother having sacrificed for our sake so that she could support us financially.

Even at a young age in the Philippines, Jane had already acknowledged the sacrifices made by her parents, particularly her mother, and had been secure with the knowledge that her parents sought employment abroad not just for their personal interest but for the collective interest of the family. In contrast to Evelyn, Jane does not resent her mother for visiting the family infrequently but in fact sees that her few visits, the first being when Jane was already ten years old, entailed financial struggles that she undertook for the sake of her children.

The extended family provides tremendous support to transnational families. Among my interviewees, it is mostly other relatives and not fathers who care for the children left behind in the Philippines. Of those in Los Angeles with young dependents, seven have their children cared for by other relatives, usually grandparents or female relatives, and five by fathers. In Rome, nine women left their children with fathers and seventeen with other relatives.

Even with the presence of other relatives, insecurities still arise among children left behind in the Philippines. As shown by the stories of Cesar Gregorio and Gay Villarama, children entertain feelings of anxiety and abandonment and feel deprived of parental love. Cesar Gregorio, a college student, migrated to the United States with his brother in 1990 —five years after his parents. Left in the Philippines with his grandparents at the age of five, Cesar recalls feeling insecure growing up, not knowing when he was going to see his parents again.

> For a long time, I was questioning the love of my parents. . . . Finally, when I got to go this country, I was looking forward to establishing a relationship with my parents and receiving affection, you know. So I just fell when I saw the baby. The least they could have done was to make sure that my brother and I were brought over before the baby was born. It would have made a difference. The fact that they can do this when they had two sons they have not spent time with for more than four years in another continent . . . I don't know. So, my wanting to make sure they really cared was impossible. But at least they took us out and did a lot of things with us our first few years, but there is still this question about what they were thinking and feeling about us while putting all this energy to their new child.

Although his feelings of insecurity were compensated by the material benefits given by his parents, Cesar still cannot resolve the fact that his parents had another child before he and his brother reunited with their parents. Moreover, Cesar is still saddened by the emotional distance brought by the knowledge that his parents missed what he considers an important stage of his growing years.

> My parents and I are close. That's not weird because I have lived more with them than I have been separated from them. So, they have seen me grow up. But [there are] a few things in our relationship that [have] a gap, but it doesn't make us not close. It's more like this absence in that period of my life that should have included them but didn't. . . . Okay, like my first day in school or my first Holy Communion, important events that they did not see, that I do not remember, that an adult is not there to tell me about what I was like, what stuff I did that [is], I guess, funny kids' stuff we hear about once in a while.

For Cesar, the lost memories from the years he spent apart from his family can never be recovered.

Besides emotional distance in parent-child ties or feelings of insecurity among children, vulnerability also plagues the experiences of children in transnational households. Sensationalist stories circulate around Filipino migrant communities about abandoned, lost, and abused children of overseas workers. Although an extreme case—but definitely not unheard of in the field—the life of Gay Villarama in the Philippines before following her mother to Rome at the age of twelve illustrates the heightened vulnerability of children in transnational households. Describing her life in the Philippines, Gay believes that the cost of family separation had been the ebbing moral values of her unmarried older sisters.

> My mother has been here for fifteen years, and she left me in the Philippines when I was only five years old. . . . It was OK because she came home every year, sometimes on Christmas and other times during our school vacation when we weren't doing much so she was able to take us out a lot. However, we did miss her. It is true that life is sweeter when you are with your whole family, even if you are experiencing hardships. At this point, you can't really say that we are rich. You can only say that we went up just a little bit. However, this was at the cost of my family separating. What happened was that my sisters got married very young. I am the only one not yet married. My two siblings here are living with their partners, and so they are not actually married-married. One has two children and met her partner in the Philippines. The other one met her partner here in Rome.

While this had been Gay's response to my question concerning the costs of family separation, one could definitely say that another cost had been her vulnerability to an abusive father, whose relationships with other women had been the significant push factor for her mother to consider employment outside of the Philippines in the first place.

> I matured very fast when my mother left us. I grew up with my father, but he was very irresponsible. He did not really look after us well. [Pauses.] When I was ten years old, I was a victim of rape. [Pauses.] I was raped by my father. That's why I decided I had to come here. I could not take what my father did to me any longer. [Pauses.] You know why he did it? I look like my mother when she was younger. My father told me that when he sees me, he sees my mother when she was still young. That is why he did that to me. For me, I wonder why? I am his own child. I am not someone that he just found somewhere. For me, I wish he did it to someone else. During the time that he did that to me . . . the youngest in our family saw it and that is why he has had some psychological problems since then. . . . I think my father has a lot of anger towards us, his children . . . . Our life is messy. [Laughs.] Thank God my brother has somewhat recovered. I sent him to a doctor when I went home. In school, he does well. He wants revenge and wants to be a lawyer.
>
> When my mother and I went back to the Philippines, we took the case to the authorities. I did not take it to Manila but just in the provinces.

When I saw my father, I told him that I was grateful that I am in this world but I am just unlucky to have him as a father. I told him that if I really wanted to kill him, I could do it, but I was just going to go through it legally for the sake of his [second] family and his new children. I feel sorry for his kids. I told him that I hope to God that he does not do what he did to me to his young daughter. . . .

But can you imagine what he did to me? I was only ten years old when he hurt me. And to top it all off, he pointed a gun at me. He tied my feet at the edge of the bed that he slept on. I couldn't tell my mother immediately after I came here. I counted three years until I told her . . . . It was all too much for me, so I finally told her. . . . I was actually scared, though, because my father told me that if I told anyone, he was going to kill me.

Gay had been very stoic when describing her experience with her father, leaving me speechless and even more surprised when she told me that she "moved the lawsuit" to grant him an early release from prison (ironically, for the sake of his younger children).

The stories of Cesar, Evelyn, and Gay illustrate the emotional insecurities of children in transnational families. Although an extreme case, the experience of Gay does indicate the vulnerability of children with absentee parents. Inasmuch as "growing up without a parent" imposes emotional strains on children, how do they cope with their situation? Gay, even with all the heart-wrenching struggles she has gone through, copes with the consolation of her family's slight class mobility and her early maturity and independence.

I have experienced the hardships of the Philippines in [their] extreme. I experienced [this] when I was so young. I remember not eating throughout the afternoon and evening. We wouldn't eat. Then, the following day, we would eat old bread. [Laughs.] We would fry it and top it with sugar. That was what I would take to school for lunch. Our life in the Philippines was difficult. Even though my mother was already here, it was hard because at first she could not send us any money. She was still new then, and she was saving money then because she really wanted to build our own house. Now, we have a house there. . . . *Our life slightly improved since we came here. . . . You have to understand that when my mother left us, we matured immediately. We learned to live without our mother being around for us. We learned to make do with what we had, and we did not, could not, rely on our father. We bought our own food and made money when we could. That's what is nice about our sit-uation. We learned to survive without her.* (my emphasis)

But one has to ask whether early maturity should be celebrated or instead considered a tragic loss of childhood. Claribelle Ignacio, who was raised by her grandfather while her mother worked in the United States, sees the "pain and hardships" of her childhood as positive lessons that better prepared her for the harsh realities of adulthood.

> It is better I realized to experience pain and hardships instead of just re-lying on my mother always. They say that a mother should protect [her] children from all the pain and hardships, but I realized that it is also good for children to experience some pain and suffering. For me, it made me a better person afterwards. Instead of just being irresponsible your whole life, I realized that if you get used to a life without problems, when you do have your first problem, you fall flat on your face. It's bet-ter to be exposed to some suffering while you are young. It makes you a better person when you get older.

Women like Claribelle Ignacio and Gay Villarama can only make the best out of their situation and, as a coping strategy, have to convince themselves that some good comes out of "suffering while you are young."

Because of her "early maturity" and "independence," Gay started work-ing as a domestic worker in Rome at the age of thirteen. Even after reunit-ing with her mother, Gay had still been denied a secure childhood free of adult responsibility.

> I got my first job from my mother when I was almost thirteen. I would give my mom money at the end of the month, but I would keep some for myself to go shopping with. When I was young, the employers did not want to take me because of my age. I had to look after this child, and they were worried that I wasn't going to be able to look after the child properly. They did not care about the housework. The child is the most important. . . . I was making 1,200,000 [U.S.$800] a month working a "day job" from 8 a.m. to 7 p.m. or to 8 p.m. Then I went to [language] school at around 8:30 p.m.
> *You were only twelve, and you were already attending evening school?*
> Yes.
> *You were riding the buses on your own?*
> Yes. I would get home at midnight because it was almost a two-hour bus

ride from the school to my house. When I got home, I would not talk to
anyone. I would just eat and then go to sleep. [Laughs.] . . . It was not
regular school because I did not want to be a burden on my mother if I
could earn my own money. She only insisted that I go to school once, but
I had tasted how good it feels to make money. [Laughs.] I can buy what I
want and do what I want to do. What is important is there be a limit.

While at the very least surprised by her independence, I had been even more
stricken by her attitude and priorities. Although Gay could finally have had
a "regular" childhood in Rome—especially after her personal struggles with
her father in the Philippines—she continues to set aside her own needs and,
first and foremost, gives priority to pleasing her mother. Wanting to ease her
mother's parental responsibilities, Gay takes advantage of the financial assistance her presence in Rome can provide the family and works so as not to become a burden on her mother.

Other children, such as Rodney Catorce, cope by emphasizing the material gains that they have been able to achieve as a family.

I have always thought about it, my dad being so far away from us for
more than ten years now. I mean, how could he? I was barely eight
years old when he left us to work abroad. He had to because he and
Mom were having a hard time trying to make both ends meet for our
family. . . . The night after he departed, I could sense the feeling of emptiness in our home, despite the fact that everybody was trying to pre-
tend that nobody left. . . . But while we were praying the rosary, the
tears rolled down from my mother's cheeks. She wept, and it was all my
dad's fault. Days after that memorable night (memorable because that
was the first time I saw my mom cry), we learned to accept that Daddy
was away, had to be away. And for us here, life had to continue. From
now on, pen and paper would be our means of communication. . . .
Sometimes I wonder what if Dad didn't gamble his luck abroad? What
if he didn't pursue his dream of giving us a bright future? What would
have happened if he preferred to stay with us? Well, undoubtedly, we
would not have missed him that much. He would not have missed us that
much. He would have celebrated the Christmases and New Years with
us. He would have been present through all those birthdays. He would
have attended all those graduations. He would have seen us grow up. Too
bad, he was not able to. But then again, we would not be where we are
now. We would not be living in our own house. . . . I and my brothers
and sisters would not be studying in great schools. Daddy would not

have been a good provider. . . . Worst, we would not have been eating three meals a day. All these considered, I am glad he did. True, he is away, but so what? (1995: 9).

By highlighting the material gains of the family, children can withstand the "feelings of emptiness" brought by missing their parents. While children can say, "True, he is away, but so what?" they do not deny the emotional difficulties wrought by separation nor do they replace its emotional costs with material gains but only camouflage them.

Children also tolerate transnational households by repressing their priorities for those of their parents. By putting aside feelings of emotional distance and by bearing the insecurities aroused by parental absence, children tolerate a transnational household arrangement and sacrifice relentlessly for its success and ease. Yet children like Junelyn Gonzaga also want parents to recognize the relentless sacrifice that they provide and commit to keep the family intact through separation.

> But I don't blame my parents for my fate today, because they both sacrifice just to give us our needs and I just got my part. . . . And now, I realize that having a parent abroad may be a financial relief. But it also means a lot more. The overseas contract worker suffers lots of pain. They really sacrifice a lot. *But, hey, please don't forget that your kids also have lots of sacrifices to give, aside from growing up without a parent. Specifically, for those who thought that sending money is enough and they've already done their responsibilities, well, think again, because there are more than this. Your children need your love, support, attention, and affection.* You can still be with your children although you really are not. You can let them feel you can be their best friends. And that you're still beside them no matter what, because distance is not a hindrance to a better relationship. . . . *It's not only one person who suffers when an overseas contract worker leaves for abroad. All his or her loved-ones do. And the children are the first on the list. The whole family bears the aches and pains just to achieve a better future.* (Gonzaga, 1995: 13; my emphasis)

Growing up in transnational families does not just entail receiving the perquisites of monthly remittances but includes the often-unrecognized hardship of "growing up without a parent" and being deprived of "love, support, attention, and affection." To amend the insecurities brought by geographical distance, children need concrete reinforcements of parental love. According to Junelyn, parents can do just that by creating "bridges" of constant communication.

When describing their position and experience growing up in a transnational household, children are stoic—foregoing their pain and desires for those of parents and the material gains of the family. Children explain: "My parents had to do what they had to do" or "I understand why they had to leave us." The attitudes of children in transnational families reflect those of the working-class children in *Worlds of Pain*, Lillian Rubin's (1976) study of working-class American family life. As opposed to middle-class children, Rubin found "no complaints from the working-class child. . . . Children in all families frequently are 'lonely or scared,' or both. But the child in the working class family understands that often there's nothing his parents can do about it" (1976: 27). Finding consolation in the belief that separation is not a preferred choice but a parental sacrifice for the reproduction of the family, children in transnational households, like the working-class children in Rubin's study, feel an immense gratitude to migrant parents and recognize the hardships that they endure "for the sake of the children." Now parents just need to acknowledge the equally relentless sacrifice of children in transnational families.

Even though children recognize the efforts of their mothers to provide emotional and material care from afar and even though they appreciate the monthly remittances and frequent telephone calls made by their mothers, the bottom line is they still want their mothers to return to the Philippines. This is regardless of their mothers' efforts to maintain ties with them. For example, both Claribelle Ignacio—whose mother returned to the Philippines every year—and Evelyn Binas—whose mother returned far less frequently—share the opinion that they would have rather had their mothers work in the Philippines. They both insist that by not returning home, mothers are being materially inclined and are not recognizing the emotional difficulties wrought by their prolonged geographical separation.

Based on the writings in *Tinig Filipino* and my interviews with children, it seems that children are not convinced that emotional care can be totally provided by the support of extended kin, the financial support of migrant mothers, and weekly telephone conversations. As an eighteen-year-old female college student in Paz Cruz's survey suggests, "guidance, attention, love, and care" can only be completely given by "family togetherness":

> I will tell my friend to convince her mother not to go abroad but to look for a profitable means of livelihood such as planting, embroidery, etc.

Two years being with the family is more worthy compared to the dollars she might earn abroad. Is it enough to show our love in terms of wealth? I think it's not. We need the warmth of love of our fellowmen, especially our parents. We need their guidance, attention, love, and care to live happily and contented. I will make her mother realize the value of family togetherness. . . . If only all Filipinos aim to have a simple life, not the luxurious one, then, there is no need to leave our country to earn more money. (1987: 42)

Despite the fact that children seem to recognize the efforts of their mothers to provide love and care from afar, for the most part they have this ingrained desire that their mothers return "home." Underlying this demand is the suggestion that their mothers are somehow at fault for working abroad. In the next section, I further deconstruct the emotional insecurities of children so as to explain why. My analysis shows that the tendency of children to view transnational mothering as an insufficient strategy for the provision of emotional care in the family emerges from socialized expectations of traditional mothering. I argue that the traditional ideological system of the patriarchal nuclear family aggravates the intergenerational conflicts engendered by emotional tensions in transnational households.

Gender and Pain in Transnational Families

The thrust of the problem is to ask to what degree the central emotional and material moment found in each society is ideology, to what degree the ideology is accepted and plays a role in sorting out material and emotional interests of the participants. . . . (Medick and Sabean, 1984: 19)

As Medick and Sabean postulate, the material and emotional interests in the social institution of the family are shaped and guided by an underlying ideological system. Ideology, according to Stuart Hall, refers "to those images, concepts, and premises which provide the frameworks through which we represent, interpret, understand, and 'make sense' of some aspect of social existence" (Hall in Espiritu, 1997: 12). In this section, I propose that emotional interests are ideologically determined. This is a springboard to further explore the feelings of pain, which I have mapped out for parents and children in transnational households.

I specifically wish to excavate the dynamics of the social category of gender in family ideology and map its influence on the emotional tensions affecting parents and children in transnational families. In this section, I argue that patriarchal gender norms in the Filipino family, with its basic framework being the division of labor between fathers economically sustaining the family and mothers reproducing family life, fuel the emotional stress in transnational families. While it is true that feelings of pain in transnational families are fostered by separation, they are undoubtedly intensified by the failure in a great number of families to meet children's gender-based expectations for mothers (and not fathers) to nurture them and also the self-imposed expectations of mothers to follow culturally and ideologically inscribed duties in the family.

As more women leave the Philippines and relegate traditional responsibilities of mothering to fathers (who do not necessarily perform them) or other relatives, the family, community, and the nation judge and scorn migrant women—especially the mothers who constitute a visible portion of female migrants—on the basis of their performance, or lack thereof, of their ideologically determined family work. In fact, the denial of maternal love is regarded as child abuse in the diaspora. As a domestic worker states: "Just [by] leaving [children] in the custody of fathers or relatives, we have already abused them. We have denied them their right of a motherly love and care" (Mariano, 1995: 26).

To downplay the formation of "broken homes," the Philippine government claims that most of its "economic heroes" are in fact nonmothers (that is, men or single women). It was only in the mid-1980s, with the larger flow of female migration, that the "problem" of the "broken home" turned into a national crisis. Between the early 1970s and 1980s, when men still dominated the flow of migration, the traditional ideological foundation of the family remained stable. Migration did not question the division of labor in the family, as husbands continued to economically sustain family life while mothers reproduced it. The spatial division of labor remained unchanged, with the father earning wages outside the home and the mother nurturing the protective environment of this space. An outmigration of women that included many mothers caused the family arrangement to topple over, with the most often asked question being how could women possibly leave fathers as the primary parent responsible for reproducing the family, considering that such an "abnormal" arrangement clearly illustrates that the Filipino family is in fact now "broken" because it no longer fits the ideal nuclear household model?

A striking image on the December 1994 cover of *Tinig Filipino* shows a

Filipino family surrounded with traditional holiday decor. The father, clutching a sleeping baby with his right hand, raises the traditional Christmas lantern by the window as his other son, who looks about five years old and holds on to a stuffed animal, is next to his older sister in her early teens. The family portrait evokes a feeling of holiday celebration as the caption states: "Pamilya'y Masaya Kung Sama-Sama" (The family is happy when everyone is together). Yet the picture is not supposed to call forth an image of celebration but directs viewers to think of a "broken family," as a very small highlighted subcaption strategically placed next to the family portrait asks in Italian "peró dov'é mamma?" (but where is mama?). The subcaption reminds readers that a mother, not a father, is supposed to be rocking her children to sleep. The image is supposed to invoke a feeling of loss as the man, not the woman, cares for the family. The magazine's editor, Linda Layosa, confirms this negative construction of the transnational family.

> I am certain, all of us have experienced similar incidents wherein abnormalities in our relationship with the members of our family are felt. A [*Tinig Filipino*] contributor stated that her son, instead of asking his [overseas contract worker] mother to sew his pants, he called his father instead. And since he is used to utter the word "Papa," he always said the same word even if he meant "Mama." (1994: 13)

Because the formation of female-headed transnational households leads to the reconfiguration of gender relations in the family, such households are generally considered "broken" and "abnormal," even in migrant communities. This is regardless of the fact that the family now can and does hire domestic workers and, more often that not, rely on other female relatives to reproduce the family.

While the prolonged absence of either a father or a mother has negative consequences on intergenerational relations, for example, emotional distance, the transnational family of women working outside of the Philippines is often construed as more pathological. Paz Cruz (1987) found that 82.8 percent of the 302 students in her survey would advise their friends to "allow your parents to work abroad," but the breakdown of responses actually shows that 59.5 percent would advise friends to allow their fathers to go abroad, 19.7 percent would advise friends to allow both parents to migrate, and only 3.6 percent would advise friends to allow their mothers to work abroad (1987: 38). As established earlier, children are able to reason that the wage earnings of a parent abroad can provide the entire family economic security and material comforts otherwise inaccessible in the insecure labor market of the Philippines. Yet they are clearly less comfortable growing up with an absentee mother, as most of them would not allow their mother to work abroad and would not advise friends to allow their mothers to work abroad. Paz Cruz's finding that most children "would allow parents to work abroad" should therefore be clarified. Most children seem to be only comfortable with the idea of a father working abroad.

The responses given by the youth to the question of what advice they would give friends whose parents are considering employment outside the country also seem to fall within the grid of traditional gender norms in the family.

Mother as nurturer:
I'll advise my friend not to allow her mother to go abroad. It's better that her father go because mothers can't do what fathers do. Mothers are closer to their children than the father. She's always present in times of difficulties and problems. (eighteen-year-old in Paz Cruz, 1987: 42)

Father as breadwinner:
I'll try to make her understand that it is the obligation of the father to provide for the family. With the present situation of the country, it's understandable that the father will look for greener pastures. They want the best for their children. I'll tell her she's lucky—her father is sacrificing to give them a good education and a good home. (seventeen-year-old in Paz Cruz, 1987: 40)

It's good that the father will be the one to go abroad because he is the man. He will manage our money. He is stronger than a girl and man is the one who is talented. (thirteen-year-old in Paz Cruz, 1987: 40)

In defining their expectations, wants, and desires, children follow the well-defined division of gender roles in the family. Importantly, the ideological construction of the family controls not just their opinions but also feelings and emotions concerning family separation.

In my study, most families with young children fall under the category of one parent abroad transnational households. Yet based on interviews with children and writings published in *Tinig Filipino*, children in transnational families generally claim that parental absence has denied them the emotional care expected of the family. Claribelle Ignacio's earlier comments—"If a child wants material goods, they also want maternal love. That is still important"—emphasize the interplay of emotions and gender. A mother's emotional care, in other words "maternal love," is what is denied to an increasing number of children in the Philippines. Moreover, feelings of emotional insecurity, even with the presence of fathers in the Philippines, suggest that fathers have failed to respond equally to the efforts of mothers to sustain the family economically. This should not be surprising when in fact it is the "irresponsibility") of fathers that has instigated the migration of most married women whom I have interviewed in Rome. The question then is whether fathers in the Philippines are able to provide the "maternal love" sorely missing from the lives of children, if women are capable of assisting them with their ideologically prescribed role as income-producer. Fathers seem to avoid giving emotional care. As I noted, fathers are less apt to care for their children than are female relatives.

What happens if fathers do provide emotional care to their children? Although I do not want to underplay the pain of children in transnational households, I question the poignant pleas for emotional security of those whose fathers are present in their everyday lives. Begging her mother to finally return to the Philippines, Nina Rea, the young child who has grown up without her mother since the time she was still too young to read and write, mentions having been left in the Philippines with her father.

> Mom, I was still very young when you left me with Kuya [older brother], Ate [older sister] and Dad. . . . Mom, . . . I am getting older and I need someone guiding and supporting me and that is you. I don't want to be rich. Instead I want you with me, Mom. (my emphasis)

As she asks her mother to return to the Philippines and finally give the guidance and support she has long been denied, I have to wonder what the father in the Philippines is doing. Why does he not give her the much-needed support? Why can she not turn to him for the guidance expected of parents? Is he not even trying to provide care, or does his daughter not recognize the care that he gives?

Unlike Nina Rea, Evelyn Binas recognizes the fact that her father has nurtured and emotionally cared for her since the fourth grade but nonetheless fails to appreciate her mother for economically sustaining the family with her earnings as a domestic worker in Rome.

> Since the fourth grade, my mother has been here in Rome. My father looked after me. I remember when there were school functions with mothers. I would worry about not being able to participate. I always thought that I was different. Everyone had a mother while I was the

only one without one. It was only my father around for me. Like in
graduation, it would be my father putting the medals on me. I remember my father always being there for me. During lunch, he would bring
me over some food.

Did he work?

No. He sometimes did some work. We had some land with fruits and
vegetables. He would go there to harvest. . . . So, he would do that work
but not all the time.

Beneath her long enumeration of all the family work done by her very caring father is her silence about the contributions of her mother to the family
and the underlying suggestion that her mother somehow failed to perform
the work that she should have done. Evelyn scorns all the material benefits
that she had gained from her mother and wishes that her mother had returned to the Philippines more frequently so that she could have received the
"maternal love" that her very caring father had been unable to give her. Evelyn insists that her family is "broken" and "incomplete." In families such as
Evelyn's, I have to wonder whether a shift or breakdown of ideological norms
would lead to a different take on the emotional costs of separation.

In sharp contrast to Evelyn's continued resentment of her mother, even
though she was raised by a very loving father, is the more blasé attitude of
Rodney Catorce, the young man whose article about his experiences growing up in the Philippines appeared in *Tinig Filipino* (Catorce 1995). Recognizing the economic contributions of his father to the family and having
been secure with the presence of his mother in the Philippines, Rodney did
not undergo a breakdown of the traditional division of labor in the family, a
fact that seems to allow him to pose the question "My dad is away, but so
what?" quite easily.

The reconstitution of gender ideologies of the family would not lessen the
sacrifices of children in transnational families but would temper the pain of
separation. By this I do not mean to imply that a shift in gender ideology
would eliminate the emotional difficulties of separation. Instead, I wish to
suggest that children may come to appreciate more fully the efforts of mothers to provide material care and a reconstituted form of emotional care from
a distance. Moreover, they may begin to demand less family labor from their
migrant mothers. For instance, they would not expect mothers to be primarily responsible for both the material and emotional care of the family. At
the same time, they may achieve greater emotional security from the care
provided by extended kin and from some fathers left behind in the Philip-

pines. The impassioned pleas of children for emotional care have to be understood within their ideological framework, which surprisingly has remained intensely patriarchal even through the drastic shifts in the gender division of labor instigated by the migration of women in so many families.

Conclusion

While enabling Filipina domestic workers to maximize their earnings, the formation of transnational households also involves emotional upheaval in their lives and those of the children whom they have left behind in the Philippines. A central paradox in the maintenance of transnational families is the fact that the achievement of financial security for the sake of the children goes hand-in-hand with an increase in emotional insecurity, an impact that nonetheless could be softened by a breakdown of the persisting ideology of patriarchy in the family. Material rewards contradict starkly the loss of intimacy in many families in Filipino migrant communities. Yet migrants continually suppress this contradiction, either by denying the emotional tensions in transnational families or by overriding emotional costs with material gains.

By repressing the emotional tensions wrought in transnational households, parents are denying the intergenerational strains resulting from the pain of family separation. Notably, emotional repression as a means of easing this dislocation is premised on the belief of their temporary sojourn: family separation, while painful, is only temporary. However, emotional repression enables parents to delay the reunification of their families. The longer they delay reunification, the more they aggravate the intergenerational strains of transnational household formation and the harder it is for them to return to the Philippines, face their children, and confront the tensions that migration has caused the family. These tensions do not disappear in time and are not voided by the material security brought by transnational household formation. Overall, this shows that the means by which migrant Filipina domestic workers confront the pain of family separation for the most part maintain this dislocation.

CHAPTER 6

Contradictory Class Mobility:
The Politics of Domestic Work in Globalization

Migrant Filipina domestic workers define their sense of self and place in the global labor market from the contentious subject-position of contradictory class mobility. This contentious location refers to their simultaneous experience of upward and downward mobility in migration. More specifically, it refers to their decline in social status and increase in financial status. This is the central dislocation that defines their experience of domestic work.[1] As such, my analysis of the performance of domestic work as a process of subject formation focuses on the constitution of this dislocation and the turn taken by domestic workers against this dislocation.

What does it mean for migrant Filipina domestic workers to be dislocated as such? First, they have great difficulty accepting the low labor market status conferred upon them by paid domestic work. In the process, they struggle to resolve the discrepancy between the social status of their current job and actual training. In addition, they are frequently reminded of the contradiction of having a "maid" and being one.

> I was crying all the time. [Laughs.] When my employer gave me the bucket for cleaning, I did not know where I had to start. Of course we are not so rich in the Philippines, but we had maids. I did not know how to start cleaning, and my feelings were of self-pity. I kept on thinking that I just came to the United States to be a maid. So that was that. I would just cry, and I wanted to go home. I did not imagine that this was the kind of work that I would end up doing. (Genny O'Connor, Los Angeles)

For migrant Filipina domestic workers, the sharp decline in their occupational and social status aggravates the stigma of domestic work.

Second, they consider domestic work to be a de-skilling process.

> I regret not using my education. I invested years to my studies, and for what? The only thing that's going to happen to me is be a maid . . . . If you don't use your education, you lose it, and you become stupid after a while. The only thing in your mind is mopping and mopping and mopping. You become stupid from your work. You don't use your brain. (Vanessa Dulang, Rome)

Further capturing this anguish is the view of domestic work as *nakakabobo*, meaning a process of making someone stupid.

Third, they carry a tremendous sense of loss for failing to utilize their educational achievements.

> Sometimes I say that I am tired. It's very different when you don't get to use your education. It gets rusty. [Laughs.] I plan to review my accounting when I go back to the Philippines. I miss what I had left. I want to review my knowledge of the subject, and I want to see if I still remember my training. What you learn just does not stay with you forever. It has been a long time. Since 1985, I have only been a domestic worker who has not done anything but scrub and scrub. You don't use what you learn in college. . . . Even here sometimes, I don't remember my English. If I am not speaking to someone who is fluent, I am not able to speak English. (Giselle Aragon, Rome)

Without doubt, underemployment is such an excruciatingly painful experience that migrant Filipina domestic workers even spoke of this experience with much greater bitterness than the denial of mothering.

The dislocation of contradictory class mobility is a concrete effect of the larger structural forces of globalization. It emerges from the unequal development of regions, including the nation-based hierarchy of educational qualifications, the lesser accreditation granted degrees from the Third World, and the limits of mobility in the Philippines. As described by Vanessa Dulang of Rome, migrant Filipina domestic workers gain and lose from the limited options of either staying in the Philippines or working as a domestic worker outside of the country.

> Life is hard in the Philippines. You don't earn enough. Nothing will happen to you if you stay there. Even though you are a maid here, at least you are earning money. What I couldn't buy in the Philippines, I could buy here. . . . You can buy something you really want, but there you can't.

> But work here is difficult. You bend your back scrubbing. You experience
> what you would never experience in the Philippines. [There], your work
> is light, but you don't have any money. Here you make money, but your
> body is exhausted.

In the spatial politics of globalization—unequal development of regions—
the achievement of material security in the Philippines entails the experience of downward mobility in other countries. This dislocation, one of contradictory class mobility, indicates that migrant Filipina domestic workers
inhabit a transnational terrain. Shifts in status from sending to receiving nations define their sense of place in the global labor market. Mobility from
their immobility in the Philippine labor market is at the cost of the downward mobility accorded by their limited choices in the transnational labor
market. Moreover, at the cost of their professional careers, domestic workers enable female employers to utilize their labor market skills as well as
solve the household problems engendered by their entrance into the workforce. This demonstrates that the unequal relations between migrant Filipina domestic workers and their employers are rooted in the hierarchies of
global capitalism, which include the marginality of the invisible women—
the poorer women—left in the Philippines.

If domestic work is a disturbingly painful experience, then why do migrant
Filipinas not quit their jobs sooner? They usually do not because of their
need to accumulate capital. For them, the pain of contradictory class mobility
is tempered by the financial gains brought by the higher wages of low-wage
service work in more developed nations. They are willing to suffer a decline
in labor market status, because in the developing country of the Philippines,
explains Lorna Fernandez, who has cared for the elderly for almost ten years
in Rome, the middle class does not have and cannot achieve financial security.

> You have to understand that our money has no value. It is very low. In
> the Philippines, I was making almost 10,000 pesos a month [U.S.$400],
> and that was even in the provinces. I lived with my parents, and I had no
> housing expenses, but still I was not able to save any money. If I had not
> left the Philippines, I would not have been able to have a house built for
> my parents. You might be able to save 2000 or 3000 pesos [U.S.$80 or
> $120] here or there but still goods are very expensive in the Philippines.

Wanting to hold on to their financial gains, migrant Filipina domestic workers negotiate the dislocation of contradictory class mobility by maximizing
its material advantages and rectifying its emotional disadvantages.[2]

As a result, migrant Filipina domestic workers find various means by which they reconcile the contradictions in status embodied in their performance of domestic work. They ease the pain of contradictory class mobility in four important ways: (1) performing servitude under the fantasy of reversal, in other words, the fantasy of eventually returning to the Philippines to be served by their own domestic workers; (2) downplaying servitude by emphasizing the higher racial status that employers accord them than their black and Latina counterparts; (3) de-emphasizing servitude by embracing intimacy, which ironically is a source of authority for employers (Bakan and Stasiulis, 1997b; Cock, 1980; Colen, 1989; Gregson and Lowe, 1994; Rollins, 1985; Romero, 1992); and (4) following the script of "deference and maternalism" (Rollins, 1985) with minimal interjection against their subservient characterization. The tactics that migrant Filipina domestic workers deploy against the dislocation of contradictory class mobility, in other words the process by which they desensitize themselves to the pain engendered by this dislocation, does not involve a struggle against its sources. Instead, they acquiesce to the larger structural inequalities placing them in a position of contradictory class mobility.[3]

My discussion of the experience of contradictory class mobility is divided into two main parts.[4] I first describe the aggravation of this dislocation by relations of power between domestics and their employers. Then I examine the ways that migrant Filipina domestic workers reconcile this dislocation. My analysis shows that they tend to diffuse their experience of contradictory class mobility by using and manipulating to their advantage various signifiers of inequality in the organization of paid domestic work, including the myth of domestics being one of the family.

The Everyday Routine of Domestic Work: Part-time Work, Elderly Care, and Live-in Housekeeping

I begin my examination of the experience of contradictory class mobility by identifying and describing the three types of domestic work performed by my interviewees: part-time work, elderly care, and live-in housekeeping. In the process, I enumerate the particular difficulties and satisfactions that they identify with each job. Providers of elderly care generally believe that they hold the most respected job because of their greater autonomy and the special medical skills required of them. Live-in housekeepers, while they may not like the social isolation of domestic work, often claim to be averse to elderly care or the added pressures of part-time work—running from one job to the next—and prefer this job for the opportunity it gives them to save money. Finally, part-time workers claim to have the most rewarding job of the three because of their higher earnings and freedom from the social isolation of live-in work.

PART-TIME WORKERS

Part-time workers are domestics who hold a series of day jobs or part-time jobs with a number of employers. I prefer to call them part-time workers instead of day workers because they are referred to as such by Filipina domestic workers. Unlike live-in workers, they are usually paid by the hour. Not physically trapped in the workplace, they also have greater control of their work schedule. Because there is a larger concentration of migrant Filipina part-time workers in Rome than in Los Angeles, I focus my discussion of its work culture in Rome.[5]

In Rome, most part-time workers had started as live-in workers but later sought part-time work to gain greater control of their time and labor. For instance, Nilda Cortes, a mother of three working in Rome since 1992, left live-in work because of the absence of a clear demarcation between working and nonworking hours in this job arrangement.

> I worked as a live-in, but I did not like it. I got sick from being awake at midnight. You can't go to sleep until they do. You have to be awake before they are because you have to bring them coffee to their rooms. . . .

In part-time work, when their shift ends, so does their work. As Ruby Mercado notes:

> Part-time is better. You work for three hours, and at the end of the three-hours you are done no matter what, even if the job is not done.

By having control over their work hours, part-time workers are able to set their schedules, maximize the number of their employers, and in turn increase their earnings.

Yet part-time workers discussed the physical tolls of their labor much more than did any other group of domestic workers. This is not surprising given the faster pace and greater load involved in this type of job. Part-time workers generally have more floors to scrub and more clothes to wash and iron than do live-in workers. For example, Rowena Chavez, once a bank teller in the Philippines and now a part-time worker for three families in Rome, describes the load expected of her to complete for each of her jobs.

> I wash their clothes, wash the plates, clean the house. I mop the floor on my knees. See employers here have a disease, it's a disease of cleanliness. Everything has to be clean. They're too much. There are employers that look for something to clean even when the house is already clean. For example, this morning, the woman had to point out that I still had to wipe this one table even though I was already on my way out. I told her: "Signora, I'll just do it tomorrow because I am already running late." She then told me that it was okay as long as I don't forget about it tomorrow.

Part-time work generally entails intensive cleaning. As Ana Vengco describes, each of the numerous cleaning tasks expected of them is strenuous on its own.

> I do cleaning, and this is from morning until early evening. Every day is the same. It is physically exhausting. Especially when I am mopping, my back aches and I get calluses on my hands. After ironing, you are just exhausted, and then you do something strenuous again like washing piles of dishes. Sometimes you feel numb all over from your hands to your feet. You are standing the whole day. We also do lifting like heavy chairs, mattresses, rugs. You have to roll those rugs and take [them] outside to the balcony and bang on [them.]

A few employers also require childcare but often as an additional responsibility to the already laborious cleaning tasks of part-time workers.

Further intensifying the routine of part-time work is the hustle and bustle of running from one job to the next, especially for domestics like Ruth Mercado, whose employers live a great distance from each other.

> I am so sick of it. I get up at seven in the morning and leave for work, which starts at 8:30. I am there until 12:30. Afterwards, I go to my next job, which is an hour away by bus. It starts at two in the afternoon and ends at six. Most days I can't go home to eat lunch. So, I always eat pizza for lunch. Then, when I go home at seven or 7:30, that is when I cook to eat a real meal. That's it.

The distance between jobs consumes any time for rest and extends an eight-and-a-half-hour work schedule, such as Ruth's, to twelve hours. This added pressure intensifies the physical ailments of domestic work. Vanessa Dulang, who works for eight employers, complains:

> You don't have time to eat. For example, you start at eight and that's four hours, let's say, so you get off at twelve noon. Then right afterwards, you have to chase your other employer where you start at twelve and end at three. At three o'clock, you have to chase another employer where you have to start at three. That is what is hard. You forget to eat because the only thing you think about is getting to your next employer on time. The work is exhausting, but I am used to it.

Despite its more onerous routine, part-time work is preferred by a great number of women for its rewards of autonomy. In the migrant community in Rome, there is a consensus among part-time workers that even though their jobs are more "exhausting" and "expensive" (due to living expenses), they at the very least are not "boring" like live-in work.

Who are the women who choose part-time work? I had expected to find a concentration of younger women in part-time work, assuming that they would not mind its physical tolls or would value freedom from the enclosure of the work setting more than would older domestic workers. Yet there was no age difference between live-in and part-time workers. In contrast, younger domestic workers seem to have an aversion to elderly caregiving, as the youngest woman holding such a job is thirty-six years old.[6]

PROVIDERS OF ELDERLY CARE

Elderly care is a somewhat specialized domestic job. Its primary duties include the provision of companionship and/or care to an elder. The tasks expected of those who care for the elderly include the traditional housework associated with domestic employment such as cooking and cleaning. Like other domestic workers, providers of elderly care face a physically demanding workload. Unlike part-time work, isolation and loneliness compound this load. Still, providers of elderly care tend to make a concerted effort to distinguish their jobs from other types of domestic work on two counts. First, they claim that the physical dependence of employers gives them greater control of their work routine. Second, this dependence garners them more autonomy. On these bases, they believe that elderly care is more respectable, requires more skills, and involves a more egalitarian relationship with employers. It is a job that they prefer and use to negotiate the decline in their status upon migration.

The formation of an immigrant niche in nursing among Filipino Americans has led to the conception of elderly care as a skilled job in Los Angeles, one requiring special "medical" skills such as the monitoring of blood pressure. In the community, any job in the medical field, including those in the lower ranks, is considered respectable. Further supporting the conception of elderly care as a skilled occupation is the possibility of receiving certification as a nurse's aide. Many Filipina workers who care for the elderly in Los Angeles use a nurse's aide certificate to negotiate for higher wage rates. Some women claim that after they became certified their minimum wage requirements increased from $60 to $90 a day.

In Rome, providers of elderly care agree that their duties require more skills than do other domestic jobs. In contrast to their counterparts in Los Angeles, however, they believe that they, along with other domestics, still occupy a low position in society because of their segregation from the formal labor market. For example, Lorna Fernandez, not unlike other care providers in Rome, is keenly aware of her subordinate status.

> They still see me as a maid. There is no improvement. You make good money, but they still call you a *ragazza* [girl]. When you are a *ragazza*, you are a maid.

Yet in both Rome and Los Angeles, the perception of elderly care as a job requiring more skills is supported by the fact that cleaning is actually secondary to the primary responsibility of providing care. For this reason, Eva Regalado, who has worked in Rome for more than ten years, limits her job selection to elderly care.

> Now I only get work with an older person because . . . it is not compulsory to clean. There is not too much to clean. Caretaking is more skilled.

Reflecting their higher self-perception, those who care for the elderly often refer to wards as "patients" to emphasize their higher level of responsibility. Not surprising then is the fact that in Rome trained medical workers—nurses and midwives—prefer elderly care over other types of domestic work. In Los Angeles, trained medical workers, in contrast to their counterparts in Rome, are not likely to pursue any type of domestic work for long periods of time, because of the demand for their skills and the greater integration of immigrants in the United States labor market.[7]

Without the same opportunities as migrants in Los Angeles, trained medical workers in Rome find compensation from underemployment in elderly care. They achieve dignity in this job from being able to utilize some of their skills and training. However, employers benefit much more than they do, considering that employers receive services, for example, physical therapy, that they otherwise would have to purchase at a much higher price. Employers take advantage of the skills of migrant Filipina domestic workers often without increasing their wages. Judy Reyes, for example, saves her employers in Rome at least U.S.$390 a week.

> They have actually saved a lot of money. They don't pay me to give the man therapy, but before, they were paying an actual therapist 200,000 lira per visit [approximately U.S.$130]. The therapist used to visit three times a week. Now I massage him twice a day—evening and morning— for one hour. . . . Their children love me.

Judy claims that she does not mind the absence of financial compensation for her added services because the similarities between her duties as a nurse in the Philippines and care provider in Rome make her "feel better" about doing domestic work.

Providers of elderly care in both Rome and Los Angeles are also more satisfied with their jobs because such work offers greater autonomy than does other types of domestic work. Elderly wards often depend on the physical assistance of care providers. Explains Lorna Fernandez, who was once a midwife in the Philippines:

> With my present employer, I wake up at seven in the morning. . . . By eight o'clock, I have to give everything to the older person. I wake her up, feed her, clean her, bathe her, change her. She is totally dependent on me. She can still walk, but she can only do so when you hold on to her. You have to assist her.

Employers usually acknowledge this dependency. Thus, providers of elderly care believe that, compared to other domestic workers, they are treated with greater respect by employers.

Those who care for the elderly also believe that they have greater control of their labor, because decision making, unlike in other domestic jobs, is usually reserved for the judgment of the caregiver.

> I only choose elderly care. What I don't like are jobs with children. No, I don't like that because you are required to do the work they are requiring of you. It is not like that with an elderly, because it is just you and the elder. You know when to feed them, bathe them. . . . These people are easy to adjust to, you just have to get to know their attitude and per-

sonality. The one I am taking care of is ninety-six years old, and so you have to kind of discipline [her,] saying "no, no, no"... I am the one who decides everything, if I should take her to the hospital, if I need to call the doctor. (Maya Areza, Los Angeles)

While domestic workers have to take orders in other jobs frequently, authority in elderly care is much more fluid. Comparing her previous job as a live-in housekeeper to her present job caring for the elderly, Judy Reyes, for instance, describes the former as having been much worse for her ego and psyche: "They never run out of orders, they do not want to lose any money but get their money's worth." In elderly care, she sets her own schedule and has more knowledge of the needs of her "patient" than do his children, and thus she has more autonomy. Mimi Baclayon of Los Angeles concurs with Judy's preference for providing elderly care. As she states, "No matter what, there is no god telling you what to do. You are the one deciding what you should be doing."

However, elderly care also has its pitfalls. In comparison to other kinds of domestic work, this job often requires twenty-four hours of labor. For example, Trinidad Borromeo, a sixty-eight-year-old woman in Rome, describes having to take care of a bedridden woman in her late eighties nonstop.

I begin at seven in the morning. I change her, feed her, give her all of her injections and medication. Then I clean the apartment. When you take care of an elder, the first thing you have to have is patience. If you don't have it, you won't last. For example, when you feed her, it can take up to an hour. It gets hard when they don't want to open their mouth or swallow the food. But taking care of an elder like this one is better than a mobile one. Those ones are demanding. You wipe them already, then they want you to wipe them again. They have no shame. These types are better.... You just move them around from the bed to the chair. You have to just clean her bed everyday because it will smell like pee around the house if you don't.... I wake up at four in the morning just to check that the woman is still alive. Then if there is no problem, I sleep until a little bit before seven, and I am done with her by nine. I just serve her coffee and biscuits. I sleep around midnight or one in the morning.

While the greatest stress of providing elderly care is its demands in time, a distant second is the absence of privacy. As Lorna Fernandez explains:

I do everything. I brush her teeth, brush her hair, clean her Pampers. I do everything. The job is nonstop.... Our beds are next to each other, and if she cannot sleep then I cannot sleep. I sleep when she starts snoring. Her snoring is music to my ears.

Becoming an extension of the dependent employer, providers of elderly care do not usually have a space to call their own.

LIVE-IN HOUSEKEEPERS

In my categorization of domestic employment, live-in housekeepers include housecleaners and childcare providers. I place them in one category because more than half of my interviewees who "live" with their employers, excluding providers of elderly care, have the dual responsibility of childcare and housecleaning. Of the three types of domestic work, live-in housekeeping offers the least rewards. Live-in domestics have less control of their schedules. Like those who care for the elderly, they are subject to social isolation and an unset work schedule. Yet unlike those who care for the elderly, they are also subject to the much greater authority of employers.

Most migrant Filipina domestic workers in Los Angeles, as mentioned, are live-in workers. None of them would even consider part-time work because the living expenses incurred in such a work arrangement would result in lesser remittances for their families in the Philippines and/or lesser savings. In Rome, live-in workers are often deterred from part-time work by its faster pace and greater workload. Michelle Alvarez, for example, switched to live-in work because the more strenuous physical demands of part-time work aggravated her heart problem: "I really can't do part-time work. I've always had a heart problem in the Philippines, and when I came here, it was made worse by my workload." In Rome, women without children also seem to be averse to the isolation of live-in employment. While there is a mixture of women with and without children among part-time workers, only four women without children in Rome have chosen live-in work.

In both Rome and Los Angeles, the routine of live-in housekeeping usually allows women to set a slower pace for themselves. Live-in work is often described as less strenuous, with specific responsibilities delineated as primary tasks. Cleaning is usually a secondary responsibility for childcare providers. Marilou Ilagan, a domestic worker for more than twenty years in Los Angeles, gives most of her attention to her two wards and does not have to worry about other domestic responsibilities such as cleaning and cooking.

I wake up in the morning, around 6 a.m., and I take a shower. By 6:45 I am in the kitchen, fixing the children's lunch. They just have sandwiches.

I check if they are getting dressed. Then when they are ready, we leave. They don't have breakfast usually, but sometimes they do. Then, I drive both of them to school. Afterwards, I come back here and clean their rooms. After that, I come down here [the kitchen]. It is not too hard to clean their rooms. . . . Then I pick them up from school. Usually, they have after school activities, like one has a tutor three times a week . . . and then the younger one has acting classes every Tuesday. Then, when they have doctor or dentist appointments, I take them. When they want to go shopping, I take them. Then we go home, and I [am] done with my work. I don't have to worry about their dinner. I am free at night.

Luzviminda Ancheta, also working for a wealthy family in Los Angeles, only worries about her main tasks of cooking and cleaning.

I wake up at 5:30, and I heat the heater in the Japanese teahouse [located in the gardens of her employers' home] because the woman [a psychiatrist] usually has a patient there by 6:30 in the morning. . . . Then, one hour later, I prepare their breakfast, but usually it is only cereal. That's it. Then I clean when I feel like cleaning. It is [up to] you to know what and when you need to clean. No one tells you how and when you are supposed to clean what. There are a lot of employers like that, but not mine. You know your routine, and so it is just right that they don't tell you what to do. I clean in the mornings and cook in the afternoons. That is my routine. For dinner, I usually cook them fish—just salmon. They don't like a variety, just salmon, and they like it tasteless. . . . Besides cooking, I fix up their room everyday. I fix their bed. I also take care of their laundry. I don't think it is difficult. They are not fancy like other bosses. Some want their sheets ironed, and here they don't. They don't expect me to iron the polyester. [Laughs.]

Designated certain tasks as the primary responsibilities of their jobs, Marilou and Luzviminda appreciate the willingness of employers to ease their load. Yet as most families only hire one domestic worker, the everyday routine of most women entails a fairly demanding schedule. Nonetheless, live-in workers still tend to have a less physically demanding work routine than do part-time workers, because they are often expected by employers to concentrate on certain tasks.

Live-in domestic workers, however, have to cope with the social isolation of working in a private home much more than part-time workers. Often feeling trapped, they cannot help but see the enclosed space of the employer's home as a prison. Without an outlet for communication, Lelanie Quezon, a sixty-eight-year-old grandmother who has been working for a middle-class Filipino family in Los Angeles for more than four years, cannot help but describe her employer's home as such.

> I felt like I was in prison. I wanted to cry. . . . Now I have gotten used to it. But I used to look out the window and wonder why I never see a single person in the middle of the day. It is just a bunch of houses. But after a while, the baby got older and now I have someone to talk to. Her grandmother was telling me that now I have someone to talk to and I won't get bored anymore. I have someone to talk to no matter what.

Considering that many women's outlet for communication is limited to their very young wards, who needless to say are often too young to hold deep conversations, it is not surprising to hear that women consider counting the days until their days off as part of the everyday routine of live-in work.

Domestic work is described as painstakingly boring by all of the women in my study but more so by live-in workers. Vicky Diaz of Los Angeles, for example, describes the emotional assault of isolation that she felt when employed as a live-in domestic for three years: "A housekeeping job—there are times at night when you cannot sleep from crying and crying the whole night. The job is boring. You do not see anything except your employer sitting there in front of you. . . . It is boring." The social isolation of domestic work highlights the mundane nature of the job. Consequently, it more than reminds them of their decline in status upon migration.

Live-in workers complained about the authority of employers more than others did. Without set working hours, live-in workers are subject to receiving orders from employers during all hours of the day. While they may develop a certain amount of control over their work routine, they cannot fully deter employers from imposing more tasks. Analin Mahusay of Rome, for instance, complains of having to work until one in the morning when her employers entertain guests.

> As a live-in, one works from eight o'clock in the morning until 9:30 in the evening. But if there are guests, one can be working until one in the morning, washing the heavy silvers and putting them back in their place.

Analin's complaint shows that the lack of regulation in domestic work leaves live-in workers in the position of having to bear and tolerate the idiosyncratic behavior of employers more than do other domestics.

DISCUSSION

In summary, various conditions in the everyday work routine of each of the three types of domestic employment stress domestic workers' experience of underemployment. For part-time workers, the laborious monotony of cleaning more than reminds them that they are not utilizing their educational training. While providers of elderly care can claim to utilize a certain degree of their training, the loneliness and isolation of their job emphasize their decline in status upon migration. These conditions contrast quite sharply with their more socially fulfilling occupations as teachers, students, business owners, and office workers in the Philippines. Finally, live-in workers contend with their decline in authority when coping with their isolation and the idiosyncratic behavior of employers. For childcare workers, the authority of young wards over them further aggravates this decline. For instance, Jerissa Lim of Los Angeles expresses the humiliation of this reality: "Would you believe, you would hold onto him in public and he would say, 'No. Stupid, idiot.' I could not take that, being told off by a little kid in public. I had to tolerate it. I was so patient for that one year."[8] All in all, every routine in each type of domestic work that I have described contrasts quite starkly with their more socially and intellectually fulfilling, though less financially rewarding, occupations in the Philippines.

The Aggravation of Contradictory Class Mobility

Documenting the inequalities reflected in the work process, the employer-employee relationship, and in the actual labor, many studies have concluded that paid domestic work is an inherently oppressive occupation, whether because of the feudal roots of domestic service (Rollins, 1985), the ghettoization of women of color into domestic work (Cock, 1980; Glenn, 1986), the social construction of employers as superior (Rollins, 1985; Constable, 1997), or the "structure of exploitation" (Romero, 1992: 142) implicit in employer-employee relations under capitalism.[9] Furthermore, they agree that domestic workers generally feel the lingering stigma of servitude. Migrant Filipina domestic workers also feel this lingering stigma. It is a stigma that heightens the pain inflicted by contradictory class mobility.

In this section, I establish that unequal relations of power between domestics and their employers aggravate the experience of contradictory class mobility. Building from other studies on domestic work, I show how its current work organization, which is similar in the United States and Italy, exacerbates the pain inflicted by this dislocation. The organization of domestic work—set as wage employment in a private home—creates an incongruent distribution of authority in the workplace. Under this work organization, there is no set standard of employment. Domestic workers are left vulnerable to arbitrary working conditions. As Mary Romero states, "Private household workers lack authority and must therefore rely on the employers' cooperation to change the structure of the work and social relationships" (1992: 158). My analysis shows that the authority of employers stresses the pain of underemployment for migrant Filipina domestic workers. For one, it increases their vulnerability in the workplace. As a result, they are subject to the idiosyncrasies of employers. Such conditions reinforce their subordinate position and consequently intensify their experience of downward mobility.

THE ABSENCE OF REGULATION

The enclosure of the work setting in a private home results in the absence of regulation. Employers of domestic workers usually have "enormous leeway to determine the working conditions by setting wages, establishing job descriptions and determining the work structure" (Romero, 1992: 120). Live-in domestic workers, for example, often complain about the absence of set parameters between their work and rest hours. However, in Italy, employers usually recognize the two-hour-long "rest hour" required by Italian labor laws. In Los Angeles, except when they are entertaining guests, employers usually leave their domestics alone after dinner. Though employers have become increasingly sensitive to limiting the hours of employees, the dependency of employees on their sensitivity still indicates that it is up to employers to monitor their own authority.

Consequently, migrant Filipina domestic workers are put in the position of having to find accommodating employers in order to secure fair standards of employment. Like the African American domestic workers in Dill's (1994) study, Filipina domestic workers consider the attitude of employers to be a measure of working conditions. They are more content with work if fortunate to have found "nice" and "good" employers, meaning employers who are not exceedingly demanding. Notably, domestic workers who claim not to have any work-related problems attribute their general satisfaction to having found "good" employers. In response to the question "What problems have you encountered at work?" those content with their jobs gave an answer similar to Michelle Alvarez's: "Nothing really because my employers have been very nice." Having "nice" employers is so important that some women have even accepted a lower salary in exchange for "good" employers.

However, migrant Filipina domestic workers generally have had great difficulty finding accommodating employers. This is true in both Rome and Los Angeles. During the first few years, they often change jobs periodically. Following the principle of supply and demand, supply is definitely on the side of employers. While there has been a significant increase in the number of Filipino migrants in Rome in the last ten years, Filipina domestic workers in Los Angeles have always had to contend with the competition posed by the large pool of Latina workers. Though the domestic workers whom I interviewed tend to be satisfied with their employers, they at one point had to tolerate stricter and more demanding employers, especially during the early years of settlement when they had not yet developed a support network in the community.

To a certain extent, migrant Filipina domestic workers have come to view their employers as "nice" because these workers have accepted certain low standards of employment. One of these standards is what Judith Rollins refers to as "spatial deference" in the workplace, meaning "the unequal rights of the domestic and the employer to the space around the other's body and the controlling of the domestic's use of house space" (1985: 171). Without doubt, employers control the spatial movements of domestic workers in the workplace as they decide upon the domestic worker's integration in or segregation from the family. More often than not, they prefer segregation as they tend to hire those "who will demand very few of their resources, in terms of time, money, space or interaction" (Wrigley, 1995: 26). The access of domestic workers to household space is usually far more contained than for the rest of the family.

This spatial inequality signifies the lesser social status of the domestic worker in relation to employers. Consequently, it reminds them of their decline in labor market status. In both Los Angeles and Rome, Filipina domestic workers, including nannies and providers of elderly care, have regularly found themselves subject to food rationing, prevented from sitting on the couch, provided with a separate set of utensils, and told when to get food from the refrigerator and when to retreat to their bedrooms. These attempts by employers to regulate their bodies are described by domestic workers as part of the larger effort by employers to own them.

With spatial deference so established in domestic work, Filipina domestic workers are often startled when employers fail to enforce segregation. Luzviminda Ancheta in Los Angeles relates this expectation in her surprise over what she sees as the "odd" behavior of her employers.

> Here they are very nice. In other households, the plates of the maids and the cups and glasses are different from the employers. Here, it is not. We use the same utensils and plates. They don't care. . . . They even use the cup that I have. They don't care. [Laughs.]

Her astonishment over her employer's lack of concern over crossing the boundaries of spatial deference is telling of the established pattern of spatial segregation in the workplace.

Notwithstanding its reflections of inequality, spatial segregation is also a source of comfort for Filipina domestic workers. Efforts by employers to rupture patterns of spatial deference are not always viewed favorably by domestic workers. For example, Marilou Ilagan, a domestic worker for a family in the exclusive neighborhood of Brentwood, expresses her discomfort over eating with her employers.

> I don't want to eat with them, and that is why I eat here [the breakfast room] on my own while they eat in the dining room. But we eat at the same time and the same food. My employer asked me if I wanted to eat with them, but I told her that I would be so much more comfortable if I were just by myself. I would rather be by myself. That was OK with her. She told me that was fine with them if that was what I preferred.
> *Why are you not comfortable?*
> I don't know. . . . This is where I sleep, but it is not the same as being in your own home. You cannot feel as comfortable as being in your own home.

The constant discomfort of domestics such as Marilou is possibly caused by their consciousness of their lesser status in race and class hierarchies.[10] According to Shellee Colen, "Eating is a materially and symbolically important arena for dehumanization and lack of consideration" (1989: 181), reflected most clearly in the "classic" situation of domestic workers eating separately from the rest of the family. Though choosing to eat on their own could be seen as an example of their conformity to the dehumanization of the domestic worker, it can also be seen as an act of reclaiming their own space, away from that of the employer where their identity is that of a perpetual domestic worker. Confining themselves to their own space within the workplace is possibly a creative act of retreat—a break—from their role as a worker.

Generally, Filipina domestic workers do not perceive eating on their own as a signifier of their lower status in relation to the employer. To them, it does not emphasize servitude. Instead, they view the following situations as clearer markers of dehumanization and servitude: employers expecting domestic workers to eat less expensive food; employers expecting domestic workers to stand by the dinner table during meals; and employers allowing domestic workers to eat only after they have finished their own meals. In these cases, differences in eating practices are far more extreme and more difficult or maybe even impossible for domestic workers to rationalize. The first and third enforce their lower material worth, while the second exaggerates the practice of servitude and reduces the value of their time and labor by rewarding the act of idleness. For migrant Filipina domestic workers, these are the cases in which their employer's behavior reinforces their decline in social status.

MIGRANT STATUS

Further compounding the authority of employers is the migrant status of domestics. One of the ultimate goals of migrant Filipina domestic workers in Italy and the United States is legalization, the achievement of which often depends on the cooperation of employers.[11] This leaves domestics in a more vulnerable position. In the United States, obtaining a green card through employer sponsorship has been described as "a form of state-sanctioned, indenture-like exploitation" because "the worker is obligated to stay in the sponsored position until the green card is granted (often two or more years) in spite of any abuses to which she may be subjected" (Colen, 1989: 173).[12] Obtaining a green card through employer sponsorship is a process that can take as long as six years. For example, Luzviminda Ancheta, a domestic worker in Los Angeles since 1987, was petitioned by her employer in 1990. Six years later she still only held a work permit that legally bound her service to the sponsoring employer.

In most other countries, employers can impose lower standards of employment, revoke visas without notice, and leave migrant Filipinos scrambling for new "hosts" to sponsor their stay in the country. In Italy, one of the most recent amnesties for illegal migrant workers, granted in November 1995, forced many domestic workers to settle for lower wages in exchange for a permit to stay. Because the Italian government expected sponsoring employers to pay a six-month advance of the income tax (*contributi*) required of them for the services of their employees, many employers lowered the wages of their domestic workers by 20 percent or expected domestic workers to cover the advance payment. As "guests," Filipina migrants had to pay income tax and consequently had to settle for lower standards than those given to the average Italian worker.

Unfortunately, employers sometimes take advantage of the dependency of their domestics for legal status and intentionally mislead them. In Rome, numerous domestics complained about reneged promises of employers to sponsor their stay under the November 1995 amnesty, which was going on during the time of the interviews. Many domestics were only informed by employers of their lack of intention to sponsor them near the amnesty's closing date (March 1996), hence not leaving them with much time to seek employers who were genuinely interested in granting them legal status. In Los Angeles, Cerissa Fariñas was misled by two of her employers about processing her papers. While they promised to sponsor her application for a green card, they did not inform her of their lack of intention to do so until after two years of service, during which time they had found other reasons to explain the delay in filing her application. While taking advantage of her dependency, Cerissa's employers guaranteed her loyalty and dedicated service. However, the threat of "getting caught" does loom over employers who take advantage of undocumented workers. Hence, undocumented workers are not the only ones made vulnerable by their employment.

Filipina domestic workers accompanying migrant Filipino professionals or business owners and their families to the United States are even more vulnerable than are other undocumented workers. Often of a lower class than middle-class domestic workers who enter the United States with tourist visas, their contacts in the host society are usually limited to the family sponsoring their migration. They consequently lack the resources and autonomy needed to choose jobs. As a result, they are usually more vulnerable to exploitative work conditions. Marilou Ilagan, a domestic worker in the United States since 1972, tolerated her substandard wages for more than seventeen years because of her limited social networks.

> I came in through a Filipino family . . . . The woman was pregnant and so they also wanted someone to take care of their baby.
> *How long were you with them?*
> Seventeen years.
> *They were that good to you?*
> They were OK but I couldn't just leave them. I did not know anyone

here. I had no friends. I had no outlet. I could not just go out if I wanted to because I had nowhere to go. So, I had no day off. I had no place to go to since they took me along with them. So, I did not go out. I did not know anyone.

They did not take you out with them?

Yes, they took me out here and there. When they go out as a family, they would take me with them once in a while. But just by myself, I did not go out. I was with them for seventeen years. After seventeen years, after I finally was able to legalize my stay, I left.

How did you get papers?

They helped me. This was in 1989 with the amnesty.

How much did you earn?

Very little. Unbelievably low, very, very, very low.

Five hundred dollars a month?

Not quite.

Less?

Four hundred dollars a month.

This was until 1990?

Yes.

Wow.

That was it. I made a $100 a week. No, they only paid me $300 a month for my services. That is why when I was able to leave them I was happy.

More like ecstatic?

Yes. [Laughs.] . . . That is why when I was finally able to leave them, I felt like my life was beginning. You know what I mean—my life changed. I felt free. And can you imagine the first job I got after that paid me $400 a week? Can you imagine that? And my salary with them was only $300 a month.

Although Marilou could have sought employer sponsorship, the isolation enforced by her Filipino employers ensured her dependence, guaranteed her continued service, and accordingly denied her the option of seeking higher-paying jobs. It was only after her employers' children were older, almost in college, and when her services were no longer needed did they assist her in obtaining legal status. This pattern of isolation emerged among three of the four other women who entered the United States with professional Filipino migrants. For example, one who worked in New York was expected to stay at home at all times and was given neither a coat nor winter boots by her employers in the two years she worked for them.

THE EMOTIONAL WORK OF DEFERENCE

The emotional work of deference is another aspect of the job that emphasizes the greater authority of employers over domestic workers. Judith Rollins (1985), in her insightful examination of the politics of everyday interaction between domestics and their employers, builds from Irving Goffman to identify "deference and maternalism" as the central script controlling the behavior of employers and domestic workers. Domestic workers must act with deference—they cannot talk to but must be spoken to by employers, they must engage in "ingratiating behavior," and they must perform tasks in a lively manner.[13] An employer's control penetrates into the bodily movements of domestic workers in myriad ways, including patterns of speech, gestures, spatial movements, and the "attitude and manner with which the individual performs tasks" (Rollins, 1985: 158). Concomitantly, employers validate their higher social status through maternalism, acting "protective" and "nurturing" to the "childlike" domestic worker. According to Rollins, the script of "deference and maternalism" perpetuates nonegalitarian relations in domestic work by confirming the superiority of employers.

The attitude and behavior of employers often disregard the experience and capabilities of domestic workers (Wrigley, 1995; Rollins, 1985). As a result, their actions, for example, their need to constantly supervise domestics, remind migrant Filipinas of their subordinate status. Because this tendency magnifies the inequalities between domestics and employers, it also injures the psyche of domestic workers by denigrating their intellect. Mila Tizon of Los Angeles complains:

> I know what I need to do because I know what they do not like. But before I get a chance to do what I know I need to do, the younger sister of my employer will be yapping away about how I did not clean that corner, this table, etc. etc. She always complains about everything she knows she can complain about. She criticizes me all the time.

Such behavior by employers further aggravates the sense of loss in social status for domestics. Rowena Chavez of Rome states:

> I regret not using my education especially when I am doing something and then they order me to do something else. When they order me around is when I cannot stand being here. It is not like I do not know what I need to do. Being ordered around is what I cannot accept at all.

Also exacerbating the various emotional tensions in domestic work is the "emotional labor" expected of domestic workers. Coined by Arlie Hochschild, emotional labor refers to the expectation of employers to "produce an emotional state in another person" through "face-to-face" interaction and is indicative of the employers' "control over the emotional activities of employees" (1983: 147). In domestic work, following the protocol of deference demands the emotional labor of smiling. Domestic workers have to disregard their true feelings, be it boredom, anger, or exhaustion, and carry attitudes reflecting the idealized (that is, pleasant) environment of the home.

> Even when you are fatigued, feeling feverish, feel terrible, you can't stay in bed, you have to get up and work. Then you have to be smiling and acting happy. (Girlie Belen, Rome)

> At the end of the day, you are so tired and they want you to smile. If you don't, they wonder why you are not smiling like you had been in the beginning of the day. (Evelyn Binas, Rome)

> Even when they are angry with you, you still have to be smiling. Even if they are serious, you have to joke around with them. (Michelle Fonte, Rome)

All of the women in my study complained of the strains imposed by the emotional labor of smiling. The opposite of women's genuine feelings, smiling intensifies the labor demands of and emotional tensions wrought by domestic work, including the strains brought by their experience of underemployment.

The Reconciliation of Contradictory Class Mobility

So far, I have established that migrant Filipina domestic workers experience the dislocation of contradictory class mobility. I have also shown that certain labor conditions aggravate this dislocation. These conditions include the work organization and greater authority of employers, the legal dependence of sponsored migrants, and the low standard of employment in domestic work. In this section, I enumerate the means by which migrant Filipina domestic workers negotiate their experience of downward mobility. I show that they do not passively acquiesce to the emotional tensions wrought by contradictory class mobility. Instead, they act on the need to resolve their decline in labor market status, because, as Genelin Magsaysay of Rome states, "It is so easy to feel sorry for yourself. You have the lowest job in society."

They attempt to subvert the pain inflicted by their decline in social status in numerous ways, which include surprisingly enough, accepting the racialization of domestics, embracing the setting of intimacy in the workplace, and, more expectedly, incorporating "immediate struggles" in the performance of domestic work. However, the central means by which they ease their pain do not question but instead maintain the relations of inequality established by employers in the organization of domestic work. For example, they wish to someday be just like their employers.

THE FANTASY OF REVERSAL

To reconcile the contradictions in their contradictory class mobility, migrant Filipina domestic workers emphasize the gains brought by this dislocation. While domestic work involves downward mobility, it at the same time constitutes a certain degree of upward mobility, not just because of their higher wages but also because of the higher social status that is generated in the Philippines by their status as a "migrant worker" (Goldring, 1998). Migrant Filipina domestic workers consequently ease the pain engendered in the dislocation of contradictory class mobility by stressing their higher status than those held by poorer women in the Philippines.

They do this through the fantasy of reversal, the fantasy of someday having and being personally served by their own domestics once they return to the Philippines. By basing their identities within the discursive terrain of transnationalism, they are able to resolve the discrepancy in class status enforced by migration with the assurance of the greater standing that they will have in the Philippines. As Joy Manlapit of Los Angeles told me:

> When I go back, I want to experience being able to be my own boss in the house. I want to be able to order someone to make me coffee, to serve me food. That is good. That is how you can take back all of the hardships you experienced before. That is something you struggled for.

Gloria Yogore, her counterpart in Rome, finds similar comfort in the knowledge of the higher social status she will possess once she returns to the Philippines.

> In the Philippines, I have maids. When I came here, I kept on thinking that in the Philippines, I have maids and here I am one. I thought to

myself that once I go back to the Philippines, I will not lift my finger and I will be the signora. [Laughs.] My hands will be rested and manicured, and I will wake up at twelve o'clock noon.

Ironically, they find comfort from the experience of contradictory class mobility by stressing the greater privilege that they have in relation to poorer women in the Philippines. Acknowledging the option they have to participate in global capitalism as transnational players is therefore critical to understanding the structural position of migrant Filipina domestic workers. Their option of securing access to the higher wages of migrant employment is in direct contrast to the insecurity of those unable to afford the option of working outside the Philippines.

Migrant Filipina domestic workers also resolve the class discrepancy embodied in the dislocation of contradictory class mobility by stressing the greater material rewards of migrating to be low-wage workers than they would receive working as professionals in the Philippines.

> I came right after graduation. I could have worked but my salary would have just been enough for me. I would not have been able to help my parents. At first, I regretted coming here. I cried a lot. I could not accept being a maid . . . . It was only after a year when I could finally look at my situation as something good. I thought about how my income here is pretty good compared to what it would be in the Philippines even though I am a college graduate. (Michelle Alvarez, Rome)

In Italy, many domestic workers make themselves feel better by reminding themselves that a bank manager in the Philippines is not earning as much as they are. They find comfort in the knowledge that many "professionals in the Philippines . . . earn less than (they) do in Italy."

The fantasy of migrant Filipina domestic workers operates in other realms. Some imagine the house they clean to be their own. Others are able to bear underemployment by constantly reminding themselves of the financial needs of their families in the Philippines. As one woman said, "I force myself to do it just so that I could help my family." Some simply do it for survival, including another woman who told me, "The idea of being a maid was very hard to accept. . . . I have to say that I liked the money though. I had to work to have an income and to survive in the United States. There was no way to get another job because I did not have papers at the time. I could not get a better job." Finally, other women are able to withstand the downward mobility in domestic work by consciously reinforcing the job's temporary length. Patricia Baclayon of Los Angeles told me that she is willing to "clean the dirt of an elderly person" only because she knows that she is doing it temporarily, only until she returns to the Philippines.

RACE AND CLASS: DIFFERENCES BETWEEN FILIPINA
AND BLACK AND LATINA DOMESTIC WORKERS

Race and class differences between Filipina domestics and their employers result in the heightening of servitude. Despite this fact, migrant Filipina domestic workers utilize racialization as a means of negotiating their decline in status. They do so by claiming and embracing their racial differentiation from Latinas and blacks and highlighting their specific distinction as the "educated domestics."

Numerous scholars have illustrated the production and reproduction of race and class inequalities between women in the daily practices of paid household work (Cock, 1980; Glenn, 1986; Palmer, 1989; Rollins, 1985; Romero, 1992). Documenting the hierarchization of womanhood in the United States in the pre–World War II period, Phyllis Palmer (1989) describes the reflection of race and class hierarchies in the division of labor between "clean mistresses" and "dirty servants." According to Palmer, the more physically strenuous labor of the servant enabled the mistress to attain the markers of ideal femininity—fragility and cleanliness. This hierarchization actually continues today, as the most demanding physical labor in the household is still relegated to the paid domestic worker.

To enhance their own status, employers often assign tasks that they would not want to undertake to their domestics (Rollins, 1985; Romero, 1992). In Italy, domestic workers are expected to scrub the floor on their knees. When performing the same task themselves, employers, the domestic workers noticed, enforce a different standard: they do not scrub but instead mop the floor. The distinction of appropriate household labor for domestic workers and employers enforces race and class hierarchies between women as tasks unacceptable for employers are rendered acceptable for domestic workers, most of whom are women of color. This division of labor is also reflected in childcare. In a study of childcare providers and their employers in New York and Los Angeles, Julia Wrigley (1995) found that employers usually assign the most demanding childcare duties to domestics and keep physically lighter work, for example, reading and shopping, to themselves. The relegation of physically demanding tasks to domestics denotes the inequality rendered by the distinction of appropriate physical labor for employers and domestics.

Another employer strategy for reinforcing racial and class differentiation is the preference for hiring "less-educated and poor domestics" (Rollins, 1985: 195), because less-educated women are expected to be more deferent.[14] Yet while employers seem to prefer black domestic workers to be less educated, Filipina domestic workers claim that their employers would rather hire educated domestic workers. Giselle Aragon, a housecleaner in Rome, states, "Filipinos are much preferred in domestic work because employers say that we are . . . educated. Other nationalities are looked at differently. I consider them underdogs." In Los Angeles, many women also made similar claims. This discrepancy raised numerous questions about the difference between African Americans and Filipina migrants in either the United States and Italy, where Filipinas are supposedly preferred over other domestic workers of color. Are employers' expectations of domestic workers determined by the different racial construction of Filipinos in both Italy and the United States? For example, do the "controlling images" of Filipino Americans as meek and compliant vitiate any possible threat of their high educational level? Are they made less threatening by an undocumented or "guest worker" status? Or are these claims of Filipina domestic workers even true? Are they just a fantasy that they hold on to so as to differentiate themselves from other women of color domestic workers? Regardless of whether these claims are true, the fact is migrant Filipina domestic workers in both Rome and Los Angeles believe that they are racially distinguished from other domestic workers by employers, because this belief helps ease their pain of underemployment.

Assuming that the racial differentiation of Filipinos is true, I now turn to Wrigley's (1995) discussion of the two-tier paid childcare system in the United States in order to explain the discrepancy between the preference of employers for less-educated black domestic workers and their seeming preference for educated Filipina domestic workers. I specifically show that this bifurcation extends to domestics generally.[15]

Wrigley distinguishes two main types of childcare workers in the United States—low-status and high-status employees. Low-status employees are considered "socially subordinate" workers who are generally assumed to be noneducated migrant women from developing countries. The services that they provide are considered "low quality," because these workers are perceived to have minimal skills and inferior cultural practices and beliefs. In contrast, "quality care" is provided by "educated, culturally similar caregivers" (1995: 48). Some employers seek "high-quality" domestic workers, usually European au pairs who demand higher wages, in order to avoid cultural conflicts with migrant women from developing countries.

Failing to recognize the high level of education achieved by most Filipina domestic workers, Wrigley, in her discussion of one Filipina domestic worker in her sample, categorically places their services under "low-quality care."[16] In recognition of their high level of education, I believe that it is more accurate to place them in-between high- and low-status caregivers. While Filipina domestic workers in Rome and Los Angeles do not have the autonomy and racial equality granted high-quality caregivers, they claim that employers distinguish them from other migrant domestic workers. For instance, Genelin Magsaysay describes the in-between location that they inhabit in Italy.

> Italians have a low opinion of us Filipinos because we are all domestic workers and we are foreigners. That's why you can't blame them for not looking at us as their equals. Filipinos look better than other foreigners do though. My employers have said that Filipinos compared to other foreigners in Italy are better. One time when my employer was hospitalized, the doctor told me that Filipinos are the best and that there's nothing bad to be said about them.

While Filipina domestic workers in Italy cannot be recognized as peers by Italians, they still seem to be distinguished from and placed above other migrant groups. This suggests that the experiences of domestic workers vary considerably depending on their racialization, colonial histories (as seen through language acquisition), and structural location. These factors affect the employer's perception of the domestic worker.

In Italy, Filipina domestic workers claim that they are preferred over other immigrant domestic workers because they are hardworking, honest, clean, and educated. By embracing these stereotypes to be true, by default, they imply that other domestic workers are not. Thus, they distinguish themselves racially from their Latina and African counterparts and support the hierarchization of racial subordinates in society. Paralleling the discrepant wages of European au pairs and domestic workers from developing countries in the United States (Wrigley, 1995), Filipinas in Italy receive on average the higher rate of 10,000 to 12,000 lira (U.S.$6.67 to $8.00) an hour for day work in comparison to the 8000 lira (U.S.$5.33) hourly rate given to women from Peru, Cape Verde, and Poland.[17] Significantly, the nation-based racial categorization in Italy distinguishes Polish women as "lesser whites" and marks them as socially inferior to Italians and Northern Europeans.

How do migrant Filipina domestic workers in Italy justify their higher wage rates? Vanessa Dulang credits the higher wage rate of Filipinas to their supposedly better work ethic.

> Italians prefer Filipinos to others because we are supposedly hardworking, trustworthy, and nice. We are clean and we are not robbers. Even though Filipinos ask for a higher rate, they still prefer us Filipinos. For example, Polish workers ask for 8000 [U.S.$5.33] an hour and Filipinos ask for 12,000 [U.S.$8.00], and Italians will still hire the Filipinos even if they have to pay more. It's because they say they trust us more and they are more satisfied with our work.

While it is highly unlikely that Filipinas are nicer and more hardworking than other domestic workers, the attachment of these stereotypes to Filipinos has made them a "status symbol" for employers. Explains Jennifer Jeremillo:

> *Compare Filipinos to other foreigners in Italy.*
> We have the same kind of work; we work in the house. The employers much prefer Filipinos because they see Filipinos as honest and dependable. They much prefer them to other nationalities that are stereotyped as the types who would steal. Here, if a family employs a Filipina, it shows that they are rich because Filipinos get paid a lot more than Bangladeshis and Peruvians, for example. Other groups would work for as little as 700,000 lira (U.S.$467). A friend of my employer for example told my employer that she was rich when my employer told her about me. She asked my employer why not pick a Peruvian or Polish, why did she need to get one that asked for a high salary? Filipinos are a status symbol.

According to migrant Filipina domestic workers, although not considered peers by Italian employers, they are distinguished from other migrant groups because they are expected to provide better-quality services. Often unable to speak English, employers are impressed by their command of the English language. Employers with children usually rely on Filipina domestic workers to tutor their children and to assist them with homework, tasks that are, following Wrigley's definition, never entrusted to low-status domestic workers. This differentiation does point to a certain racialization of Filipinos, one that is segmented by a glass ceiling and one that should not be celebrated by migrant Filipina domestic workers. At most, a high level of educational attainment has only taken them to the status of "better-than-low-quality" domestic workers, which is only a slight differentiation from other groups of migrant domestics.

Just as Filipinos in Italy claim to be the Mercedes Benz of domestic workers, those in Los Angeles similarly profess to provide better services than do Latina domestic workers. Moreover, they contend that the "higher-quality" services that they offer—from housecleaning to providing elderly care—are reflected in their higher pay rate.

> *Do you think that employers respect your education?*
> I really think so. I really think it just shows in the pay rate. With Mexicans usually, they work for a lower rate, like $250 a week. Once in the bus stop in Bel Air, there was this group of women speaking Spanish, and I know how to speak Spanish. They were telling stories about how much they made—comparing salaries. One was happy with $250 a week, and one was $120 a week, and she had to clean every corner in the house. Then she works for longer hours. It was just abuse! I think that here they have tremendous respect for Filipinos because they know that most of us are educated. Often, when they look for employees, they ask for Filipinos. (Genny O'Connor)

A recent survey of Latina domestic workers in Los Angeles shows that live-in domestic workers only receive the mean hourly wage of $3.79 for sixty-four hours of work per week. They earn approximately $242 a week, much less than the women in my study (Hondagneu-Sotelo and Avila, 1997). This wage discrepancy is perhaps partially due to the greater English-language skills of migrant Filipinas, because greater language skills often translate to higher earnings for migrants (Chiswick and Miller, 1996).

Other domestic workers second the claim of Genny O'Connor, attributing the preference for Filipinos to their higher level of education and greater command of the English language. Joy Manlapit, for example, explains that it is critical for providers of elderly care to know the English language in case of medical emergencies.

> As a caregiver, you have a lot of responsibility. You have to have knowledge and skills. You have to know what to do in case of emergency. You have to be able to call a doctor and explain what happened. That is why they do not hire someone who cannot speak English. The only thing they care about when hiring is that you know how to speak English.

That is what they like. I am also proud to tell you that they prefer Filipinos [over] Latinas. It is because the second language of Filipinos is English. That is why we don't have a hard time speaking English and understand them right away. It is also because most of the Filipinos are professionals, even if we enter domestic work.

Based on these comments, it is possible that employers meet the higher wage rates of Filipina domestics because they find some sort of reassurance in their belief that they are receiving higher-quality service from these workers.

The different reception and the distinction of Filipina domestic workers from blacks and Latinas in Rome, which also seems to hold true for those in Los Angeles, point to their different racialization. In her article on cultural citizenship, Aihwa Ong identifies the "bifurcation of Asian immigrants" in the contemporary United States, where Hmongs, constructed as "undesirable citizens," are "ideologically blackened subjects manipulating state structures in order to gain better access to resources" and middle-class Chinese immigrants, as "desirable citizens," are "caught between whitening social practices and the consumer power that spells citizenship in the global economy" (1996: 751). The pattern of racial differentiation that Ong found among Hmong refugees and Chinese immigrants parallels the differentiation of Filipina domestic workers from Latina and black domestic workers in Rome and Latina domestic workers in Los Angeles. There seems to be a bifurcation of domestic workers of color into better-than-low-quality and low-quality workers. It is a differentiation that Filipinas openly accept due to its rewards of greater respect and higher wage rates. Moreover, it is one that they emphasize to give notice to their high level of educational attainment. This bifurcation thus consoles them over their experience of contradictory class mobility.[18]

THE USE OF "LIKE ONE OF THE FAMILY"

There is a consensus in the literature on domestic work that the perception of domestic workers as "one of the family" enforces, aggravates, and perpetuates unequal relations of power between domestic workers and their employers (Bakan and Stasiulis, 1997a, 1997b; Cock, 1980; Gregson and Lowe, 1994; Romero, 1992; Wrigley, 1995; Young, 1987). First and foremost, it is rooted in the feudalistic conception of domestic workers as servants bound to the master for life. Second, it clouds the status of the domestic worker as a paid laborer, so employees are less able to negotiate for better working con-

ditions. Their duties become conflated with "family" obligation and considered by employers a "labor of love" because of their close relationship (Gregson and Lowe, 1994; Romero, 1992). Third, employers can manipulate the
use of family ideologies for the extraction of unpaid labor, for example, the
emotional labor of affection and attachment to their wards (Romero, 1992).
Lastly, it obscures the existence of their own families (Bakan and Stasiulis,
1997b).

While I do agree that the myth of being "like one of the family" perpetuates inequalities, I found that domestic workers can also use this myth to
manipulate employers and resist the inequalities that this myth perpetuates
in the workplace (Young, 1987). In fact, migrant Filipina domestic workers
in Rome and Los Angeles embrace the notion of "like one of the family" and
the intimacy resulting from this construction. Though intimacy increases the
authority of employers in the workplace and concomitantly stresses the decline in status of migrant Filipina domestic workers, the women in my study
still use intimacy to de-emphasize servitude. They reason that as "one of the
family," they are not servants but more like the more respected au pairs in
Wrigley's (1995) study. Moreover, they use intimacy to increase the material advantages of domestic work and in the process maximize the benefits of
their contradictory class mobility. Thus, domestic workers have a dual purpose for the use of intimacy. The first is to decrease the emotional pitfalls of
contradictory class mobility, and the second is to increase this dislocation's
corresponding material benefits. In making this assertion, I do not intend to
argue that domestic workers achieve egalitarian working conditions when
embracing the intimacy that is selectively promoted by employers. Instead,
I want to give notice to the agency of domestics workers and at the same time
provide an empirical illustration of power's complex operation; as Foucault
has argued, it does not operate only in a descending order. Thus, I wish to
show, as the migrant Filipina domestic workers whom I observed and interviewed revealed to me, that various emblems of inequality in domestic work
have not simply imposed adversities on them.

BEING "LIKE ONE OF THE FAMILY" MEANS
BEING CONSIDERED A HUMAN BEING

I am lucky that I have good employers now. They are professors. They don't look
down at us. So, I am very happy with my present employers because I am treated
like a human being. (Helen Gambaya, domestic worker in Los Angeles 1988–89
and in Rome since 1990)

Like the Chicana domestic workers interviewed by Romero (1992) and the black domestic workers in Dill's (1994) study, Filipina domestic workers "feel like a person" when considered "one of the family." A domestic worker in Los Angeles states, "I like my job because my employers treat me like a human being." As domestic workers weigh their jobs according to how employers treat them, those who treat them "like a human being" are considered the best employers.

In response to my question of what it means to be treated "like a human being," the women enumerated the following criteria: (1) recognizing their skills and "brain" by not being ordered around constantly or by giving them the option to decide whether to wear a uniform; (2) recognizing their social needs by allowing them to have visitors and permitting partners to spend the night; (3) recognizing their physical needs by making sure that they rest, for example, by advising day workers to ease their pace; and (4) recognizing their presence, for example, by offering food to day workers when they first come in and asking them to sit down and chat (while they are getting paid). Lastly, being treated "like a human being" also means being considered as "one of the family."

Domestic workers consider distinguishing them as not "one of the family" to be a marker of their lesser status as a person. Claribelle Ignacio of Rome, for example, considers being "treated like a slave" the opposite of being treated "like one of the family."

Do you like your job?
Yes. Because my employer right now is a very good employer. They are kindhearted and treat me like one of the family. That is the one thing that is important to me. I want to be treated like a person. Not all employers are good; some are very bad. You can have a high salary but get treated like a slave. I don't care about the high salary as long as I am treated as a person, part of the family, and I get along well with my employer. It is important to have a good rapport and work relationship. What I found among us in Italy, many are unhappy and not content with their employers.

Why do Filipina domestic workers equate being a human being with being "one of the family"? Romero found that Chicana domestic workers have a tendency to contrast "treatment as a 'non-person' versus treatment as a 'family member'" because they seek respect and dignity in the workplace, a psychological desire that makes them more vulnerable, as efforts to please em-

ployers usually take them "above and beyond the standard contractual relationship" (1992: 125, 126). Diverging from Romero's observation, I found
that migrant Filipina domestic workers consider treatment as not "one of the
family" inhumane simply because being treated more coldly in the intimate
space of a private home contrasts with the established norms of interactions
among other inhabitants of the home and by default labels them as inferior.

Migrant Filipina domestic workers actively seek to be treated "like one of
the family." Reminiscing about an elderly employer who had recently passed
away, Jovita Gacutan of Los Angeles proudly describes the conditional familial relationship she had had with her employer.

> We were like a mother and daughter. We had our fights. We would have
> different opinions. But of course I could not look at her as a mother
> completely because no matter what she was still my employer. But our
> relationship was one of honesty and compassion. Like a family.

Because domestics work in the private space of the home, they desire a less
rigid work environment and much prefer the intimate environment of being
treated "like one of the family."

Although aware of the possibility of being manipulated when demanding
to be treated "like one of the family," Filipina domestic workers still prefer to
be accorded this treatment than the emotional distancing found by Romero
(1992) among Chicana domestic workers. A less rigid work environment does
give them flexible work standards. Domestic workers are able to get away with
occasional slip-ups. The informal environment that they achieve from the
myth of "like one of the family" also accords them a more lax work routine.
Day workers might enjoy occasional breaks while still on the clock (for example, having tea with employers). Live-in workers can ease their work pace
and workload. For these reasons, Filipina domestic workers do not enforce
distance but instead seek intimacy. However, without a set work standard,
domestic workers are left more vulnerable to the authority of employers.

Despite this danger, migrant Filipina domestic workers still turn to the notion of "like one of the family," because in the process of doing so they never
lose sight of their status as a worker. For instance, migrant Filipina caregivers
tend to measure the quality of their labor in terms of their personal expectations for their own families. In Rome, Girlie Belen's case is an example.

> I had an employer with two young children. . . . They called me "zia"
> (aunt) because they could not pronounce my name. . . . I took care of
> them for two years. . . . The love that I had for my child [in the Philip-

pines], I poured to these two young children. . . . I clothed them, bathed them, taught them how to pray. . . . [Because] I was paid to do it, I gave the children all of my love and attention.

Many domestic workers are like Girlie, as they tend to describe the very familial act of "pouring love" as a central duty of caretaking. Yet the tendency of migrant Filipina domestic workers to "pour love" is not an emotional bond that is easy for employers to manipulate. As it is only part of the job, domestic workers are able to maintain a certain degree of emotional distance from this emotional labor. More often than not, the act of pouring love leaves them physically exhausted. This, in turn, serves as a strong reminder of their wage-based relationship.

I would wake up at 6:30. I make breakfast, feed the baby, then after they have breakfast and leave for the offices, I take care of the baby, take the baby to the park, and then when I go back, I cook and bathe the baby. . . . There is a seven-year-old daughter that I have to pick up from school every afternoon at 4:30. Even if the baby is sleeping, I have to wake the baby up to pick up the sister. I cannot sleep. I cannot rest. I cannot breathe at night anymore. I can hardly feel my heart pumping. I am exhausted; from the baby to the household cleaning, doing it at the same time is a hard job. . . . (Gloria Yogore, Rome)

The physical exhaustion imposed by domestic work is difficult to ignore. Thus, in the field, I was not surprised to never hear domestic workers talk about the employing family with affection or reverence. Instead, I often heard complaints.

Another reminder of their status as a paid employee amid their emotional attachment to the employing family is the clear difference between their physical state of exhaustion and the female employer's well-rested body.

It was very difficult. If the child is awake, you have to be awake as well. Sometimes I worked for over sixteen hours. I would wake up at six or seven in the morning. That is when the boy wakes up, and so I have to watch over the boy and make him breakfast and see to his other needs. I start cleaning the kitchen. My employers would wake up at around twelve or one. . . . When they woke up, they would just shower and leave. (Jerissa Lim, Los Angeles)

The woman was a spoiled brat. She can sleep until ten, eleven, twelve in the afternoon without thinking about her two children. I am the one that looked after the children—did everything, spoon-fed them. . . . When she woke up, I even brought her breakfast in bed. (Luisa Balila, Rome)

Domestic workers often cannot help but compare their activities to those of their employer's and in the process usually notice that one of their main duties is to free them of time for leisure, rest, and relaxation. They are subsequently reminded of their status as an employee of the family.

While never foolish enough to believe that they are actually a member of the family, migrant Filipina domestic workers still only consider employers who treat them "like one of the family" to be "good employers." In recognition of the agency of domestic workers, this attitude should not be seen as one that is too dangerous for them to hold. Behind their incorporation into the family lies the knowledge that they are paid employees. This is a status that is hard for them to forget, because they know that beneath the positive attitude of employers lies high expectations. As one interviewee told me, "They love you if they are satisfied with your work, and when they cannot get everything they want from you, they become very dissatisfied."

As Wrigley has argued, it is in the best interest of employers to treat domestic workers with dignity and respect: "Just as sociologists have found that the kind of work people do affects the behavior they encourage in their children, so too this can apply among caregivers" (1995: 19). There seems to be a cycle of dependency defining employer-employee relations in domestic work. By treating domestic workers "like a human being," employers can induce domestic workers to "do a good job." Domestic workers may similarly attain the treatment they so desire to be "like one of the family" by "doing a good job." Some Filipina domestic workers, such as Ana Vengco of Rome, also recognize this cycle of dependency in domestic work: "They treat me well because they need me." Generally, Filipina domestic workers with "good employers" credit the positive attitudes of employers to the quality of their work. However, when they are not accorded the treatment of a human being, they do not consider it to be a sign of doing a bad job.

An employer's terrible attitude, without doubt, makes domestics less invested in their work. Mimi Baclayon of Los Angeles, for example, did not think twice about leaving her difficult employers in a lurch.

They were too strict with the caregiver, and that is not the kind of environment you would appreciate. You would want your work, even though it is just that, you would want your environment to be right. So, I gave up that job even though the pay was good. It was for $100 a day . . . so after my cousins picked me up for my day off one day, I decided not to return anymore.

While it can be argued that power inequalities in domestic work would make domestic workers more dependent on employers, employers also have a great deal invested in treating domestic workers "like one of the family." For example, employers are made extremely vulnerable by the threats wrought by intimacy, including child neglect and property violations. Thus, employers may find themselves having to treat domestic workers "like human beings" and not just as labor-producing machines.

Still, not all of the efforts of domestic workers to do a good job are rewarded by employers. In Rome and Los Angeles, a great number of employers actually do not accord domestic workers treatment that reflects the quality of their labor. Explains Jennifer Jeremillo of Rome:

> Sometimes I wish all of them are like my employers. . . . I often hear
> from my friends about problems that they have with their employers,
> how their employers refused to pay them at the end of the month. . . .
> Some complain about how they did not get out on their day off because
> their employer had work for them to do. Many of us live-in workers
> don't stay with our employers for a long time because we are not treated
> well; for example, in eating, we do not get to eat the same food.

Supporting Romero's (1992) observations that authority clearly lies with employers, the efforts of many migrant Filipina domestics to do a good job do not always lead to trust, respect, or humane treatment. This indicates that the turn taken by migrant Filipina domestic workers toward the use of the myth of "like one of the family" to mitigate the pain of contradictory class mobility maintains the authority of employers, which is one of the greatest factors that aggravate this dislocation.

AFFECTION — DEBILITATING OR REWARDING?

Regardless of the notion of "like one of the family" being a myth, domestic workers—in particular, live-in workers—may manipulate the attachment that develops from the closeness between domestic workers and employers. While critics of the notion illustrate the greater susceptibility generated by the "attachment" of domestic workers, they often forget that wards and employers can also become attached to the domestic workers, as Jovita Gacutan's and Maria Batung's stories show.

They (the children of her elderly ward and her ward) kept on calling me in the Philippines, and after I came back, she was already different. She had been affected by the separation. I realized then that it is not advisable for your ward to get too attached to you. (Jovita Gacutan, Los Angeles)

If you could have only seen them when I was about to go home. In the airport, all the other passengers were looking over at us because one was hugging me, one was tugging me [on] the right. They were all crying . . . . My employers told me that they had to take the children out so that they would not cry. . . . It was such a big drama when I went on vacation. Then, when I was in the Philippines, soon after I landed they started calling me long distance. They asked me when I was coming back, and I told them that I just got there. (Maria Batung, Los Angeles)

As Dill (1994) has observed, intimacy gives rise to a "familial" attachment that domestic workers can take advantage of to cope with the demands in the workplace. An example is the story of Gelli Padit, a domestic worker in Rome. Even after a huge argument ensued between Gelli and her employer of four years in which Gelli scared her employer "by hitting the wall in (her) room" and "screaming out on the terrace," the employer begged her not to leave when she started packing that evening. The employer told her to just take a few days off but not to take any of her belongings. While the employer could have been threatened by Gelli's violent reaction, the familiarity intimacy breeds may have influenced her to suppress any desire to fire Gelli. In both Rome and Los Angeles, numerous domestic workers mentioned how employers who considered them "like one of the family" did not replace them with other domestic workers when they extended their vacations in the Philippines, even up to six months.

However, as other scholars have pointed out, the danger of holding affection for their wards is that it makes it difficult for domestics to negotiate for fair wages or even leave. Lelanie Quezon of Los Angeles wanted to leave her job but felt guilty about leaving her employers in a tight situation. In a similar situation, Valentina Diamante wanted to quit her live-in job but was restrained by her close attachment to the two young girls she had taken care of for more than four years. However, Valentina and Lelanie were not completely hindered by their attachment, which only delayed their departure. Having waited to leave until their employers found suitable replacements, they do not believe that their attachment adversely affected them but only made them more considerate. In addition, Valentina, who even with her higher salary had not been satisfied with her new employers, was immediately rehired by her former employers without any grudge over her decision to leave them.

Many studies of domestic work dismiss gifts given by employers to domestic workers as acts of "benevolent maternalism" (Cock, 1980; Rollins, 1985; Romero, 1992). As Romero states:

> When employers grant favors, make promises and give gifts, the employee becomes ensnared in a web of debt and obligation that masks considerations of the employee's rights. . . . Gift-giving is simply another employer tactic for keeping wages low and for extracting additional unpaid labor [from] the employee. (1992: 131)

Though employers may intend to use gifts as a tactic of control, domestic workers have gained tremendous material benefits from the inclination of employers to give gifts.

Numerous examples show that gifts bestowed by employers do not have to ultimately increase the power of employers but can actually also work to the advantage of employees. Considered "like one of the family," a domestic worker in Los Angeles inherited enough money to retire comfortably in the Philippines from an elderly employer. At least two domestic workers persuaded their employers to invest in business ventures in the Philippines. The trust that comes from the intimacy of being "like one of the family" led Jovita Gacutan's employer to cosign a loan she used to purchase a house in Los Angeles. Consuelo Cabrido of Rome was given two-years' advance payment by one of her four employers so that she could have a house built for her family in the Philippines. One can easily argue that, because Consuelo is bound to work for her employer, the loan translates to indentured labor. However, Consuelo, who is consequently freed of rent, considers the loan from her employer a much better option than her only other choice of borrowing money from a migrant Filipina in Italy. While the standard monthly interest rate for loans in the Filipino-Italian migrant community is 10 percent, her employer is not charging her any interest.

Employers have also helped domestic workers legalize their status. Girlie Macabalo of Rome, for example, could not convince her new employers to sponsor her legalization by attaching their names to her permit to stay. They did not want to sponsor her legalization because they were not willing to be liable to taxation. As a personal favor, a former employer agreed to sponsor Girlie. Michelle Fonte of Rome found her permit to stay threatened after a squabble with her sponsoring employers led her to leave and seek other employment. The employers later reported her to the authorities as an illegal worker, as her work permit required her to work for them for another year. While her new employers did not want to get involved, a former employer willingly took over the sponsorship of her permit to stay. In both cases, Girlie and Michelle were not obligated to return to their old employers.

All of the preceding examples indicate that the practice of gift giving does not necessarily signify benevolent maternalism. They also suggest that the intimacy of the family engenders the employers placing a great level of trust in employees, which consequently can result in tangible improvements and greater material benefits in employees' lives.

CONTROLLING THE SCRIPT OF DOMESTIC WORK WITH CONSCIOUS EMOTIONAL DISPLAYS

Migrant Filipina domestic workers in Rome and Los Angeles have not invested in large-scale efforts of mobilization. While this is true, I neither lament the absence of traditional means of resistance nor see this absence as an indication of complacency. As they do with other dislocations, migrant Filipina domestic workers take a turn against contradictory class mobility and the other inconsistencies in domestic work, such as the authority of employers, by means of "immediate struggles." Importantly, the notion of immediate struggles cannot be equated with coping strategies. An example of the latter is the act of keeping busy to pass time in hopes of easing the boredom of social isolation or the pain of subservience. Not merely relying on this sort of coping behavior, migrant Filipina domestic workers incorporate immediate struggles in their everyday work routine in an attempt to subvert the authority of employers, improve work conditions, and gain control of their labor. They do all of these to reduce their position of subservience and to temper the contradictions in their contradictory class mobility.

This is not a surprising observation. Numerous studies of domestic work have made similar claims. Both Hunter (1997) and Dill (1988, 1994) establish that the everyday acts of subversion incorporated by domestic workers pose a constant threat to the authority of employers. Dill shows that African American domestic workers enforce measures of control over working conditions through the incorporation of various individual acts of subversion, including "chicanery, cajolery, and negotiation" (1994: 50). Likewise, migrant

Filipina domestic workers in both Rome and Los Angeles manipulate the script of deference and maternalism as an act of immediate struggle. Performing a balancing act, they simultaneously follow and question the script of deference and maternalism. While Nicole Constable claims that Filipina domestic workers "internalize a sense of inferiority" when performing the script, I found them to be more conscious beings (1997: 69). As conscious beings, they are somewhat removed from the emotional script of domestic work. Consequently, they are able to hold feelings of attachment for and detachment from their employers simultaneously and in the process attempt to subvert the script within the routine of domestic work.

How are migrant Filipina domestic workers able to subvert the script of deference and maternalism while simultaneously abiding by it? Individuals, according to De Certeau, function as "consumers" in society as their everyday practices follow rules and social orders inculcated through the use of "the products imposed by a dominant economic order" (1984: xix). At the same *De Certeau* time, individuals are not always inclined to abide by the disciplining measures disseminated in society but subvert them through the use of strategies, defined as the visible reconstruction of the proper order, or tactics, defined as the incorporation of subversive activities manipulating the proper order in the rituals of everyday life.[19] Tactics and strategies are differentiated by time and place. Tactics occur in the place of oppression and involve the manipulation of time through key moments of intervention, while strategies require the resource of a place, a space in which to strategize and retreat.

Domestic workers, as consumers, are hammered in by rules, particularly the script of deference and maternalism, and as part of the "weak" more often develop tactics when subverting the authority of employers. Strategies, for example, collective bargaining, have long been elusive measures of resistance for domestic workers. Tactics, such as "chicanery" and "cajolery" are "victories of the 'weak' over the 'strong'" and are incorporated within the boundaries of the rules and order of domestic work through "clever tricks, knowing how to get away with things, 'hunter's cunning,' maneuvers, polymorphic simulations, joyful discoveries, poetic as well as warlike" (De Certeau, 1984: xix). Through tactics, domestic workers take advantage of opportune moments within the daily rituals of domestic work by creatively interjecting subversive acts into everyday routines so as to resist the tedium and disciplinary measures that normalize inequalities between employers and employees.

In the script of deference and maternalism, employers are said to use emotions to control domestic workers (Rollins, 1985). They manipulate the af-

fective aspects of the relationship to elicit additional labor, for instance, acting kind to make domestics more willing to comply with substandard wages.
As a tactic to subvert the control of employers, migrant Filipina domestic
workers have also realized their ability to manipulate the emotions of employers. For example, by complying with the expectations of employers for
domestic workers to constantly act happy, they normalize the deferent behavior demanded by employers. They are then able to manipulate its nor-
malization, because the smallest detour away from the script is noticeable to
employers.

> In domestic work, I always had to be happy. I had to make them laugh,
> tell stories. They were happy with that, and that is why they liked me.
> Once in a while I had to frown because the mood of a person is never
> the same. . . . Sometimes I just wanted to get mad. . . . When [my em-
> ployer] [saw] that I [was] lonely, she would ask me if I wanted to go
> shopping. I would say sure. (Vicky Diaz, Los Angeles)

> Sometimes we chat with our employers. They talk to you if you have a
> sense of humor. You have to be in a light mood and cheerful, then they
> talk to you. When you work, you always have to be smiling so that your
> employers think you are sweet. Even if I am in a bad mood, I am smil-
> ing. If I am not smiling, they know that I have a problem because I am
> always smiling. (Ruby Mercado, Rome)

Aware of the emotional script they are expected to follow, domestic workers
have come to realize that they have the ability to subvert the authority of employers through the manipulation of this script.

Doing just that, migrant Filipina domestic workers utilize the tactic of
conscious emotional displays, the tactical projection of emotions as a means
of negotiating working conditions. They go against the script of deference
and maternalism by crying, showing anger, projecting a somber mood, becoming very quiet and unresponsive to employers, or by simply talking
back. Emotional deviation in domestic work has to be rare for it to be effective, since it loses its punch when utilized frequently. Nonetheless, domestic
workers have still been able to bargain effectively using this tactic.

As Rowena Chavez of Rome explains, the emotional script of smiling is
so well established that it is very clear to employers when domestic workers
fail to follow the script.

> They always want you to be smiling even when you are really tired. They
> always want you to be smiling. If you are not smiling, they always bug

you, ask you what's wrong, if you have a problem. If you're frowning because they said something offensive, they feel guilty and apologize.

Through the calculated projection of emotions, domestic workers are able to make demands on employers. They are particularly able to do so by eliciting emotional discomfort in employers, such as unease and guilt. Moreover, they manipulate the maternalism of employers by putting employers in the position of having to make domestic workers feel better. In utilizing conscious emotional displays, they not only challenge the script of deference and maternalism but in doing so ease various challenges of domestic work such as boredom, a heavy workload, or the demeaning attitude of employers.

Genny O'Connor, for example, relies on frowning as a way to ease her workload.

> Oh, you have to be smiling all the time. If you are not smiling, they
> don't like it. They want you to have a jolly face all the time. They don't
> want to see you frown, but once in while I just have to show them that I
> am frowning from all the work that I have to do. Especially when I am
> not used to it and they give me so much work.

Genny claims that her attempts to ease her workload are usually successful, for instance, leading to the extension of the number of hours that the employer expects for her to complete a task. Like other domestic workers, however, she is only able to manipulate the rituals of deference to her advantage by going against them sparingly. The women whom I interviewed did not rely only on the emotional manipulation of employers to ease their workload; they also incorporated other subversive acts, such as working at a slow pace. Yet when given an unreasonable load by employers, they more often relied on the tactical display of emotions.

Other challenging aspects of domestic work are also met through this tactic. In order to relieve the loneliness and boredom engendered by social isolation, Janet Sapida of Rome would sometimes cry to intimate her desire to visit friends during a working day while still a live-in domestic.

> When my [previous] employer would come home, sometimes I would
> be bawling. I would still continue my work but I would be crying while I
> did it. I would tell them that I was missing my parents. So, they would
> take me to the house of a friend.

By manipulating the maternalism of her employer with the calculated projection of crying, Janet was able to arrange subversively a visit with a friend during a working day. More often than not, however, the women whom I interviewed usually cope with social isolation by keeping busy (for example, watching television).

Other times, domestic workers feel compelled to reveal their anger, irritation, and frustration over a demanding workload or an employer's demeaning treatment more directly. They might do this by banging pots and pans.

> I always frown and bang things around when I'm mad . . . . It's funny that my employers always try to appease me by giving me presents. (Claribelle Ignacio, Rome)

Emotional outbursts contradict the expectations of employers so starkly that employers are caught off guard, made uneasy, and consequently left easier to manipulate when responding to the unexpected emotions projected by domestic workers. Employers accommodate domestic workers so as to return to the script immediately.

While one may wonder why domestic workers do not attempt to speak rationally to employers, power inequalities between domestic workers and employers often prevent them from being able to do so. Moreover, domestic workers find the projection of emotions to involve less effort.

> When I do get mad, I just keep it to myself. I don't show it. But when I get quiet, they know it affected me. They know when they offend me. They offend me when they ask me why I have not cleaned something that I have cleaned already. After they know that I am offended, they leave me alone and then talk to me again later. (Incarnacion Molina, Rome)

Incarnacion's story reveals that she does not have to exert the effort of explaining her dissatisfaction to her employer as she can instead choose to display particular emotions.

If displaying emotions does not successfully inform employers of their problems over working conditions, domestic workers resort to talking back, which is a more direct form of arbitration and one that puts their job security at greater risk. Helen Gambaya is one domestic worker who tends to talk back.

> My employers always shouted at me. But in a book, I had read "When in Rome, do what the Romans do." So, I did what the Romans did, I screamed back at them.

Because domestic workers talk back so sporadically, when they do, it often leaves employers surprised and compelled to listen. Michelle Fonte of Rome finally talked back to her employers when they slammed the phone down while she was speaking to her mother in the Philippines.

> That old employer of mine used to slam the phone on my mother when my mother called me. That's when I got mad at them, and that's when I started fighting back. . . . Then my employer told me I was being disrespectful. I told her that I am disrespectful when she is disrespectful. I am nice when she is nice.

According to Michelle, her employers did not dramatically change for the better, but they did recognize her action by never slamming the phone on her mother again. While none of the women who rely on displaying emotions were let go for doing so, a few women were fired for daring to talk back to employers. Talking back contradicts the script of deference but also questions and threatens the authority of employers more directly. Thus, some employers are less tolerant of it.

To reduce the risk of being fired, other domestic workers, like Rowena Chavez, use a softer approach of communication. They take advantage of the expectations of employers for domestic workers to "entertain" them with conversation by sometimes inserting information that would elicit feelings of guilt.

> I told my signora, "Signora, you think that this is the only kind of job that we know how to do." Then she asked me: "What kind of job did you used to have?" I told her: "I used to work in a bank." Then she asked: "Well, why did you come here then?" I told her: "The salary there is enough to support yourself, but it's not enough if you want to help your family. Even though I did not know that this is what I was going to experience here, it's fine as long as I can help my family."

Many educated domestic workers are like Rowena and often insist on letting their employers know of their educational qualifications. They tend to share this information when they are responding to an insult made by an employer against migrants or Filipinos.

If talking back or displays of emotional discontent do not transform working conditions for the better, migrant Filipina domestic workers—not unlike the domestic workers in Dill's (1994) study—rely on quitting as a last resort. Quitting, however, is not a very accessible option. Because their families rely on their earnings, they often cannot risk losing even a month's salary. Many of them do not always have the resources that they need to quit. This is true despite the social networks and sentiments of collectivism that have developed in the migrant communities in Rome and Los Angeles.

THE HIDDEN TRANSCRIPT

The individual acts of immediate struggles that I have enumerated in this chapter are in fact collective acts. They do not reside at the level of the individual but are rooted in the collective consciousness of a shared struggle among domestic workers. When domestic workers do complain, it is highly likely that they had heard or articulated those same complaints to another domestic worker before they did so to their employers. Domestic workers find the strength to incorporate tactics in the daily activities of domestic work from the "hidden transcript" that they maintain with other domestic workers, those with whom they share experiences in migration and at work. Coined by James Scott to explain the ability of the "weak" to develop a consciousness of collective struggle, the "hidden transcript" refers to the "discourse that takes place 'offstage,' beyond direct observation by powerholders" (1990: 5). In the case of domestic workers, the "hidden transcript" refers to the discourse that they maintain outside of the view of employers. In sites of the "hidden transcript," migrant Filipina domestic workers brew tactics, as defined by De Certeau (1984), using the very limited resources available to them.

In addition to the multinational space of the magazine *Tinig Filipino*, migrant Filipina domestic workers produce the "hidden transcript" in numerous local sites. These include churches, community centers, and buses. In these sites, they speak of difficulties encountered in the workplace and complain about the unreasonable demands and abusive behavior of employers. They reveal their true feelings in these sites. Consequently, the "hidden transcript" becomes an outlet for the built-up frustrations that domestics have accumulated in the workplace.

From the "hidden transcript," migrant Filipina domestic workers garner the information and resources that they need to lessen their dependence on employers and secure the option of quitting. As Mila Tizon of Los Angeles states:

> Most of the people that I ride the bus with every morning are domestic workers. There are many of us [Filipinos]. There we compare our salaries to know the going rate. We also ask each other for possible job referrals. We often exchange phone numbers and contact each other.

Providing domestic workers a consciousness of a collective struggle from their shared experiences of domination, the "hidden transcript" enables them to establish standards of wages, evaluate the fairness of their working conditions, validate suspicions, and finally garner the strength to disobey the script of the dominant order. They might feel more empowered to demand higher wages from employers, because the knowledge that they have gained from the "hidden transcript" establishes standards different from those set by employers. Consequently, it is an alternative space that they actively seek to create.[20]

The functions of the "hidden transcript" have been acknowledged in the literature of domestic work. Though not quite like the "hidden transcript," which is a discourse and not an institution, the notion of social networks has been observed by scholars such as Hondagneu-Sotelo (1994) and Hunter (1997) to be a resource created by domestic workers to increase their control of their labor. Like the "hidden transcript," social networks give domestic workers access to job referrals and knowledge of established labor standards. My purpose for turning to the concept of the "hidden transcript" is not to present its functions but instead to argue that the individual acts of resistance that have been identified in domestic work are in fact not individual but instead are collective, an observation that has yet to be made in the literature of domestic work.

Conclusion

Domestic workers neither passively acquiesce to the disciplining mechanisms of employers nor do they internalize the pain inflicted by contradictory class mobility. They contest them through the manipulation of the very same mechanisms of control used by employers, such as the script of deference and maternalism and the myth of "like one of the family." Their use of established emblems of inequality suggests the fluid operation of power in society; that is, power is not simply imposed by "those on the top at those at the bottom" (Dreyfus and Rabinow, 1983: 186). This occurs for the simple reason that domestic workers, or generally anyone on whom power is exercised, are acting subjects (Foucault, 1980, 1983). At the same time, it points to the acquiescence of migrant Filipina domestic workers to the structural inequalities defining relations in domestic work. Clearly, they do not attempt to subvert the structures, which place them in a position of subservience. They only manipulate the direct results of these larger systems of inequal-

ity. However, the "immediate struggles" that they deploy have brought concrete change, such as the decrease of emotional adversities and increase of
material rewards in the dislocation of contradictory class mobility. These
struggles have also threatened the authority of employers, but not to the extent of questioning the subservience of domestic workers.

In light of their dislocated class position, how do they feel about domestic
work and settlement? Both groups of women in my study did not necessarily develop "a highly critical perception of the host society" as speculated by
Portes and Rumbaut (1996) of migrants who experience downward mobility
upon migration. The different "contexts of reception" that welcome them
have led to two very distinct sentiments about domestic work and settlement
for women in Rome and Los Angeles. In Rome, they are resigned to domestic work and have settled with the job. In Los Angeles, they do not underplay
their dissatisfaction and abhor domestic work. They voice their definite re-
pulsion against domestic work and, unlike their counterparts in Rome, have
not resigned to it completely. Mila Tizon's sentiments reflect those of the
women in Los Angeles:

> Actually, I do not like the kind of work that I do. I am here and I cannot
> do anything about it. So, I just have to do it and work. You cannot ex-
> pect anything good with domestic work. You can never be content with
> yourself doing housekeeping work.

Patricia Baclayon echoes these bitter sentiments: "When I worked in the
home, I realized that this is the United Mistakes of America. I had never
thought that this was what I was going to experience here."

While women in Rome share the bitterness of their counterparts in Los
Angeles, they are more resigned to accepting domestic work. Their resolu-
tion is probably influenced by the fact that they are all domestic workers in
Rome. In contrast, domestic workers in Los Angeles have to cope with the
added pressures of seeing more "successful" Filipino migrants, such as the
slew of health professionals migrating in the last three decades. Only one
woman in Los Angeles holds an attitude that mirrors the more resolved attitude of women in Rome. Dorothy Espiritu, once a domestic worker in Saudi
Arabia, sounds like the women in Rome when she states, "Any kind of job
would do, but at this point this is the only kind of job that I can find. I am not
mad or angry about it. It's just the way it is."

The Dislocation of Nonbelonging: Domestic Workers in the Filipino Migrant Communities of Rome and Los Angeles

The dislocation of nonbelonging defines the community life of Filipina domestic workers in both Rome and Los Angeles.[1] By describing their community life as such, I emphasize that a sense of constant discomfort characterizes their lived experience in the migrant community. Nonbelonging results from two distinct sources of social exclusion for these two groups of women. For women in Los Angeles, it stems from the Filipino migrant community, and for women in Rome, from the dominant Italian society. Despite its different sources, nonbelonging is a shared localized dislocation for these two groups of female migrant workers. It is a discomfort that constantly affects their behavior, attitudes, and feelings in the community. As such, my analysis of the migrant community centers on this dislocation.

My discussion focuses on the culture of the community, which refers to the "sharing of modes of behaviour and outlook within the community" (Wilson 1996: 66). In this way, my analysis of the community concentrates on the perspective of the migrant subject, which in both Rome and Los Angeles is determined by the dislocation of nonbelonging. In doing so I take note of Rouse's observation that migration scholars still "know very little that is analytically significant about the ways in which recent settlers have made sense of their lives" (1992: 27).

In both Rome and Los Angeles, the migrant community maintains coexisting cultures of collectivism and competition. In other words, migrant Filipina domestic workers find not just support but also alienation from the migrant community. Explained by the state of nonbelonging of the migrant subject, the coexistence of "anomie" and "solidarity" for migrant Filipina domestic workers in Rome and Los Angeles summarizes my depiction of their community life (Mahler, 1995).[2]

197

I move away from solely depicting the migrant community as a supportive niche from dominant society.[3] My wariness against doing so is influenced by the work of Sarah Mahler (1995), who, in a rich ethnographic study
of Salvadoran and Peruvian refugees in Long Island, questions the long-
standing tendency in migration studies to romanticize migrant communities
when she establishes that anomie often plagues feelings of solidarity among
migrants.[4] According to Mahler, the social and labor market restriction of
migrant groups into a segregated community characteristically results in
anomie, because segregation limits the migrant's source of mobility to coethnic exploitation.[5]

While on the one hand I follow Mahler's course of argument concerning
anomie, on the other hand I diverge from her seeming bias against solidarity, which she purports to be a "product of romanticism and outsider analysis." Unlike Mahler, I found that the practices of migrant domestic workers
in Rome, who are plagued with immobility like Salvadorans in Long Island,
not only result in anomie but also manage to simultaneously build solidarity. At the same time, in Los Angeles, migrant Filipina domestic workers do
not experience less co-ethnic conflict, as would be expected from the community's access to the mainstream. Instead, anomie results from class inequalities in the community, while solidarity emerges only among the subgroup of domestic workers and not the community as a whole. Contesting
Mahler's claims that finding solidarity is a result of "outsider analysis" and
"romantic views" of migrant communities, my discussion illustrates the coexistence of anomie and solidarity in the outlook and behavior of migrant
Filipina domestic workers in Rome and Los Angeles.

In this chapter I analyze the community life in Rome and Los Angeles
separately. Following the same logic of analysis in each discussion, I begin by
first explaining the conditions that foster the dislocation of nonbelonging;
second, I describe the geographic constitution of the community; third, I analyze the shared modes of behavior that are prompted by nonbelonging; and
finally I assess the implications of these practices on community relations.

Rome: A Segregated Community

Despite arguments that European states accord "postnational" membership
to guest workers through the provision of rights and protection grounded in
the principles of human rights (Soysal, 1994), the official policies of the newly
emerged receiving state of Italy allow only a quasi-membership that remains

stunted by the restrictive incorporation of its growing number of migrants. In *Limits of Citizenship*, Yasemin Nuhoglu Soysal concludes that migrants in Europe have realized their rightful membership in the host polity because of their experience of "a shared public social space; a set of abstract principles and responsibilities (such as human rights, respect for justice . . . and a 'productive life'); and the rationalized organization and routine of everyday praxis" (1994: 166). Though these experiences are technically applicable to migrant Filipina domestic workers in Italy, they, as "guest workers," would not agree with Soysal, as they have yet to realize their right to membership in this state.

Many societal constraints, most of which I have addressed in previous chapters, promote feelings of nonmembership among migrant Filipina domestic workers. One factor is their segregation in domestic service. In the community, mobility from low-wage service work is understood as an unrealistic goal. In fact, employment in the formal service sector, for example, as a fast-food clerk at McDonald's, is construed as mobility in the community.[6] The segregation of Filipinos in domestic work is also reflected in the media, as shown by the case of the actress Barbara Jane Ricassa, who finds herself cast only as a domestic worker. Though not an actress in the Philippines, Barbara got her break in Italian cinema playing the lead role in *Comincia Tutto Per Caso* (1993), a film partly about the interracial relationship between a Filipina domestic worker and an Italian plumber. The fact that she only plays domestic workers on the screen is not too surprising. What is most ironic about Barbara's situation is that she is employed as a domestic worker when not playing one on the screen. Because there is not a great demand for actresses to portray domestic workers in film and television, Barbara cannot depend on acting as her only source of income. Describing her dual life as a domestic worker, Barbara states:

> To me, acting is just fun. After being stuck in housecleaning, I get to face the camera, and it's fun. . . . Let's say I have a cue call. I am told I have to be at some place, at some time, at some day. I excuse myself from my work. They like it. My employers encourage me, and they are proud of me. They get a kick out of the fact that their domestic is an actress. It's OK, but it's also hard. What happens is they [the producers] speak to my employers and ask what month I could be free, and they try to do my scenes around that time.

More than signifying the segregation of migrant Filipinas in domestic work, Barbara's labor market activities—as a domestic worker and an actress— render a surreal incorporation in the labor market. Barbara's two roles as a domestic worker carry the highest and lowest levels of labor market prestige. Italians have even approached Barbara for her autograph between her shifts from one domestic job to another. Considering the "high status" that she has achieved as an actress, it is quite surprising that Barbara, who has tried to find a job in retail, has not found other forms of employment besides domestic work. Barbara's dual position in the labor market, as it encompasses bipolar extremities of status, embodies the constriction that Filipinos face in the labor market. This immobility is a central factor that instills feelings of curbed membership among them.

Sentiments of nonmembership also result from the restricted social integration allowed migrants in a xenophobic society such as that of Italy. This segregation is reflected in Filipinos' avoidance of public spaces of leisure. For example, of forty-six female interviewees, only two have ever gone to the movies on their own, that is, without employers or young wards. My own experiences also demonstrated the segregation of Filipinos. To my discomfort, Italians often vocalized their surprise or just stared at me when I entered higher-end clothing stores or even neighborhood Italian restaurants. I was not accorded this treatment when accompanied by my white friends, that is, Italians or Americans, as their presence established my identity as a "tourist" whose purchasing power abated my racial othering as a Filipino. While interviewees explain that they restrict their leisure activities in public social spaces so as to minimize their expenses (for example, not eating in Italian restaurants), without doubt the "self-imposed" restriction of leisure space among Filipinos is also influenced by their construction as perpetual foreigners in Italy. Hence, it is not surprising that settlement is driven by an intense desire to return to the Philippines, where not only would they reunite with the children whom they wish to protect from the immobility of life in Rome but where they would also attain the higher social status that they economically garner in migration.

Thus, in response to Soysal's claim that the universalistic rights of individuals transcend citizenship, I would argue that personhood does not transcend citizenship if integration is constrained by legal measures that limit the person's labor market activities to particular low-wage sectors or restrict the person's legal status to "guest workers" ineligible for permanent settlement. Instead, the conditions of citizenship (that is, incorporation) would still determine the migrants' sense of membership. For the most part, the conditions of settlement for migrant Filipina domestic workers in Italy have not fostered feelings of membership but instead those of nonmembership in this host society.

The Dislocation of Nonbelonging

In Italy, the material conditions of settlement essentially institute the consciousness of nonbelonging on the migrant subject. Discussions of the community—its formation and character—require a shift in the focus of analysis from the objects constituting the conditions of settlement to the (emotional, mental, and physical) state of the migrant subject. Only by doing so can we determine the actual experience of migration. This logic of analysis follows the concept of the "structure of feeling" (Williams, 1977).[7]

I specifically turn to this concept to make sense of the actions, in other words, modes of behavior, constituting the community life of domestic workers. According to Williams, a "structure of feeling" refers to "the experiences to which the fixed forms do not speak at all, which indeed they do not recognize" (1977: 130). It moves beyond the reiteration of objects to the subjective, meaning "what is actually being lived, and not only what is thought to be lived" (Williams, 1977: 131). In this case, nonbelonging is "actually being lived," and, in turn, this lived experience transforms to a consciousness that conditions the behavior and outlook of migrant Filipina domestic workers in the community. A structure of feeling is the "affective elements of consciousness and relationships; not feeling against thought; but thought as felt and feeling as thought; practical consciousness of a present kind, in a living and interrelating continuity" (Williams, 1977: 132). It is the "thought as felt and feeling as thought" of nonbelonging that characterizes the lived experience of the community. The experience of settlement, while structurally determined by legal, social, and political conditions, constitutes the practical consciousness of nonbelonging.

The practical consciousness of nonbelonging generates two outlooks in the community: the urgency to leave Italy and the urgency to create a local supportive niche within the dominant society. Hence, the practical consciousness of nonbelonging translates to a liminal state of settlement, particularly one encompassing the contradiction of settling to expedite one's departure. In turn, this liminal state of settlement produces contradictory feelings in the community: migrant Filipina domestic workers simultaneously experience solidarity and anomie.

The geography of the community helps make sense of how and why this liminality produces anomie and solidarity. Nonbelonging translates to the segregation of migrant Filipina domestic workers from the dominant society. Segregation, in turn, delimits their options of mobility to profiting from

other members of the community (Mahler, 1995). In light of the urgency of
Filipinos to leave Italy, segregation instills anomie with the rise of competition over the accumulation of capital among migrant Filipina domestic workers. At the same time, segregation creates interdependency. They can turn
only to each other for the support that they urgently need in settlement.
Thus, segregation also promotes solidarity, that is, the sense of personal responsibility of domestic workers to one another. The practices of the community engender solidarity and anomie simultaneously, as the dual urgencies promoted by nonbelonging mean that they depend on solidarity to
create a supportive niche, and instill anomie in competition to expedite their
departure from Italy. The coexistence of solidarity and anomie, which is explained by the state of nonbelonging of the migrant subject, is the central
contradiction characterizing settlement for migrant Filipina domestic workers in Rome.

Having established the dual outlook of the Filipino migrant community
of Rome, I now evaluate the implications of this duality to the geographic
constitution of the community and examine the shared modes of behavior
that this duality engenders in community life.

The Pockets of Gathering

In Rome, the community is geographically situated in what I refer to as isolated pockets of gathering, pockets which are located in both public and private spaces. Migrant Filipina domestic workers congregate on their day off in
the private domain, at church centers and apartments, and in the public domain, at bus stops and train stations. The term *pockets* aptly describes the
community's geographic organization as it captures the following central
characteristics: the segregated social space of migrant Filipina domestic workers; the enclosed interactions among Filipino migrants in these spaces; and
the proliferation of Filipinos into multiple geographic sites in the city.

Though migrant Filipina domestic workers congregate in public spaces, I
still describe the community's geography as one that is isolated. The public
spaces where they gather are arguably not so public; if not removed from the
view of the dominant society, these spaces have minimal impacts on the public domain. For example, one of the main sites where Filipina domestic workers gather in public is located underneath an overpass by the Tiber River and
is not visible from the street level. Other main gathering sites in the community are located in the periphery of the city, in places with not many pe-

destrian activities. Thus, the community's pockets of gathering, even in public spaces, are arguably segregated from the public social space of the dominant society.

The Filipino migrant community in Rome differs from the usual spatial distribution of migrant communities. Migrant communities typically form around particular sections of the city. Ethnic enclaves, for example, Little Havana in Miami or Koreatown in Los Angeles, are usually spatial segments of the city (Portes and Stepick, 1993). In Rome, the formal economy of Filipino migrants is composed only of a dozen remittance centers, which are not concentrated in one area but are dispersed throughout the city and are controlled by business firms in the Philippines, not by local migrants.

The distinct geographic constitution of the Filipino migrant community is not necessarily due to the small number of formal businesses that make up its ethnic economy. While Haitian migrants in Miami are like Filipinos in that they also have few formal businesses in the ethnic community, the geographic constitution of their community mirrors those of most other migrant groups as they are concentrated in Little Haiti (Portes and Stepick, 1993). The spatial segmentation of Filipino migrants in Rome emerges as pockets of gathering most likely because their labor market segregation in domestic work residentially disperses them throughout the city. Targeting workers in particular areas, remittance centers are located in various neighborhoods. The informal economies of the community are also dispersed in various neighborhoods, creating pockets that are conveniently located in multiple areas of employment. The dispersal of the migrant community in Rome to various isolated locations contrasts with the community of their counterparts in Hong Kong, who take over a central public social space during their day off (Constable, 1997).

Though Filipino migrants in Rome are concentrated in isolated pockets of gathering, their dispersal does not signify their invisibility. Their daily interactions with Italians in various public venues are unavoidable, and they constitute a recognizable population in the city. Visible in the daily activities of the city, they are identifiable in buses, supermarkets, bars, and other public venues. Though they gather in the public domain, there is still a clear limit to their social incorporation. While they may compose a visible population, their movements in public spaces are often fleeting. They inhabit public spaces on their way to private spaces and do not spend long periods of time in public spaces.

In Rome, the geographic organization of their community symbolizes their separation from the dominant society. The physical contours of the terrain of the community are shaped by the very conditions of settlement—the restricted integration of Filipinos in society. The concentration of migrant Filipina domestic workers in "hidden locations" and their geographic dispersal minimize the impact of their presence. On the one hand, the spatial organization of their community into isolated pockets of gathering eases their process of settlement by limiting their interactions with the dominant society. The formation of these pockets, on the other hand, demonstrates that the spatial deference expected of migrant Filipina domestic workers in the workplace extends to a societal level. Thus, the constriction of the community into pockets dispersed throughout the city of Rome is also telling of the limits of Filipino integration into Italian society.

PRIVATE DOMAIN: CHURCH CENTERS AND APARTMENTS

On their day off, migrant Filipina domestic workers gain access to the private domain in church centers and apartments. In Rome, there are at least five churches (four Catholic and one Baptist) that house centers established for the specific purpose of providing shelter for migrant Filipina domestic workers. While the first center opened its doors as early as 1985, the option of congregating in apartments did not come until the early 1990s, when a sizable number of migrant Filipina domestic workers switched from live-in to part-time work. Church centers and apartments are valued in the community. Prior to the opening of church centers, migrant Filipina domestic workers often spent their day off at parks or train stations. Removed from the dominant society, the private spaces of church centers and apartments give Filipina domestic workers safe places to meet other migrants. Apartments provide migrant Filipina domestic workers an intimate environment where they can spend many hours watching Filipino movies, playing mah jong and card games, and cooking Filipino dishes.

Reflecting the growing number of migrant Filipinos, approximately twenty Catholic churches in Rome hold at least one mass in the Tagalog language on Sundays.[8] Of all the migrant groups in the city, the Filipino community receives the most formal assistance from the Catholic Diocese of Rome. For example, they are the only migrant group officially recognized as a local constituent, and the diocese has not granted other large migrant populations with the same religious background, for example, Peruvians, church centers or an official parish. While the greater assistance to the Filipino community is explained partially by its larger population, it is also due to the efforts of the Filipino clergy stationed in Rome to formalize ties between the diocese and Filipino migrant community.

Coordinating activities for Filipino migrants throughout the city, the Filipino Chaplaincy, established in 1991, represents a coalition of twenty-eight local churches whose leaders include clergy and community members. It is the largest association in the community and serves as the strongest advocate of migrant Filipino workers.[9] The local office of the Overseas Workers Welfare Administration (OWWA) is a less prominent advocacy group than the chaplaincy. It mostly oversees services and programs assisting with return migration.[10] The formation of the chaplaincy, and ironically not OWWA, institutionalized the presence of migrant Filipinos in Rome. The chaplaincy is the official gateway to the community for various outsiders, such as academic and government researchers, the media, and city officials. For instance, the chaplaincy (and not OWWA) publishes a directory of religious, government, and civic organizations representing the community.

As the most pressing concern of church leaders is to maintain the deep faith of migrant workers, the chaplaincy organizes a number of spiritual activities in its parish church, Santa Prudenziana. In the facilities of the parish, migrants may join the prayer group Legion of Mary or participate actively in church services through the groups Commentators and Lectors Guild and Knights of the Altar. Extending beyond the realm of spiritual services, the chaplaincy's activities also concern the social issues of migrant workers. A variety of social services are offered at Santa Prudenziana, including legal assistance, free medical care, job placement referrals, and Italian-language classes. In addition, migrant workers can take part in cultural groups such as choirs, dance troupes, and a theater group. One of its largest groups is the Filipino Youth Ministry, which in addition to coordinating catechism classes arranges various social activities such as volleyball and basketball tournaments in the summer. Largely supported by the entire community, the chaplaincy, though dependent on the presence of the Filipino clergy, relies on the generosity of churchgoers for its funding.

Large numbers of Filipinos seek shelter on their day off at Santa Prudenziana as well as at other church centers. In these centers, domestic workers may choose not to partake in spiritual activities. For example, one center mainly provides entertainment. It is equipped with a wide-screen television set, stereo, and karaoke machine, all of which were purchased using the annual dues of members. Another attraction drawing scores of Filipinos into these centers is the meals, which they can purchase for extremely reasonable prices (usually 5000 lira [U.S.$3.30]). In at least two of the centers, there are regular vendors who have made special arrangements with the church to sell meals to domestic workers. In designated corners of the center's dining area, vendors staff long tables filled with industrial-sized pots of home-cooked dishes and trays of assorted desserts. Behind each table, menus written on cardboard boxes display a selection that includes at least five dishes served with rice, *pancit* (noodles) and in the winter *arroz caldo* (chicken rice soup).

Church centers usually formed with the assistance of local priests, in particular parish priests who recognized that Filipinos were the largest constituents of their church. The only Baptist church in the city of Rome established a center for its "unexpected" ninety Filipino constituents soon after it officially opened in the early 1990s to cater primarily to American expatriates. The formation of church centers depended not solely on local ties but in some cases also on the transnational networks of religious orders. While sometimes local priests of the churches regularly attended by Filipinos (usually those offering English-language church services) had sometimes recognized the need for day-off shelters in the community, networks between the local churches of sending communities and local churches in Rome also initiated the formation of centers. Eva Regalado, a founder of one of the centers, explains that, through letters, she had sought the assistance of nuns in the Philippines (that is, her former teachers) in locating a local church sponsor in Rome. They, in turn, contacted and referred her to nuns in their religious order who were affiliated with local churches in the city.

PUBLIC DOMAIN: BUS STOPS AND TRAIN STATIONS

Filipinos—the largest group of legal migrants in Rome ("Official Report" of the Philippine Embassy in Rome, 1995)—have an unavoidable impact on the city's public life, especially during the days that they leave the confinement of their employers' homes to attend to their errands, meet social obligations, and fulfill their religious obligations. On their way to a remittance agency, church, friend's apartment, or back to their employer's home, they usually stop by one of the train stations and bus stops where Filipinos are known to gather in Rome. The three largest pockets of gathering in the public domain are Eur Fermi, Mancini, and Termini. Located in the southern periphery of the city, Eur Fermi is a popular site of detour. Up the stairs from the Metro station Eur Fermi, hundreds of Filipinos congregate on what could be described as a wide sidewalk that extends to a length of about 100 yards. In the northeastern corner of the city, Filipinos gather in even greater numbers near the bus stop Mancini. Situated in the city center, Termini, the central train station and bus transfer point of the city, is an ideal meeting place, as they can conveniently head to any destination from the station—a friend's house, a party, a church center, or a remittance center.

Termini is the only site in the city center where Filipinos gather in public and where they impose on the public space of Italians. It is an imposition I am sure that Italians resent, as even I have been yelled at by bus drivers at Termini to get off the public phones that they had wanted to use. On any given day off, the bus stops of Termini are never congested with Filipinos in the morning and afternoon; they seem to congregate there only in the evening. One can imagine that the women crowding Termini at night are just delaying their return to their employer's home, staying a little bit longer, hoping they might run into a friend whom they have not seen in weeks. In general, most women do not spend an extended amount of time in pockets of gathering in the public domain. Nevertheless, they do regularly extend their short visits to these public pockets, especially in the summer when most Romans escape the city's sweltering heat for the cooler areas by the beaches or mountains. Authorities particularly discourage migrant Filipina domestic workers from gathering in the central location of Termini. Sometimes they are literally shooed away. As it is made uncomfortable for them to spend the day in the public domain, they understandably minimize their time in these places.

The preference for particular pockets of gathering among migrant Filipina domestic workers is often determined by convenience to their place of work as well as by the women's regional background. Women from Northern Luzon congregate more often at Termini. Their counterparts from Southern Luzon dominate Eur Fermi. Women from the Visayan province of Samar compose the majority of domestic workers who spend their day off at the Redemptorist Church. Vendors also become magnets, drawing their townsfolk to particular pockets. For example, a group of migrants from Iloilo, a province not very well represented in the community, are drawn to one particular pocket by the presence of an Ilonggo vendor.

Taking advantage of the demands created by the concentration of Filipinos in particular locations, entrepreneurs of the community sell meals in every pocket of gathering, including apartments. In each pocket of gathering, vendors are quite distinguishable. At Termini, Filipinos carrying large duffel bags offer a selection of *merienda* (snacks)—various sweets, noodles, and even dishes over rice. Meals are prewrapped in plastic bags so they are convenient to take home but are also served on a paper plate for those wishing to eat right there. At Eur Fermi, hidden in cars with slightly opened trunks are industrial-sized pots carrying a selection of dishes to eat for lunch or dinner. The presence of vendors essentially establishes particular locations as official pockets of gathering in the public domain. Migrants often head to these sites just to grab a bite to eat from their favorite cook.[11]

In the public domain, the actions of domestic workers are controlled to avoid harassment from the authorities, who, many women informed me, barely tolerate the impact of their presence in pockets of gathering. For example, I was repeatedly told that any attention at Eur Fermi from the authorities would jeopardize their access to this public domain. Ironically, as this particular public pocket is situated in the periphery of the city, its imposition on the public space of Italians, to begin with, is quite minimal. Though Filipino pedestrian traffic on the sidewalk at Eur Fermi is not at all congested, it is still visible to the public. Consequently, feelings of constant surveillance control the actions of domestic workers in this space, as in other pockets of gathering, including those in the private domain. For example, Filipinos are very conscious of the impression that they make on the religious clergy in charge of church centers. In apartments, Filipinos worry about the opinion of their Italian neighbors. As such, they avoid cooking "smelly" Filipino food and often keep their noise level down. At Eur Fermi, Filipinos clean up after themselves, since littering is looked upon negatively by everyone in the community. Migrants monitor their own activities as well as police the activities of other migrants.

The self-monitored actions at Eur Fermi most likely come as a lesson learned from the experiences of vendors in other public pockets of gathering. At Termini, vendors have been fined up to 1,400,000 lira (U.S.$933) on the grounds of health code violations. For the same reason, vendors who used to congregate at the bus stop of Mancini were forced to relocate after being constantly harassed by police, who would not only impose fines but also confiscate all of their goods (including canned food). As one of these vendors describes, they believe that the motive behind the harassment had been the anger of Italians over the presence of Filipinos in "their" public space.

> We were near the bus stop for four years. There were many Filipinos who went there, but the Italians started getting mad at us because Filipinos would fill up the plaza. They complained to the police, and so the police started coming after us. That place was ideal because many Filipinos transferred buses there.

As the actions of the police informed them that they could not impose on the public domain of Italians, these vendors literally had to find a hidden space in a public place, meaning a site that, while in the public domain, does not have a felt presence in the public social space of Italians. To stop the harassment by the police and to avoid Italians, they consequently moved to a new site in the area, one assuredly not at all imposing, as it is located underneath an overpass by the Tiber River. The site is an abandoned shanty of Albanian refugees. Its very closeness to the rat-infested Tiber River makes it quite an unsanitary location. I was told that, as the area had once been filled with garbage and tall weeds, it took dozens of vendors at least five months to clear the area and set up the generator to power the lights during the winter.

This "public domain" has since been cleared, though it remains unpaved, and now houses fifteen informal business enterprises, including restaurants, food stores, tailoring shops, and hair salons. These informal businesses are set up in wooden stands along the two structures of the overpass. There are also wooden benches scattered throughout the area that food vendors have built for their customers. Because there is no running water at Mancini, vendors—in particular cooks and hairdressers—use the drinking fountains located up the stairs and near the bus stop for their water supply. In the evening, the stoves and portable gas tanks of restaurants, the sewing machines of the tailors, and the goods of the food stores are stored in padlocked wooden cabinets built at the premises. Because no one lives there, security is fairly lax at night, and some businesses have been ransacked at least two times since they opened.

Mancini is a one-stop shopping bazaar. At least a hundred Filipinos patronize these businesses each day, while an even greater number do so on their day off. In the summers, vendors at Mancini host a volleyball tournament that attracts scores of additional patrons to their subcommunity. Besides stopping to grab a bite to eat between part-time shifts, migrant Filipinos can get a manicure and a perm and shop for imported canned goods from the Philippines as well as fruits and vegetables (including homegrown Filipino vegetables such as *ampalaya*). Though two Middle Eastern food stores in the city have begun to stock Filipino food products, most Filipinos still prefer to visit this pocket of gathering and patronize the informal businesses of their compatriots, probably because they are more likely to run into other migrant Filipina domestic workers at Mancini. This place of gathering under the bridge has given Filipino migrants of Rome a haven from the public domain in the public domain. Nonetheless, their very presence under the bridge serves as a reminder in the community that they do not belong in the public social space of Italian society.

The Dual Culture of Pockets of Gathering: Anomie and Solidarity

Demonstrating the removal of Filipinos from the dominant society, the topography of the migrant community reflects and reinforces the practical consciousness of nonbelonging among Filipino migrants. The very constitution of pockets of gathering reminds migrant Filipina domestic workers of their discomfort in the social spaces of the dominant society and promotes the role of the community as a base of both solidarity and anomie. In this section, I describe the activities in these pockets of gathering to illustrate the dual culture of solidarity and anomie in the community.

SOLIDARITY: PRACTICES OF MUTUAL ASSISTANCE

The concentration of Filipinos in pockets of gathering strengthens social networks and the level of personal responsibility in the community. Various shared modes of behavior in the community attest to the culture of solidarity, including the practices of sharing information, providing assistance to newer migrants, and smiling at every single Filipino one sees in public. In the community, migrant Filipina domestic workers expect practices of mutual assistance, and those who do not accordingly participate in these customs stand out. For instance, Filipinos who withhold information about jobs are blacklisted as *hindi matulungin* (unhelpful), *mayabang* (boastful or snobbish), or *madamot* (greedy). Filipinos who do not smile at other Filipinos in public are considered *mayabang*.

An example of a practice of solidarity in the community is the use of pockets of gathering as a base of support from the workplace. Conversations in pockets of gathering often concern their problems at work. Women voice complaints about demanding, inconsiderate, or pestering employers. While some wistfully sigh and wish that they could tell their employers off, others brag about having fought back or tell stories of how they ignored direct orders. Stories also relate verbal battles that they have had in public social spaces, such as fights over a snide remark directed at them on the bus. Pockets of gathering essentially function as their main site of support. It is where women can find release from the stress of the work week and relief from their discomfort in the social spaces of Italians. Thus, migrant Filipina domestic workers create and use pockets of gathering not only to avoid Italians but also to create a base of support in Rome. Hence, the formation of pockets of gathering fulfills one of the urgencies promoted by the practical consciousness of nonbelonging, that is, the need to create a supportive niche away from the dominant society.

Pockets of gathering function as the geographical base of the social networks that migrants use to ease their settlement in the host society. Considering that employers usually turn to their domestic workers for help with finding a potential employee, job referrals circulate among migrants in pockets of gathering. In the field, I often noticed pieces of paper with an employer's name and number regularly passed from one migrant to another. In addition, I often heard inquires made about available housing.

Another common practice instilling solidarity is Filipina domestic workers' participation in rotating credit associations, which are often place-based in a particular pocket of gathering. Every woman whom I interviewed had at one point been part of a rotating credit association. In the Philippines, rotating credit associations are referred to as *paluwagan,* which derives from the word *luwagan,* meaning "to loosen" or "to ease." One can infer that the term *paluwagan* signifies the purpose of rotating credits, which is "to loosen" or "to ease" one's financial difficulty. In the community, *paluwagan* runs for a year. At the beginning of each month, participants are required to deposit a specified monthly payment, which is then given to the participant who drew that specified month as their collection date. Like Asian migrants in the United States, migrant Filipina domestic workers in Rome turn to *paluwagan* to obtain a substantial amount of money otherwise made inaccessible by their ineligibility for loans from local banks (Glenn, 1986). They might use the money for investment in a small business, for instance, to purchase a passenger jeepney in the Philippines.

In pockets of gathering, solidarity among migrant Filipina domestic workers is bolstered by other practices of mutual assistance, such as the sharing of information. Older migrants familiarize newcomers with the bureaucratic process of extending permits to stay (for example, having to show one's *libretto di lavoro* [booklet of employment] at two offices). They also offer financial assistance, including to those whom they barely know. Because older migrants understand that securing one's first job can take as long as a month, they sometimes give newly arrived migrants a small amount of money (usually no more than U.S.$20) to hold them over until they secure their first job. Because most migrants had to abandon all of their possessions when crossing the border of Italy clandestinely, clothes (perhaps hand-me-downs from employers) are also given to new migrants. More surprising is the practice in the community of giving strangers a place to stay. Some women told me that Filipinos whom they had met at the train station upon their arrival (and after being abandoned by their coyote) offered them assistance with finding a place to stay their first few days in Rome.

As demonstrated by these practices of mutual assistance, the solidarity among migrant Filipinos is visible to anyone inhabiting a pocket of gathering. This shared mode of behavior and outlook is manifested in the expectation that assistance can be requested from anyone in the community. Though an "outsider," I also received this particular benefit of solidarity. In the field, I frequently relied on the help of strangers whom I met in the streets. On buses, especially during the time I conducted preliminary fieldwork, I often would ask Filipinos for directions. The knowledge that I was bound to run into another Filipino on the bus eased my worries about getting lost. I also accompanied women to various pockets of gathering for the purpose of asking any Filipino for job referrals. This was a common practice, as I often encountered jobless women who asked me if I knew of any employment opportunities.

The physical concentration of the community in pockets of gathering strengthens the camaraderie among migrant Filipina domestic workers to the point that this camaraderie extends to their interactions in the public spaces of the dominant society. Though their position in the labor market as domestic workers isolates them from each other, they still manage to create social networks by utilizing the solidarity fostered by the practical consciousness of nonbelonging and the spatial politics of their community formation.[12] Two particular features of the geography of the community promote solidarity. First, isolation in domestic work promotes feelings of interdependency. Second, segregation from the dominant society fosters the solidarity of domestic workers. Mutual assistance is a practice collectively expected in the community. It consequently manifests itself as part of the daily rituals of community life for Filipina domestic workers in Rome.

ANOMIE: COMPETITION AND CAPITALIST ACTIVITIES IN THE COMMUNITY

So far, I have described the spatial formation of the community only as fostering camaraderie. Yet not all of the activities in the community strengthen camaraderie. The same women who told me that strangers assisted them in the early stages of settlement also warned me against trusting anyone in the community. Many of my informants told me that they do not have any friends in the community, including Christina Manansala, who states, "There is no such thing as a friend here. In Rome, Filipinos cannot have friends." An extremely high level of distrust plagues relationships among Filipinos. Friends are considered dangerous, a source of pain, and consequently a threat from whom one must protect oneself. I was informed that migrant Filipina domestic workers, who are only concerned with their own advancement, do not care about the expense of their actions to others in the community. In light of the practices that demonstrate solidarity in the community, how do we make sense of these assertions? What practices in the community, while coexisting with solidarity, still manage to instill anomie?

The segregation of Filipina domestic workers, while reminding them of their temporary stay in Rome, accentuates the purpose of their migration, that is, the accumulation of capital. From their segregated position, the fulfillment of their goal of accumulating capital can most conveniently be expedited through profits obtained in the community.[13] Thus, in the reiteration of nonbelonging to the dual outlook of migrant domestic workers, the goal of accumulated capital exceeds, though does not subsume, solidarity to impose anomie in the community with the rise of competition and capitalist activities.

Competition over the accumulation of capital is an underlying feature of the migrant community. Though most migrant Filipina domestic workers acknowledge the existence of this competition, they also deny their active participation in it. Instead, as most of my interviewees did, they portray themselves as victims of competitive domestic workers, particularly those who are jealous of their success in the labor market. Workers describe two types of "bad seeds" tainting the culture of solidarity in the community: women who hoard jobs and women who practice *sulutan*, which means to undermine or betray for personal gain. Women who hoard jobs are those who charge a fee for job referrals and those who do not share with other domestic workers jobs that they cannot maintain. For example, some domestic workers with a full schedule, when offered additional jobs that they cannot accommodate, would rather not share their load with another domestic worker but would prefer to reduce their hours in their other jobs so as to hoard the new job.

Sulutan also refers to the practice of offering employers a lower rate than what they are paying their current domestic worker. Four of forty-six interviewees told me they were victims of *sulutan*. Usually, domestic workers with highly paid jobs are those who are *sinulutan* (undermined), most often by their friends, as they are the ones likely to know the salary rate and phone number of the employer. If the employer rejects their offer, domestic workers who attempt *sulutan* do not usually concede the failure of their efforts. According to domestic workers, these women are more often overcome by such an intense level of jealousy over the "success" of another domestic worker that they resort to harassing the employer with repeated phone calls until the current employee is let go. One live-in domestic worker told me that her employer, who paid twice as much as the average rate, received phone calls from another domestic worker for more than one month and that this employer eventually let her go. The practice of *sulutan* is, however, uncommon in the community. Like the practice of hoarding jobs, it is for the most part adversely regarded by migrant Filipina domestic workers. Thus, no one would admit to doing it. Its threat, however, unavoidably instills mistrust among migrant Filipina domestic workers. For example, no one would admit to earning more than the average salary of domestic workers in the community.[14]

Besides competition, the other feature of community life instilling anomie for migrant Filipina domestic workers is the prevalence of microbusinesses. This instills anomie because it inadvertently commercializes the friendships of migrant Filipina domestic workers. Compelled by the urgency to leave Rome, most migrant Filipina domestic workers engage in capitalist activities in the community in the hopes of expediently meeting their goal of capital accumulation. Profits from the community are considered a viable source of supplementary income. Consequently, financial transactions are an extensive part of the daily rituals of community life. All of the domestic workers whom I interviewed supplement their primary income as domestic workers with what they refer to as a "sideline," meaning an informal microbusiness. "Making money off the margins" (Mahler, 1995) is a characteristic feature of migrant life not exclusive to the Filipino community of Rome. It has also been identified among Mexican migrants in San Diego (Chavez, 1992), Latino refugees in Long Island (Mahler, 1995), and Haitians in Miami (Portes and Stepick, 1993; Stepick, 1989). Nonetheless, its extent among migrant Filipinos in Rome seems to be unparalleled, since almost everyone in the community maintains a sideline.

Mirroring those of other migrant communities, microbusinesses in the informal economy of Filipinos in Rome provide, though not exclusively, ethnically demanded services and goods that are not available in the local economy. The wide array of needs to which informal microbusinesses cater in the community include entertainment, commodities, telecommunication, and personal services. Meeting the entertainment needs of the community, some domestic workers supplement their income by producing concerts, sponsored by remittance centers, by well-known entertainers in the Philippines. Local rock bands cater to the community by providing entertainment at weddings and christenings. Food vendors and retailers sell ethnic goods such as movie videos, food products, and magazines. Personal services available in the local economy (such as beauty and tailoring services) are provided at a much lower rate in the community. The use of an underground telecommunication system is available in the informal economy. Finally, entrepreneurs in the community sell commodities that are also available in the local economy.

In contrast to other informal economies that compete with lower-level formal economies (for example, the garment industry), the "isolated informal economy" that can be found among Haitians in Miami and Filipinos in Rome caters solely to the migrant community (Stepick, 1989). In an "isolated informal economy," profits are obtained exclusively from other members of the migrant community. A sense of unease arises, as profiting contradicts the solidarity that they expect from one other. Informal microbusiness enterprises, which are remarkably prevalent in the community, consequently engender anomie among migrant Filipina domestic workers. They alienate domestic workers from one another with the reduction of the daily rituals of community life to financial transactions.

Reflecting the unconscious negotiation of anomie and solidarity's coexistence in the community, migrant Filipina domestic workers distinguish their capitalist ventures into two categories: they are either disdained or accepted. Disdained capitalist activities are those that contradict solidarity, because the profits achieved are at the expense of preventing the mobility of another member of the community. These activities are primarily restricted to money lending and charging fees for job referrals. Accepted activities are those that do not hinder mobility and include service-oriented microbusinesses (for example, "gypsy cabs," informal beauty salons, and tailoring), informal restaurants, housing rental enterprises, and retail-oriented businesses. While most accepted activities generate little profit, some, in particular the subleasing of housing, are extremely profitable. Though community members are aware of the large returns in the housing rental system, this enterprise is still accepted in the community because, in this system, profits from a single individual are fairly small and, as such, do not hamper the mobility of other migrants.

COMMODITIES

Retail is the most common avenue taken by domestic workers to supplement their income. These businesses tend to be small in scale and very informal, as women usually limit the range of their commodities to one product. The factors restricting the scale of retail ventures in the community include the limited capital of domestic workers and the limited amount of time that they can commit to their microbusiness. Though individually small in scale, retail is part of the daily rituals of community life due to the large number of domestic workers engaged in this practice.

Promoting its prevalence is the spatial formation of the community into pockets of gathering. The concentration of domestic workers in particular sites gives retailers a convenient venue to make sales. A typical day off in one pocket of gathering would encompass having to deal with solicitations from numerous migrants. My field notes tell of this experience.

> In one of the church centers of the community, I notice that for a span of two hours I had been approached by at least 10 individuals soliciting various commodities. I was given catalogs of Amway and Avon. I was asked to look at a bag of sweaters, which are consigned by a domestic worker for her employer who owns a boutique. I was approached by a woman about shoes and bags that she sells and orders from a manufacturer in Napoli. A man inquired if I was interested in purchasing bootleg tapes that he had recorded from compact discs. He designs the tape containers and sells the tapes for 10,000 lira (US$6.60). The selection of music ranges from artists such as Air Supply and Whitney Houston to Filipino artists such as April Boys. Another woman asked me if I was interested in looking at suits in her apartment, while another informed me that she is a supplier of canned food—specifically corned beef—to the community.

Migrant Filipina domestic workers sell various commodities, including those specific to the ethnic economy and those available in the local economy. The former include ethnic music and food while the latter include leather goods, beauty products, and clothes. Because the latter products are more easily accessible for potential entrepreneurs, most retailers sell these kinds of commodities. Domestic workers frequently purchase these products from fellow domestic workers rather than from formal stores in the city.

Ironically, most commodities are more expensive in the ethnic economy than in the local economy. Vendors usually charge 5000 lira (U.S.$3.30) more than Italian stores for commodities such as perfume. Jovan Musk costs 35,000 lira (U.S.$23.30) in a local perfume store but not less than 40,000 lira (U.S.$26.70) from a domestic worker. Why do domestic workers choose to purchase items, available at a competitive rate in the local economy, in the underground economy of the community? In other studies, underground economies of migrants are said to form not just from ethnic demands. Migrants usually turn to the alternative of informal economies to seek lower costs for goods and services (Mahler, 1995; Stepick, 1989). For example, migrants in Long Island turn to other migrants for "gypsy cabs," childcare, and telephone services (Mahler, 1995). While this is also applicable in certain cases in the Filipino underground economy of Rome, it contradicts their patronage of noneconomical microbusinesses.

Interviewees explain that they choose to patronize noneconomical microbusinesses in the community because of their greater flexibility, convenience, and accessibility.[15] First, this option is made convenient by the possible arrangement of installment plans. Women can arrange a monthly payment plan, which eases the financial burden of having to pay for the entire cost of a commodity all at once. Showing a certain degree of solidarity is the trust between the women, as such an arrangement is never put in writing.

Second, they explain that the option of visiting local businesses is too time consuming. They would rather save time than money by buying commodities in a pocket of gathering. Though they spend an average of 5000 lira (U.S.$3.30) more for a product in the community, women explain that patronizing another domestic worker does not result in a loss of 5000 lira, if one calculates the time that they save from having to visit a local business. Instead of "wasting" an hour to go to a retail store, they would rather spend their already limited free time relaxing with friends in a pocket of gathering or use the time productively to earn an extra hour of wages from domestic work. Thus, the additional costs of purchasing commodities from other domestic workers is actually construed as payment for the services of a "personal shopper."

This reasoning consequently justifies the profits earned by another domestic worker, who is often also their close friend. It also justifies the practice of women charging their friends 5000 lira for the "personal favor" of purchasing an item in a local store that is located near their own workplace but far from that of their friends. While seeming to reflect anomie by the fact that the retailer profits from another domestic worker and, moreover, a friend, this practice also reflects solidarity. Customers reward the retailer for giving them time to relax. In the same way, women who work share with their "personal shopper" the financial gains that they had incurred from her service. Hence, they do not lose 5000 lira, but actually gain 10,000 lira, which they then share with the retailer (or "personal shopper"), whose labor of visiting the local outlet, they recognize, enabled them to earn this extra income or to spend time together. In this way, the microbusiness of selling commodities is rationalized so as not to contradict solidarity. Yet this logic only works if domestic workers limit their purchases to one product per week, because the profits from more than one product would then exceed the gains of an additional hour of work. Fortunately, they usually do.

OTHER SERVICES

Besides retail, the three other types of services available in the informal economy are telecommunications, personal, and food services. From "gypsy cab" rides to the airport to haircuts and long-distance phone calls, the services available in the ethnic economy are usually more economical than those in the outside economy. They are consequently viewed as "accepted" capitalist ventures in the community.

The use of illegal telecommunications services is rampant in the community. On their day off, women form lines to use public phones located in the vicinity of various pockets of gathering. These public phones are managed by Filipino male migrants who have ties to operators of the government-owned phone company. Per-minute rates charged for long-distance calls to the Philippines in these public phones are usually 1000 lire (U.S.$.66) less than resident phone lines. Personal services are also available in the informal ethnic economy for a much lower cost. Most Filipinos do not patronize hair salons, nail salons, and tailoring businesses in the local economy. Instead, they choose to get haircuts or their nails done in a pocket of gathering, for example, underneath the bridge by Mancini or even at church centers. Hairstylists and manicurists also do home visits on their day off, usually securing at least five appointments per visit to an apartment. While the going rate for haircuts in the community had been 10,000 lira (U.S.$6.67) during my field research, it would have cost at least 30,000 lira (U.S.$20.00) in an Italian hair salon.[16]

Selling food in pockets of gathering is actually the most labor-intensive microbusiness that one can run in the informal ethnic economy. However, it is also one of the more profitable sources of surplus income. Half a month's income can be earned in one week from selling meals or *merienda* to domestic workers. Though profitable, only a few women choose this option as a sideline because many are deterred by its physical demands.

> Imagine, you stay up the whole night on Wednesday. On Thursday morning, you go to work. On Thursday afternoon, you have to heat all the food even when you are tired from working all morning. On Saturday, you don't work but go to the market and buy all the food you need. Then, when you get back home, you start cooking the food and stay up the whole night again. On Sunday morning, you have to wake up really early to heat up the food. Then, you stand around the whole day, but you have to be constantly looking around and staying alert for the police. When they come, you start running. (Tessie Mandin, a vendor at Termini)

> On Wednesdays, when we return from work, we start preparing the food at around six in the evening. We don't cook yet because it is too early. The food will just get cold. So, we half cook the food. For example, we marinate the meat. We wake up at four in the morning and cook the food. We cook until nine in the morning, then go sell the food. On Sundays, I cook until ten in the morning. Food is served from the morning until nine in the evening. (Giselle Aragon, a vendor at Eur Fermi)

Usually only part-time workers venture into selling food. Their live-in counterparts are not free the day before to make the necessary preparations. On a smaller scale, live-in workers do sometimes engage in food services as a "sideline." They usually specialize in desserts. For example, live-in workers take special orders for birthday and wedding cakes. They also prepare one dish of a Filipino rice cake, which they then consign to the food vendors already established in pockets of gathering.

MONEY LENDING

The practice of money lending is an even more lucrative business than selling food in the community. In addition to generating greater profit, it does not entail any physical labor. With the option of *paluwagan* available in the community, women usually turn to money lending only in case of emergencies, such as the hospitalization or sudden death of a family member or the need to assist relatives abandoned by their coyote in Eastern Europe.

Money lending in the community evolves from the practice of "5-6" in the Philippines, which refers to the enterprise of lending for a 20 percent monthly interest. Though still referred to as "5-6" in the migrant community, the monthly interest rate has been reduced to 10 percent because of the currency exchange from the devalued peso to the lira. Unless otherwise prearranged, monthly installments for repayment are not an option in "5-6." Instead, borrowers must pay the monthly interest until they cover the loan in its complete sum. For example, a payment of $300 for a $1000 loan covers only three monthly interest payments. It does not reduce the loan to $800, even though the interest for that given month is only $100. Loans consequently double before ever getting fully repaid. In this way, moneylenders accumulate capital for investment in a business in the Philippines at the expense of the greater hardships of other migrant Filipina domestic workers.

Each of the four moneylenders whom I interviewed is an early migrant who, during her extended stay in Rome, has managed to secure a sizable savings, which she then used as start-up funds for her business. Since getting involved with this lucrative business, they have seen their savings grow exponentially. As expected, they have the largest bank accounts among my interviewees, with one woman having saved as much as U.S.$40,000. In addition, all of them have secured small businesses in the Philippines. For instance, one owns a grocery store and another a bakery. Though they have all reached their migration goal of capital accumulation, they have decided to prolong their stay in Italy to maintain access to this profitable capitalist venture.

Despite being the clear winners of capitalism in the community, moneylenders are neither respected nor admired but instead are considered incorrigible by most migrant Filipinos. Money lending is the most disdained capitalist activity among migrant Filipina domestic workers for a number of reasons. First, it contradicts the deeply instilled expectations of shared personal responsibility in the community.

> I think of moneylenders as the oppressors of their fellow Filipinos. They just help keep down other Filipinos. *It is not help that they are giving.* When you lend for an 8 percent monthly interest, you might as well not work, because monthly, you make as much as a domestic worker. Let's say the loan was for 10,000,000 lira [U.S.$6670]. They don't need to work [because the monthly interest they earn equals another domestic worker's entire monthly wages]. (Giselle Aragon, Rome; my emphasis)

Disdainful of those who profit from someone else's difficult situation, most women consider excessive interest rates to be unjustifiable. They believe that migrants in a difficult situation, as they are the only ones who would even consider the high interest rates of "5-6," should instead be assisted with low-interest loans. Second, this practice is unacceptable for most women because the profits of money lending are at the expense of the labor of another domestic worker. Third, money lending leaves borrowers in a worse position after obtaining the loan.

> People here generally think lending money for an interest is bad. But if we really held on to our money wisely, we would not borrow any. But for me, it's not good. For me, it is terrible to lend money out for such a high interest. People know that, when they lend money, it just ensures the borrower is even in a worst position. They are already in a tight situation, and they end up in a tighter situation. (Girlie Macabalo, Rome)

In general, migrant Filipina domestic workers in Rome are strongly against money lending, because taking advantage of the needs of another domestic worker goes against the core principles of solidarity. Instead of hampering one another's success, migrant Filipina domestic workers, according to the principles of solidarity, should be assisting with one another's mobility. Thus, like *sulutan*, money lending is adversely regarded in the community.

HOUSING SYSTEM: BED-SPACERS AND DAY-OFFERS

Filipinos in Rome can make money off their apartments in two ways. First, they can cater to part-time workers by renting out beds (as opposed to rooms) in apartments. Second, they can rent out access to their apartments to live-in workers during their day off. As landlords usually require a three-month deposit, proof of legal documents, and extensive references from potential tenants, apartments are inaccessible for most migrants in the community. Acting on the housing shortage imposed on the community by the stringent requirements of landlords, those able to secure rental agreements can easily turn their apartment into a moneymaking enterprise. Like moneylenders, migrants who profit from housing in the community are older migrants. They tend to have more resources than do newer migrants, including human (for example, language) and financial capital. In general, most women are unfamiliar with the process of renting apartments in the city. Though older migrants share most other information with newer migrants, they selectively do not familiarize newer migrants with this profitable process. Reflecting the unfamiliarity over housing in the community, most interviewees responded to questions concerning the housing rental system in Rome quite vaguely:

"It's very difficult to obtain," most of them said. It is this unfamiliarity, coupled with the strict requirements of landlords, that enables the few actual tenants in the community to profit easily from the housing system.

Day-offers are live-in workers who rent the privilege of spending their day off in apartments. The going rate for women to have free access to an apartment on Thursday afternoons and Sundays is 100,000 lira (U.S.$67) a month. Day-offers are usually limited to the friends and relatives of the tenant; strangers usually cannot rent access to any apartment in the community. Personal relationships are those that are commercialized in the system of day-offers. Weekly visits to a friend's or relative's apartment require a fee. Though commercializing relationships, this system is not adversely regarded in the community. Instead, day-offers consider their access to an apartment a favor from the tenant. It gives them a safe space to spend their day off. More important, they are freed from the labor of cooking meals, as the tenant, following the Philippine cultural tradition of hosts being expected to serve food to their visitors, usually provides food to "guests." Day-offers reason that this "favor" is justifiably deserving of a fee to offset the costs.

In this commercialized cultural system, the "gracious" tenant usually amasses a significant profit. This system often relieves them of rent. One of my interviewees, a woman who rents a tiny one-bedroom apartment near the center of Rome for 700,000 lira (U.S.$467) a month, charges 100,000 (U.S.$67) lira each month to seven women who regularly visit her on Sundays. Other interviewees have as many as fifteen regular visitors. In the apartments that I frequently visited, tenants charged their "guests" flexible rates. Newer migrants, poorer women (for example, those with families still living in nipa houses in the Philippines), and women facing severe hardships (for example, those with a sick child) are usually not charged for visiting their friends. Moreover, friends are given the option of paying an amount that they can afford. This flexibility eases the rigidity of the day-offers system, a rigidity that instills anomie by the reduction of friendships to business-like arrangements.

In general, tenants consider the funds provided by day-offers only a supplement to the greater profit provided by the system of "bed-spacing." Next to money lending, the second most lucrative business in the community is the practice of renting out beds. The principle behind this system—the subcontracting of housing for a profit—is similar to the *encargado* system identified by Mahler (1995). Boarders do not just alleviate the tenant's rent, as they actually function as a source of income for the tenant, who subleases beds instead of rooms to maximize profit. In this way, the fees collected for one room can equal the monthly rental cost of the entire apartment. Tessie Mandin explains that tenants are usually freed of rent when taking on bed-spacers:

> One can live rent free and even make more money by getting people to pay 250,000 lira [U.S.$166] a month to live in their apartment. In one room, there could be four people. So, if the apartment costs 1,000,000 lira [U.S.$667], a three-bedroom for example, one can make 2,000,000 lira [U.S.$1334]. That's more than enough to pay for the whole apartment plus the utilities.

Though profitable, apartments are made extremely crowded by the presence of bed-spacers. While the tenant (and her spouse) usually occupies one room, bed-spacers are placed in rooms with four people. Thus, privacy in apartments is limited to the actual tenant. Occupied by a full house of bed-spacers, an apartment that I stayed in for a weekend was overcrowded and always bustling with activity. As I wrote in my field notes:

> The apartment is quite large with three bedrooms and one *salone* (living room) converted into a bedroom as well. Upon entering the apartment, the first thing I saw were three clothes lines hanging in the middle of the hallway. To enter the apartment, I had to walk around the wet clothes blocking the entryway.
>
> Each room is separated in the center with large armoires. On each side is either a full-size bed or two twin-size beds. Couples, I learned, sleep on the larger beds which usually fill up the entire space of their side of the room. The only space left is enough for one dresser with a TV and a VCR usually on top of it. In one room, there were even two TVs, each situated in front of the two beds separated by two armoires each facing a different side (or half) of the room. Like the other rooms, four people live in this one room.
>
> There is only one bathroom in the entire apartment while there are 14 individuals living in the apartment. The apartment was quite chaotic. There were always two sets of television on, sometimes set on the same channel, and stereos simultaneously playing from both sides of the house.
>
> The kitchen, which is their only common area, is always full. Tenants take their turn eating, as the kitchen cannot accommodate everyone at the same time. There are pots of cooked food lined up on the counters.

At night, there is always a group relaxing in the kitchen. I notice they always play cards. I was asked to live in this apartment for 350,000 lira (US$233) a month including all utilities, but I declined their offer for the reason that I wanted to have more privacy when I retreated to reflect on my day's field work at night.

In apartments, the word *privacy* is usually not in the vocabulary of occupants. For example, people cannot escape to their own bedrooms but only to their side of the room.

In the community, the housing rental system is considered a lesser disruption of solidarity than that caused by money lending, the most rewarding capitalist activity in the community. Though bed-spacers are aware of the profits accrued by the tenant, they do accept this financially unequal system but not without a certain degree of resentment. Subleasing for a profit, in general, is justified as a business opportunity fairly earned by another migrant. The housing rental system is acceptable, because profits do not stem from blocking the mobility of another migrant. Moreover, the housing system of bed-spacers secures boarders low-cost housing, as it averages only 250,000 lira (U.S.$166) a month. Nonetheless, bed-spacers are denied the privacy technically afforded to them by the average rate charged in the community for housing.

DISCUSSION

The deep-seated urgency of migrant Filipina domestic workers to leave Rome results in the hyperreality of making money. Everyone in the community maintains a sideline so they may expediently meet one of their central goals of migration, that is, the accumulation of capital. Thus, in Rome, the urgency of making money among migrant Filipinos has reached a distortedly hyperstate.

Migrant Filipina domestic workers turn to sidelines in response to the immobility of their life in Rome—socially, legally, and economically. Segregation and immobility intensify desires to expedite the accumulation of savings and in turn pressure them to produce surplus income. At the same time, segregation confines their sources of profit to the community. Profiting from each other is therefore their most viable source of supplementary income and, next to maintaining a full load of domestic work, is the second most viable source of mobility. Women seem to function on the basis that not a single day can ever pass without earning a profit. A day off is seen as a day to profit. As they sit and chat with friends only seen once or twice a week, they have to be profiting. Because women operate under this mind-set, a thriving informal economy has developed among migrant Filipina domestic workers in Rome.

The hyperreality of making money alienates migrant Filipina domestic workers from one another. It results in the commercialization of friendships and daily rituals in the community. With the hyperreality of making money, personal favors and visits to a friend's house are even attached with fees. Trust among friends is even further tainted by the threat of competition (for example, *sulutan*).

On the surface, financial transactions seem to characteristically only embody the culture of anomie. Yet they also rely on solidarity. Solidarity compels women to support one another's business ventures and to recognize the worth of each other's labor. In addition, solidarity also interrupts the hyperreality of making money in the community to temper the formation of anomie. For example, many women refuse to make a profit from those facing difficult times in the community. Vendors are known to give free food occasionally. Day-offers are sometimes not expected to pay rent. Though more sporadically, even moneylenders grant grace periods and lower interest rates to friends and a select few women facing difficult times. The distinction of microbusinesses as either "disdained" or "accepted" capitalist ventures illustrates that solidarity sets standards for the behavior of women in the community. The justification of retailing commodities as a means of sharing the wealth in the community or as a means of recognizing the worth of each other's labor also shows another interruption of anomie by solidarity. Finally, the insistence of women on charging flexible rates is another behavior instilled by solidarity to temper the alienation wrought by the commercialization of friendships in the community.

Money circulates in the community, but its circulation generally brings minimal profits. The standards of solidarity force most women to minimize the profits that they obtain from the community. Most of the women do not engage in money lending and subleasing for a profit. Some apartment tenants usually just sublease to free themselves of rent. Thus, many women do not sublease to double their salary from domestic work. At most, entrepreneurs of the community only gain "spending money." Most actually expect to earn merely supplementary income. For example, Valentina Diamante sells Amway products for this reason alone: "I thought this might be the way to make money so I can send all of my salary to the Philippines. With Amway, I will still have money for myself to keep." From the circulation of money, a monthly cycle of exchange develops: in a given month, those spending less money than others in the community are able to accumulate extra income and consequently send more of their earnings to their families in the Philippines. In turn, those spending more money than they earn from the community lack supplementary income.

The circulation of money in the community implies the turning of migrant Filipina domestic workers into microcapitalists. They resort to "sidelines" to maximize their earnings, thus to accumulate capital, but most women do not get ahead, as money only circulates within the community. The cycle of capital's circulation within the community defeats the purpose of sidelines, which is to hasten migrant Filipina domestic workers' departure from Rome, as most women do not "win." This tells us that the means by which migrant Filipina domestic workers respond to the urgencies prompted by nonbelonging aggravate this dislocation through the imposition of anomie.

There are, however, a few winners in this microcapitalist community—official tenants and moneylenders. Ironically, winning does not translate to departure. Moneylenders, for example, delay their departure so as to accumulate more profits from the community. This is at the expense of an even greater number of women having to also prolong their stay. As a large portion of earnings of domestic workers circulate within the community, only those willing to repudiate the coexisting culture of solidarity win. In other words, capitalist activities that are not at all tempered by the culture of solidarity are those that generate tremendous profit.

In the "anomie-solidarity continuum" (Mahler, 1995), the migrant Filipino community does not fall on either side but in the middle. The competition instilled by the hyperreality of making money defines the geocultural space of the community as much as camaraderie. Contradictory forces of life in Rome produce contradictory sentiments of community life. Their marginalization pushes them to engage in surplus income-generating activities but simultaneously strengthens their feelings of allegiance to one another. While the "self" exceeds "collectivity" as the top priority of migrants, the allegiances fostered by marginalization are not completely subsumed in competition. The community maintains a dual culture of camaraderie and competition. The practical consciousness of nonbelonging and its many contradictions—the reality of trying to belong but the reality of not belonging and the reality of trying to fit into the migrant life of Rome and the reality of trying to leave it—is exactly why the culture of the community results in both solidarity and anomie.

Los Angeles: A Middle-Class-Dominated
Migrant Community

In contrast to Rome, the Filipino migrant community of Los Angeles does not represent a cohesive body. First, there are more than a hundred locally based ethnic organizations serving the community. Representing a wide range of interests, they include subgroups of national organizations (such as professional associations, political groups, church organizations, and lodges), Philippine regional organizations, and alumni associations (Pido, 1986). Second, the diverse labor market activities of Filipino Americans generate multiple niches in the community. As a result, there is not an official gateway to this migrant community. The community is consequently composed of multiple intersecting subcommunities without a representative organization, thus making the community life of domestic workers more difficult to narrate and examine. In addition, the absence of literature on contemporary Filipino migration to the United States makes the subject of the community more difficult to address. On this basis, my discussion does not attempt to paint a picture of the community as a whole but instead provides a glimpse of it from the perspective of one subgroup of its low-wage workers.

The Filipino community of Los Angeles can unquestionably be referred to as an immigrant community. With its roots predominantly tracing back to the post-1965 migration of professional workers, this migrant community, from the onset has had considerable access to mainstream jobs. Returning to Mahler (1995), this should indicate a lesser degree of coethnic exploitation in this particular migrant community than in Rome, where migrant Filipinos are undoubtedly segregated from dominant society. Mahler maintains that as an immigrant group achieves greater "access to mainstream jobs," the less likely they are to be plagued by coethnic conflict. Conversely, the less access that they have to mainstream jobs, the more likely they are to exploit each other. Comparing the community activities of Filipina domestic workers in Rome and Los Angeles, this is true to a certain extent. Competition and capitalist activities do not mar relations among domestic workers in Los Angeles as much as they do in Rome. For example, none of my interviewees in Los Angeles maintain a "sideline." In addition, they claim not to experience competition against other domestic workers.

Yet even without the conspicuous presence of coethnic exploitation, anomie still defines the experience of domestic workers in this migrant community. In fact, migrant Filipina domestic workers in Rome claim to experience greater camaraderie in the community than do their counterparts in Los Angeles. The lesser extent of camaraderie among migrants in Los Angeles refutes Mahler's contention concerning the cultural outcomes that could be expected from the class constitution of migrant communities. The community's access to the mainstream does not ease anomie among domestic workers in Los Angeles.

Why do migrant Filipina domestic workers in Los Angeles believe that they do not garner support in the community? Why do they view the community as a source of anomie instead of solidarity? The particular class cleavage of this migrant community answers these questions. The class cleavage of the Filipino community can be described as bipolar, divided between the haves (the middle class) and the have-nots (the working class). Conflicting outlooks in the migrant community emerge along class lines, with those in the upper end finding less coethnic conflict, thus supporting Mahler's arguments, and those in the lower end experiencing greater conflict, though not among each other. From the perspective of domestic workers, the Filipino migrant community is centered around the middle class, which is a group not limited to those in the professional managerial class but includes those employed in "low-level professional occupations" such as records processors and office clerks. Considering that Filipinos culturally claim to be family oriented, we can assume that those in the latter group stabilize their middle-class status by maintaining two-income households.

According to domestic workers, class disparities in the migrant community of Filipinos instill anomie. Access to mainstream jobs does not result in less coethnic conflict because of the disparities that are likely to arise from this access. Thus, in a migrant community, the polarization stemming from differences in access causes anomie for those at the bottom. For the have-nots in the community, polarization serves as a constant reminder of their lesser success. Migrant Filipina domestic workers, as they are among the have-nots, experience the community from a contentious location, one that always carries a keen awareness of their lesser success. Similar to their counterparts in Rome, the practical consciousness of nonbelonging determines the experiences of migrant Filipina domestic workers in the community. However, unlike their counterparts in Rome, it is instilled not by the host society but by the host community.

Differentiating the outlook engendered by the practical consciousness of nonbelonging for domestic workers in Los Angeles from those in Rome are the greater opportunities in the United States. As demonstrated by the access of migrant Filipinos to mainstream jobs, conditions of settlement for these migrants signify the membership of Filipinos in the host society of the United States. With the basic principle of citizenship determined by jus soli, eligible migrants are accorded full membership in the host polity. Notably, many of my interviewees have gained permanent residency through marriage or the certification of their employment.

The different conditions of settlement between Italy and the United States distinguish the outlooks engendered by the practical consciousness of nonbelonging. In contrast to Italy, they do not instill the urgency to leave the United States. Instead, they generate ambivalence over settlement and taint the promise of mobility offered by the presence of the middle class. The opportunities in the United States—at the very least the possibility shown by the presence of the professional managerial class—instill desires for permanent settlement. Yet the realities of not having similar opportunities to the middle class also enforce the perspective of temporary settlement. Significantly, the realities of domestic work seem to outweigh the possibilities presented by the presence of the middle class, as most of my interviewees claim to be temporary members of the community.

In further contrast to Rome, nonbelonging does not instill the urgency of turning to the community for support. It instead promotes the avoidance of the community and particularly its dominant middle-class members. Nonbelonging consequently aggravates the isolation of domestic work, as the community becomes a site of antagonism instead of support. Nonbelonging is further established as a practical consciousness by the fact that temporary membership becomes the most viable justification of one's lesser success in the community. In Los Angeles, migrant Filipina domestic workers purport to be visitors ("outsiders") of the community so as to denote their lack of desire to achieve success. Hence, for domestic workers, the belief of one's temporary membership in the community tempers their discomfort over having lesser success.

My discussion now turns to the sources of anomie for migrant Filipina domestic workers in Los Angeles, in other words, the realities that impose their sense of place as "outsiders" of the community. I specifically look into the community's employment characteristics and geographic constitution to establish the view of domestic workers that the community is a middle-class space. I then examine the practices reflecting and instilling their "outsider" location, specifically their conscious and unconscious avoidance of the middle class.

EMPLOYMENT CHARACTERISTICS

We can begin to understand the community and the place of domestic workers in it by examining employment characteristics. Mirroring national figures, Filipinos in Los Angeles have an extremely low rate of self-employment.
In Los Angeles County, only 4 percent of women and 6 percent of men in
the Filipino community are self-employed (Ong and Azores 1994a). In contrast, other Asian ethnic groups are at least twice as likely to turn to self-
employment. For example, the Southeast Asian community has the second-
lowest percentage of self-employed workers among Asian ethnic groups in
Los Angeles: 11 percent of men and 12 percent of women. While most Filipinos pursue wage employment, they are not concentrated in one particular
sector of the labor market. In Los Angeles, 25 percent of them hold managerial and professional jobs, an equal percentage low-level professional occupations, and the rest lower-end service and manufacturing jobs (Ong and
Azores, 1994a). Engaged in a wide range of paid employment, Filipinos cannot be lumped into one particular labor sector. This consequently makes them
quite nonrepresentable, which possibly explains the absence of literature on
this particular migrant group. Nevertheless, a class cleavage defines this migrant community and determines the place of its members in it.

Among those Filipinos of working age in Los Angeles, 54 percent are
described as highly skilled, while only 9 percent are low skilled (Ong and
Azores, 1994a: 106). Though there is a sizable managerial class in the Filipino migrant community, a considerable number of highly skilled migrants
experience underemployment upon migration (Lowell, 1996). In the United
States, only 25 percent of men and 28 percent of women are in professional
and managerial occupations (U.S. Census, 1993). Highly skilled migrant Filipinos in Los Angeles have not always been able to use their education and
training, as only 27 percent of women and 17 percent of men have attained
jobs in the professional managerial class (Ong and Azores, 1994a: 106).
Though Filipinos and South Asians share an equal proportion of highly
skilled migrants, Filipinos have a much lower rate of incorporation into the
upper end of the labor market spectrum (Ong and Azores, 1994a). Facing underemployment, Filipinos have turned to low-level professional jobs in technical, sales, and administrative support occupations. In the United States,
34 percent of men and 39 percent of women are engaged in such occupations
(U.S. Census, 1993). In Los Angeles, a lesser percentage of Filipinos hold low-
level professional occupations: 21 percent of men and 27 percent of women
(Ong and Azores, 1994a). Based on these figures, we can assume that many

of the 54 percent of highly skilled migrants ended up, if not in the managerial class, in low-level professional occupations. However, my data suggests that skilled migrants also engage in occupations with a much lower level of prestige. Considering that many of my interviewees are highly educated women, we can assume that a subgroup of skilled migrants can also be found in low-wage service occupations.

The employment profile of the Filipino population of Los Angeles is quite diverse, as it includes managerial, low-level professional, blue collar, and service workers. Despite its diversity, the community is distinctly divided between the haves and have-nots, with migrants obtaining office work (even if low-level) considered the haves and migrants in low-level service occupations (for instance, hotel and domestic workers) included among the have-nots. The class disparity splitting the Filipino community mirrors the current trend in the Los Angeles economy—the "widening disparity between high skill, high paying jobs and low skill, low paying jobs" (Sabagh, 1993: 123).

The concentration of Filipinos in paid work provides a foundation for understanding the position of domestic workers in the community. From the diverse incorporation of Filipinos in the labor market develops class hierarchies determining relations in the community. In the hierarchy of paid employment, domestic workers are clearly at the bottom. This is the case even though they believe that their jobs carry a higher level of prestige than other types of low-wage service occupations, for example, fast-food clerks. Within domestic service, there is also a rank of prestige—one determined by the employer and type of employment. While the wealth of the employer determines the status of the job (because wealthy employers are likely to offer higher wages), domestic work is also ranked according to type, with elderly care deemed a higher-status job than childcare and housekeeping. Despite these variations in rank, domestic work is still a low-status occupation. It is this reality that consequently shapes the practical consciousness of my interviewees concerning their "place" in the community. In the context of the presence of higher-end workers in the community, the low level that they occupy in the labor market signifies their nonsuccess. This is especially true in light of their high level of education. Thus, it is their class-based marginal location that shapes their perspective of their place in the community.

GEOGRAPHICAL CLUSTERS

Despite the fact that Filipinos represent the second most numerous Asian immigrant group in Los Angeles, they still do not have a visible ethnic enclave economy, meaning "a locational cluster of business firms whose own-ers and employees are (largely) co-ethnics" (Light et al., 1994: 68).[17] Un-like most other Asian immigrant groups in Los Angeles, the Filipino ethnic economy is distributed throughout the city and is not contained within an identifiable enclave. The absence of a Filipino ethnic enclave economy can be attributed largely to their concentration in wage employment. On the one hand, there are small clusters of ethnic businesses concentrated in par-ticular areas. For example, many Filipino ethnic businesses are located in downtown Los Angeles. On the other hand, these businesses do not form a locational cluster, since the larger number of Korean businesses in the area surrounds them.

The geographical constitution of the Filipino community is more discern-ible by residential patterns. Residential clusters of Filipinos have developed in both the inner city and suburbs. Filipinos are the dominant ethnic group in the suburbs of Carson and West Covina. In the inner city, community in-siders identify a few neighborhoods in the vicinity of downtown, for ex-ample, certain blocks of Temple Street, as Filipino Town. This neighborhood houses a small number of video rental stores and markets that cater to its predominantly Filipino residents. The other residential clusters of the com-munity include Eagle Rock, Echo Park, Cerritos, and Long Beach.

In general, the class cleavage of the Filipino community cannot be easily demarcated according to residential patterns. For most other Asian ethnic groups, inner-city residents are usually more disadvantaged than their coun-terparts in the suburbs (Ong and Azores, 1994a). Yet urban planners have noticed that "inner-city Filipinos are the exception to this pattern. Central Los Angeles City is the home to a sizable middle-class Filipino population whose members have a fair amount of education" (Ong and Azores, 1994a: 121). Middle-class and working-class Filipinos reside alongside each other in both the inner city and suburbs. The per capita income of suburban residents is slightly higher, however. Inner-city and suburban residents are also dis-tinguished by the greater percentage of homeowners in the suburbs (Ong and Azores, 1994a). In addition, some communities are distinguishably those of the middle class, and particular neighborhoods within a residential cluster of Filipinos are determinedly class-defined.

Because sharp geographic boundaries do not reflect the class division of the Filipino population, the entrance of migrant Filipina domestic workers into the community unavoidably leads to close encounters with the middle class. Migrant Filipina domestic workers are, for the most part, denied a spa-tially demarcated working-class community that would protect them from being reminded of the greater success of their middle-class counterparts. Hence, the spatial configuration of the community inadvertently enforces their practical consciousness of nonbelonging.

Within the world of domestic workers, they are able to form now and then a subcommunity among themselves during the workweek. While pockets of gathering in Rome are the haven of domestic workers from the host society, the subcommunities of domestic workers are likewise the haven of domestic workers in Los Angeles from the host community of migrant Filipinos. Domestic workers occasionally meet in parks and playgrounds of wealthy neighborhoods, such as Bel Air and Beverly Hills. Similar to Rome, these places represent pockets of gathering for this subcommunity of migrant Filipinos. In addition, part-time domestic workers form a subcommunity with women whom they meet on buses on their way to and from work. As they are far outnumbered by Latina domestic workers, however, only a very small number of them meet in these pockets. There are also subcommunities of migrant Filipina domestic workers in retirement villages, where the isolation of domestic work is often tempered by the guaranteed proximity of other migrant Filipina domestic workers.

By creating pockets of gathering during the workweek, those who care for the elderly take advantage of their concentration in retirement villages. Jovita Gacutan describes one such subcommunity of domestic workers:

> I was able to form a group. We helped each other out. . . . We would always be in my room, which was informally referred to as the Filipino Center in the village. We gave each other moral support. It was because we were all just starting over in this country, and that is why it was in all of us to help each other out.

In other retirement villages, when employers took afternoon naps, Filipina domestic workers would meet in front of an employer's apartment or house. They would also congregate in an employer's home, though rarely, as most employers are not tolerant of domestics entertaining visitors.

Yet on their day off, Filipina domestic workers usually leave the subcommunity of domestic workers or the isolation of their employer's home for other subcommunities of Filipinos. The subcommunities that they enter as weekend visitors are rendered middle-class spaces by the spatial configuration of the community. Moreover, their entrance into subcommunities is not always guided by work-based networks (that is, the subcommunity of domestic workers) but more often by familial ties. While the foundation of contemporary chain migration to the United States from the Philippines is the labor migration of professionals in the 1970s, the movement of domestic workers into the community is likewise initiated by relatives who are more often employed in managerial and professional occupations.

On their day off, domestic workers most frequently encounter other Filipinos in ethnic businesses and private residences.[18] For the most part, domestic workers have to depend on their limited group of middle-class friends and relatives in the area to physically free them from the isolation of domestic work. This is because many of them do not drive or have access to a vehicle on the weekends. If none of their friends and relatives are available on the weekends, domestic workers are usually trapped in the homes of employers. As Lelanie Quezon states, "On Saturdays, my sister takes me out if she is around. She takes me shopping. My sister is not here this weekend. So, I am staying here [employer's home]."

Occasionally, the subcommunity of domestic workers does extend beyond workdays to provide them an outlet from the alienating spaces of the workplace and Filipino migrant community. While Mila Tizon frequently spends her day off, similar to most other domestic workers, with her sister-in-law who is employed as a nurse, she occasionally chooses to spend time at the apartment of a domestic worker she met on a bus three years ago: "I go to church and go home to my sister-in-law's. Sometimes, I come here and hang out [the apartment of a domestic worker]. We tell stories for hours and watch TV. We eat downstairs or cook here." Migrant Filipina domestic workers in Los Angeles are most comfortable in these enclosed spaces. However, these spaces are rarely available to them. Family obligations usually take them to the more common middle-class-dominated spaces of the community.

Work-based and family-based networks do not always direct migrant Filipina domestic workers to different niches of the community. Due to the geographic constitution of the community, domestic workers rarely find an enclosed working-class niche. Work-based networks more often lead them to middle-class spaces in the community. For example, work-based networks usually lead them to the frequent get-togethers drawing the multiple subcommunities of Filipinos in Los Angeles. From town fiestas and association balls to more informal family celebrations (for example, graduations, birthdays, and christenings), get-togethers are extremely popular in the community. They are the community's lifeline. Almost every weekend, I was taken to parties by domestic workers and other members of the community. Often it was for the specific purpose of helping me locate other domestic workers to interview. Letty Manlapit Xavier is one of the women who invited me to numerous parties in the community. As she describes, Filipinos usually come together in these venues: "My day off goes from Friday night to Monday morning. It depends, or Sunday nights. On my day off, I usually go shopping and go to parties. There are always a lot of parties. Filipinos always have parties. I go with friends from work. I have met a lot of people through work. You meet them at the park or on the bus." Because parties free them from the isolation of the workplace, Filipina domestic workers often look forward to attending them during their day off.

Though the entrance of Letty into parties is usually guided by work-based networks, the parties are rarely limited to her working-class niche but frequently reflect the class diversity of the community. They are usually not given by other domestic workers but more often are organized by middle-class members of the community. These parties represent the intersections of subcommunities in the community, as intersecting family-based and work-based networks guide the access of domestic workers to them. For instance, I once accompanied domestic workers to a town fiesta of one of the women's hometown in the Philippines. Invited by her sister, an office worker, she in turn invited her friends, some of whom had not known until I informed them that people from their own towns organize similar events. Thus, it seems that domestic work limits their access to and knowledge of the community. With their lack of access to networks of other migrants from their own particular regions in the Philippines, domestic workers find themselves in community spaces that emphasize their "outsider" status, at least in the particular subcommunities that they do enter. For example, considering there are more than eighty-eight dialects in the Philippines, the language barrier that they inevitably face in these festivities reinforces this "outsider" status.

Parties ultimately represent the community and its spatial configuration, as they are frequent occasions of cross-class interactions. They are consequently described by domestic workers as "middle-class" spaces. Not surprisingly, domestic workers often kept to themselves at these events. This seeming discomfort is what I describe in the next section when I discuss the outlook engendered by the community's makeup and geographical constitution for domestic workers.

THE BEHAVIOR, ATTITUDES, AND ASPIRATIONS OF DOMESTIC WORKERS: DEFENSIVE POSTURING AGAINST THE MIDDLE CLASS

So far, I have established that the practical consciousness of nonbelonging is instilled in domestic workers by their location in the labor market, the geographic constitution of the community as middle-class spaces, and finally their constitution as weekend "visitors" to the community. In this section, I illustrate its reflection in the practices of domestic workers through a discussion of their shared modes of behavior and outlook in the community. Although some domestic workers have created subcommunities through work-based networks, these subcommunities are rarely removed from the felt presence of the middle class in the community. Thus, my discussion of modes of behavior focuses on occasions of cross-line interactions, as they represent the incorporation of migrant domestic workers into this polarized community. My analysis shows that migrant Filipina domestic workers experience a constant discomfort in the community. This discomfort is manifested in their preference for enclosed spaces that are limited to other domestic workers, their avoidance of the middle class, their opinion of the community as a hostile space, and finally their constrained aspirations for mobility in the United States.

In the representative spaces of the community, the actions of domestic workers reveal their limited incorporation into the middle-class-centered community of Filipinos. For example, domestic workers do not at all seem comfortable in the frequent cross-class events of the community. At numerous get-togethers that I attended with domestic workers, their physical movements seemed to have been constrained by an invisible class line that separated them from the middle-class members of the community. In my field notes on one of the get-togethers that I had attended in the community, I describe the repressed movements of Filipina domestic workers:

> Terisita Cadiao had invited me to a birthday party at her home, where
> she rents a room from a Filipina teacher. As it is the 75th birthday party
> of her landlord, the party is quite a big celebration with more than
> 50 people in attendance. I learned that most of the guests are from the
> same province as Terisita and active in their community organization.
> For most of the party, the popular song Macarena has been playing re-
> peatedly. The guests are teaching each other the dance that coincides
> with the song. I notice it is the older women teaching the younger
> women the choreographed steps. Though some men are dancing, most
> of them are sitting around and talking. . . . Everyone seems to be inter-
> acting and enjoying him/herself, except Terisita. While everyone is
> gathered around the large oak tree in the backyard, Terisita is inside the
> house looking out through the screen door of the kitchen. Hardly ever
> stepping out of the house to join the rest of the group, she only did so to
> help clean up the place. Interestingly, she didn't step out of the house

while we were eating. She did not come out and join the rest of the group. Instead, she came out to get some food and then carried it back inside the house. I learned that among the guests were many professionals and members of prominent families from her province. . . . There seems to be an invisible class line that she is tiptoeing around. It's sad considering the other people in the party did not seem to notice the patterns of her actions, her nonparticipation in the festivities.

When I asked Terisita why she didn't want to join the rest of the group, she responded quite vaguely and told me that she didn't feel well. Terisita's behavior is, however, not uncommon among domestic workers. At another party that I attended with domestic workers, the three women I accompanied kept to themselves the whole time. They stayed at the far corner of the room, removed from the rest of the crowd, and not once did they speak to anyone else but themselves. In middle-class spaces representing the community, the physical movements of domestic workers reveal their sense of discomfort and alienation. They are clearly uncomfortable in these spaces, despite the fact that their identity as domestic workers is not physically distinguishable from the rest of the group. Avoiding the middle class, however, ensures the protection of the identity that they do not want to reveal. For domestic workers, hiding their identity lessens their discomfort in the community. As they have to segregate themselves to do so, they paradoxically heighten the discomfort that they are attempting to ease through their repressed actions.

Anomie also characterizes the attitudes and opinions of migrant Filipina domestic workers about the Filipino community of Los Angeles. Though some domestic workers describe the community as generally supportive, most interviewees feel the absence of camaraderie among Filipino migrants. Vicky Diaz echoes most of the other responses of interviewees to the question "What do you think of Filipinos in Los Angeles?": "I have felt vibes from Filipinos looking down at you just because you are walking on the street and they are driving a car. I also felt it when I told them that I was a housekeeper. It's hard to explain, but you just feel that they look at you differently." As members of the have-nots in the community, domestic workers are acutely aware of its class divisions. It is an awareness that consequently engenders their cautious behavior in the community. The access of the community to mainstream jobs does not hamper anomie, because the class disparities that are generated by this access create a hierarchy that determinedly reduces status in the community to class. Thus, domestic workers generally describe the community as insensitive and unsupportive.

In contrast, the two teachers whom I interviewed describe the community quite differently. Ligaya Smith, for example, believes there is no class segregation in the community: "I don't think they looked down at me when I was doing domestic work, even those who are not my relatives did not look down at me. I think there is no class segregation." In contrast to domestic workers, the middle class—such as Ligaya—is quite oblivious to the displacement and unease generated by class disparities in the community among its have-nots. Moreover, Ligaya's differing opinion suggests the easy shift in perspective generated by mobility from one class position to another.[19]

Domestic workers who have been employed in other countries are those most aware of the absence of camaraderie in the community. Each one of them believes that Filipinos in other countries are more supportive of each other because of the absence of class disparities in other receiving communities. For example, women who had worked in Taiwan, Hong Kong, Italy, and countries in the Middle East describe these receiving communities as extremely supportive. In contrast, they consider the culture of the Filipino community of Los Angeles to be not of solidarity but instead of competition. Jerissa Lim distinguishes Taiwan and the United States along these lines.

> In Taiwan, Filipinos were closer to each other than Filipinos are here. Instead of competing with each other, we decided to be there for each other. Of course, there would also be those who would bad-mouth you to employers, but you can count the number of those types of people with your fingers unlike in the United States. Here you succeed just a little bit, and even your fellow Filipinos would pull you down. They have no love for each other. Even if they know that you are poor and undocumented, having a hard time making ends meet, they would step all over you. That's actually why it would be hard for someone like you to interview people, because here people always threaten you that they will report you to the immigration. Any misunderstanding or conflict is followed by the threat of reporting you to immigration. That is how it is in America.

According to Jerissa, access to the mainstream does not reduce coethnic conflict. In fact, it intensifies competition at the expense of camaraderie. Hence, practices of mutual assistance are far less common in Los Angeles than in Taiwan. Mahler's (1995) claims of lesser coethnic conflict for migrant communities with access to mainstream jobs only seem to apply to those who in fact benefit from this access. While the professionals whom I interviewed believe that there is less competition than camaraderie in the community, the women who have not yet been able to leave domestic work describe the community quite differently.

For domestic workers, their experience of downward mobility is aggravated by the presence of successful migrants in the community. Cherry Jacinto states:

> There are people here who I knew in the Philippines. I used to feel terrible that they were treating me differently than how they did in the Philippines. They treat you differently just because you are in this situation [a domestic worker]. They give you attitude. They act like you are below them, telling you haughtily that you are a domestic worker. They are not sensitive and don't remember that you were not like this in the Philippines. They don't treat you the same way. . . . It really registers in my mind. One of these days, when I do some writing, I will put this all [on] paper, how people can be so careless and insensitive. . . . What I want is just a little bit of respect. There is nothing like that here.

The presence of the middle class not only intensifies their decline in status, the absence of support from the middle class also heightens the discomfort of domestic workers over their downward mobility.

As established earlier, the middle class is an unavoidable presence in the community life of migrant Filipina domestic workers. As such, class disparities shape their consciousness of their location and experience in the community. In particular, class disparities result in anomie for domestic workers. For domestic workers, community life is determinedly reduced to their nonsuccess through their unavoidable encounters with the middle class. Indeed, the actions of the middle class fail to alleviate and in fact heighten these sentiments among domestic workers. In various ways, the middle class represents to domestic workers an intense reminder of their low status in the United States.

The discomfort of community life is consequently resolved by stressing domestic workers' temporary membership in the community. Temporary membership helps rationalize their nonsuccess. Thus, most women claim not to have any aspiration for further mobility in the labor market, because they will soon return to the Philippines. While the presence of the middle class suggests the possibility of mobility, it also constrains the aspirations of domestic workers for mobility. By admitting to their aspirations, they by default would admit to their nonsuccess. Moreover, the possibility of not securing a higher-status occupation poses a threat, which further constrains their desires for mobility. Domestic workers would rather stay satisfied with domestic work so as not to concede to the possibility of failure. Yet as I discussed, most migrant Filipina domestic workers in Los Angeles abhor domestic work. By not aspiring, however, they do not fail. For example, the youngest woman whom I interviewed, Heidi Marquez, justifies her current status as a domestic worker by identifying "faults" with her aspired to occupation.

> I want to be a licensed vocational nurse or even a registered nurse to make more money than domestic work. That is why I want to do that kind of work. . . . I really want to work in a nursing home, but in a house there is no gossiping. I am alone. I can just count the days and am off before I know it. Before I know it, it is already Saturday. So, domestic work might be better. Nursing homes are difficult to enter. The Filipinas there are snobbish and ignore you when you are new.

In contrast, most other women have settled into domestic work.

> I want to be a live-in worker as long as I can do that type of work. Because you can save much more being a live-in worker. You have less expenses. Your food is covered, for example, At least you have something to spend for yourself, too. When it is your break or half day, it is the time to go and shop for your family [in the Philippines]. I have no ambition for other kinds of work. I am content with this kind of work, just to earn money and then that's it. (Mimi Baclayon, Los Angeles)

The older age of most of my interviewees is most likely a determining factor in their lack of interest in changing jobs. Among my interviewees, however, age seems to be less of a consciously articulated reason for wanting to stay in domestic work. Only two women mentioned this factor as a barrier against their aspirations for attaining higher status jobs. More than age, it seems that their ambivalence over settlement is the central factor that constrains them from pursuing another form of employment. Though many outwardly claim to be temporary members of the community, some sought my help for securing "better jobs." This pointed out to me that the ambivalence of domestic workers over settlement is mirrored in their attitude about their position in the labor market. They privately aspire for mobility but publicly claim not to have any aspiration for other jobs.

Similar to domestic workers in Rome, nonbelonging defines the community life of domestic workers in Los Angeles, though characteristically in a different way. Their particular relationship to the middle class enforces their temporary membership and discomfort in the spaces of the community. For domestic workers in Los Angeles, nonbelonging generates ambivalence about settlement and contains their feelings of solidarity to other low-wage workers.

Conclusion

A number of characteristics differentiate the migrant communities of Rome and Los Angeles. The differences include their geographical constitution, class constitution, gender constitution, and, most important, social conditions of settlement. Membership in the host society and polity is possible in the United States, while it is clearly restricted in Italy.

Though different characteristics define the geocultural space of the Filipino migrant communities of Rome and Los Angeles, they still lead to a similar dislocation among migrant Filipina domestic workers, who share a sense of dislocation from their local conditions. For women in Rome, it is a dislocation from the host society. In Los Angeles, it is from the community. In Rome, nonbelonging in the host society generates the dual outlooks of needing to leave and needing support and consequently results in the conflicting experiences of anomie and solidarity among domestic workers. In Los Angeles, nonbelonging in the community engenders feelings of nonsuccess and consequently leads to acts of defensive posturing in their behavior and aspirations (for example, temporary membership) as well as bitter attitudes toward the community. Thus, anomie and solidarity also define the community of Los Angeles. While the presence of the middle class instills anomie, domestic workers find solidarity with each other.

Migrant Filipina domestic workers in Rome and Los Angeles share with one another a localized dislocation in the community. They share hampered feelings of camaraderie and heightened feelings of temporary settlement. They also notably share an "inward" direction of resistance against their shared consciousness of dislocation and nonbelonging. Instead of turning "outward" by establishing their rightful membership in either the host society of Rome or the Filipino migrant community of Los Angeles, they both maintain their status as outsiders. Women in Rome cope with nonbelonging by engaging in microbusinesses in hopes that these capitalist ventures will expedite their departure. However, because the enclosed network of their community prevents them from truly succeeding, this negotiating strategy instills anomie and consequently aggravates the dislocation of nonbelonging. In Los Angeles, women turn against nonbelonging by further segregating themselves from the community. In the process, anomie remains a prominent characteristic of their community life.

Servants of Globalization:
Different Settings, Parallel Lives

Migrant Filipina domestic workers are the global servants of late capitalism. Located in more than 130 countries, they work in the cities of Athens, Dhahran, Kuwait City, Rome, Milan, Madrid, Paris, London, Toronto, New York, Los Angeles, Hong Kong, and Singapore. To emphasize the extent of their geographic dispersal, I have framed the understanding of their experiences in the context of the global economy because the effects of global restructuring vis-à-vis the Philippines implicitly include the constitution of this female labor diaspora.

In recognition of this diaspora, I have compared the lives of the global servants in two destinations: Rome and Los Angeles. This study has set out to show the process of settlement undergone by two distinct groups of migrant women. By containing my analysis to women, I am able to consider multiple variables that control their experiences and in the process show the imbricated relationships between race, class, gender, and citizenship. These factors inform the process of subject formation and particularly the dislocations that migrant Filipina domestic workers encounter in migration and settlement. I have thus examined their experiences by tracing their subject formation in migration and by comparing their subject-positions in four key institutions of migration: nation-state, family, labor market, and migrant community.

I began this study with the assumption that women in Rome and Los Angeles would have different experiences of migration. Though the contemporary migration of Filipina domestic workers to Rome and Los Angeles is similarly rooted in globalization, I still expected to find significant differences between them, precisely because of the varying conditions of settlement in these two destinations. Different histories of migration, disparate policies of migration, and diverse social characteristics of the Filipino migrant commu-

nity distinguish one destination from another. I initially intended to control
for the variables differentiating their experiences so as to contribute to a
broader understanding of settlement, but once I realized that the experiences
of these two groups of women were not as different as I had initially assumed, I had to redirect my analysis. Since I found striking similarities in
their experiences, I needed to account for the emergence of parallel lives
across different settings among migrant Filipina domestic workers.

Parallel Lives

What are the most striking parallel characteristics that I have identified
among the women in my study? First, they share the experience of quasi-
citizenship in relation to the nation-state at both ends of the migration spectrum. As the status of the Philippines as a sending nation of secondary-tier
workers in globalization leaves its government too weak to ensure the protection of its nationals, the incorporation of migrant Filipinas into the host
society depends mostly on the cooperation of the receiving state. Yet racial
and other forms of segmentation stunt the rights accorded to them by the receiving state, albeit to a much greater degree in Italy where legal migrants
from the Philippines are for the most part limited to domestic work.

The formation of transnational households and consequently the everyday experience of the pain of family separation represent another parallel
characteristic among migrant Filipina domestic workers. The varying conditions of settlement in the United States and Italy have not led to different
outcomes in household structure. While the right of family reunification
had only been given to migrants in Rome in 1990, the citizens of California
recently attempted to take it away from those in Los Angeles with the state
referendum Proposition 187. This shows us that in Rome the recognition of
human rights with family reunification has not strongly influenced the situation of migrants: the separation of families in the entire duration of settlement remains the norm. In Los Angeles, the attempt to deny their human
rights simply perpetuates the separation of families with the maintenance of
transnational household structures.

Another parallel characteristic that has emerged from my study is directly
related to the experience of domestic work. The high level of educational attainment of migrant Filipina domestic workers in Rome and Los Angeles results in the dislocation of contradictory class mobility. For these groups of migrant women, domestic work involves a simultaneous increase and decrease

in labor market status. They gain by earning more than they ever would in the Philippines but concomitantly lose since they can only gain at the expense of experiencing downward mobility from their higher social status in the Philippines. The relatively comfortable class standing of migrants is to be expected in light of the resources needed for emigration from the Philippines. As many scholars have noted, migrants are hardly ever the poorest of the poor in sending nations (Portes, 1989). This suggests that many more migrant groups other than Filipina domestic workers share this particular dislocation. Also, relating to the experience of domestic work, women in Rome and Los Angeles identify resoundingly similar issues in the workplace that aggravate the dislocation of contradictory class mobility. Most of the women, for example, disdain the routinization of domestic labor and describe domestic work as *nakakabobo*—a process of slowly making them stupid. In addition, they both contend with the aggravation of their routinized labor by the greater authority of employers in the workplace.

The experience of alienation in the migrant community is another similarity that I identified. Though the composition of and shared modes of behavior in the Filipino migrant communities of Rome and Los Angeles are distinguished by the presence of middle-class Filipinos in Los Angeles, I found that amid these material distinctions are similar feelings of community life. Though coexisting with solidarity, anomie similarly plagues the experiences of domestic workers in the Filipino migrant communities of Rome and Los Angeles. Anomie results from the hypercapitalist state of the migrant community in Rome and from class segmentation in Los Angeles.

In addition to the four dislocations that I have examined, the penetration of global capitalism into the lives of migrant Filipina domestic workers demonstrates more subtle parallels between the two groups. In globalization, capitalism is heightened by its penetration into the intimacies of family life. Migrant Filipina domestic workers in both Rome and Los Angeles place the material gains of the family over its emotional needs. Time with children is less important than giving money to children. I have thus argued that the formation of transnational households cannot stem solely from economic restructuring in globalization but also relies on the conscious and unconscious reworking of priorities and values in the families of Filipina domestic workers. Capitalism's determination of personal relationships in the migrant community underscores another example of their similar experiences. In the case of Rome, I have argued that personal relationships are marred by their commercialization with the prevalence of capitalist activities. In Los Angeles, I have shown that migrant Filipina domestic workers base their worth in the community primarily on their class position and determinedly reduce the basis of membership in the community to class.

Even though I have repeatedly stressed the similarities engendered by migration among Filipina domestic workers in Rome and Los Angeles, I have not disregarded the differences between their experiences. Globalization is a highly uneven process, with varying local consequences. In recognition of this well-established view, I have looked at globalization from a very localized perspective and framework. Still, I found that migrant Filipina domestic workers in Rome and Los Angeles share certain dislocations. However, these dislocations neither manifest themselves in the same way nor are they materially constituted in like fashion. For instance, partial citizenship is differentiated by varying degrees and levels of exclusion in receiving nations, with some much more restrictive than others. Nonbelonging is also a shared dislocation, but it is one that emerges from different material configurations of a migrant community. Notably, the nuances that are brought out by interrogating these differences would not eliminate these shared dislocations.

Migrant Filipina domestic workers in Rome and Los Angeles also share similar experiences with their counterparts in other regions of the world. Based on writings of domestic workers in the multinational monthly magazine *Tinig Filipino*, Filipina domestic workers in most other countries maintain transnational household structures. I nonetheless want to emphasize that the conditions of settlement for women in Rome and Los Angeles are differentiated from other domestic workers in the diaspora by the fact that they are not restricted to short-term overseas labor contracts. Moreover, the more lax migration policies in Italy and the United States grant them greater freedom to choose employers. However, the similar confinement of migrant Filipina domestic workers within the walls of private homes results in characteristically similar vulnerabilities among these women throughout the world.

Why Parallel Lives?

My findings neither override nor create ambivalence over the important theoretical contributions of Portes and Rumbaut (1996), who argue that experiences of migrants shift according to different "contexts of reception." By illustrating the parallel lives of migrant Filipina domestic workers in host societies with different contexts of reception, I have only emphasized the fact that across their different contexts they do share a similar role in various local economies. Moreover, they share a similar position in the global economy as part of the secondary tier of migrant workers in the economic bloc of postindustrial nations. At most, this study confirms the view that the macroprocesses of globalization should be given greater consideration when accounting for the influences of different contexts of reception on settlement.

Macroprocesses of globalization stunt the integration of migrant Filipina domestic workers and consequently impose upon them social, economic, and political barriers that limit their ability to develop a sense of full membership in their host societies. To name one example, the opposite turns of the "denationalization of economies" and "renationalization of politics" result in their conflicted incorporation as desired workers and yet rejected citizens of receiving nation-states (Sassen, 1996b). With its examination of dislocations situated in such macroprocesses, this study has shown that the structural location of migrant Filipina domestic workers in global restructuring propels the emergence of similarities between them in Rome and Los Angeles. Globalization and its corresponding macroprocesses initiate the emergence of parallel lives in different settings. Macroprocesses do not have an umbrella-like impact, but they do impel the confrontation of similar issues of migration among workers in similar economic locations.

Parallels therefore do not emerge out of some ontological similarity in institutions globally. They emerge from a particular process of globalization — global restructuring and its corresponding macroprocesses, which include but are not limited to the formation of the economic bloc of postindustrial nations, the feminization of labor, the unequal development of regions, the heightening of commodification in late capitalism, and the opposite turns of nationalism. As Lisa Lowe states:

> Just as these new patterns allow capital to exploit discrete sectors of the labor force in distinct ways and according to different means, the "class subject" of transnationalism cannot be politically and ideologically unified in any simple way but may be "unified" according to a process based on strategic alliances between different sectors, not on their abstract identity. (1996: 172)

Parallels come from the constitution of labor migrants within localized institutional processes in globalization. As it happens, migrant Filipina domestic workers in "different sectors" can cross-nationally and cross-continentally identify with each other on the grounds of the similar effects of global processes in their lives. These similar impacts are what I have repeatedly referred to as dislocations. Dislocations are the tropes of alliance among migrant Filipina domestic workers. In making this point, I want to emphasize that the search for dislocations fits the categorization posed by Grewal and Kaplan (1994) of transnational feminist projects. Such projects forge links on the basis of the similar impacts of particular global processes on the experiences of women across places affected by different domestic politics.

How do macroprocesses of globalization initiate the constitution of parallel lives? As I established earlier, the economic bloc of postindustrial nations more than ever demands low-wage migrant workers to expand their pool of cheap labor and particularly female migrant workers to perform low-wage service work in "global cities." Hence, low-wage migrant workers join the ranks of the working class and underclass of postindustrial host societies. Yet as the pool of cheap labor expands, the middle class of postindustrial nations correspondingly shrinks, with the formation of a two-tier labor force of highly paid professional workers and low-paid workers of routinized service and decentralized manufacturing labor. Migrants, who are easy targets because of their lesser access to the host polity of postindustrial nations, have consequently been labeled scapegoats of the turmoil caused by economic restructuring. With the rise of xenophobia, society promotes the temporary membership of migrants, their stunted incorporation into the nation-state, and the formation of transnational families. From these social realities arise numerous dislocations of migration, including migrants' status as quasi-citizens, the pain of family separation, and the feeling of nonbelonging in the migrant community. In globalization, the fact of the matter is that even though the "denationalized" economy demands the labor of migrants, the "renationalized" society neither wants the responsibility for the reproductive costs of these workers nor grants them the membership accorded by the contributions of their labor to the economic growth of postindustrial nations (Chavez, 1997).

The unequal development of regions in globalization also causes similarities between women in Rome and Los Angeles, in particular the formation of transnational households and similar experiences of domestic work. As I explained in the introduction and in Chapter 6, the unequal development of regions in the global economy means that the achievement of material security in the Philippines via overseas domestic work imposes a decline in social status. The lesser value of an educational degree from a developing country such as the Philippines translates to the relegation of developing countries as a greater source of low-wage workers rather than professional workers in the transnational workforce. This is not to say that migrants from the Philippines do not get to utilize their training in other countries. Many doubtlessly contribute their skills more so than do migrants from other nations, considering that the Philippines has been one of the largest sources of trained medical workers in the United States. My study, however, shows that not all have successfully done so. The integration of professionals is a highly selective process that is determined by the demands of the labor market in the receiving society. The experience of migration in turn comes to involve the experience of contradictory class mobility for the dislocated middle-class women who can afford to flee the economic turmoil that the unequal development of regions has caused the Philippines but only land jobs as domestic workers.

As I have shown in Chapter 4, the formation of the transnational family also results from the unequal development of regions in the global economy. To sustain the family materially, migrants form transnational households by turning to the lower costs of reproduction in sending countries. This characteristic feature of migrant life is not particular to Filipina domestic workers; it is also shared by migrants from Mexico, the Dominican Republic, and other traditional sending countries of migration. This underscores the fact that despite the different conditions of settlement in postindustrial countries such as the United States and Italy, the economic role of low-wage migrant workers promotes the similar structural constitutions of migrant households globally.

Commodification is the last key feature of globalization that I address to emphasize that macroprocesses of globalization do indeed promote the constitution of parallel characteristics among migrant Filipina domestic workers in Rome and Los Angeles. The heightening of commodification is keenly illustrated by the global commodification of caretaking, which is a process that refers to the hierarchical chain of reproductive labor in globalization. The underlying premise of the international transfer of caretaking is the commodification of the family in global restructuring, meaning the reduction of family ties to commodity-based relationships. The commodification of the family is exemplified by the practices of showing love with material goods. In transnational households, relationships in the families of migrant Filipina domestic workers are forcibly reduced to monthly remittances. Conversely, the families of their employers in Rome and Los Angeles still manage to maintain intimacy despite the commodification of reproduction. However, the privilege of maintaining some semblance of noncommodified family life for these families is at the expense of the reduction of intimacy for the families of migrant Filipina domestic workers.

From the heightening of commodification to the demand for low-wage workers in postindustrial nations, various structural and cultural features of globalization lead to the formation of parallel lives among migrant Filipina domestic workers in Rome and Los Angeles. They themselves are aware of their parallel lives and as such use these shared interests as the basis of their "imagined (global) community." Globalization is why they have parallel lives, and their parallel lives prove that there is globalization. As such, the similar features of migrant life for women in Rome and Los Angeles signify the importance of situating them in the labor diaspora constituted by global restructuring.

The similar characteristics of migrant Filipina domestic workers in Rome and Los Angeles also maintain the inequalities of globalization with the emergence of winners and losers. For example, there are winners and losers in the formation of transnational households. The losers are the family members who are denied intimacy, and the winners are the families of employers who gain intimacy at the cost of the formation of transnational households for their domestic workers. The winners also include the host societies of Italy and the United States as well as the sending country of the Philippines. While the Philippines is guaranteed its steady flow of monthly remittances by its construction as the rightful home of their less than fully incorporated migrant workers, the host societies of Italy and the United States are freed of the reproductive costs of a large segment of their productive labor force. The losers are the migrant workers who are denied the rights of membership granted to them by their economic contributions to the host society. However, the Philippines also loses along with its workers. The relegation of developing countries as a source of secondary-tier transnational workers perpetuates the status of these states as developing countries and maintains the inequalities that cause the outmigration and social decline of their educated workers.

Analyzing Migration from the Level of the Subject

By analyzing migration from the level of the subject, I have avoided giving an essential representation of the experiences of migrant Filipina domestic workers. Instead, I have described their shifting subject-positions in multiple migrant institutions in order to illustrate the process of their constitution as migrant subjects. I specifically looked at the social processes of migration from the point of view of the subject to identify the formations of subordinations, in other words, the dislocations, elicited within these processes and to examine the responses of, or as Butler has written "the turn taken by," women against these dislocations. Thus, I have not intended to provide a whole unitary picture of migrant Filipina domestic workers, one that would make it convenient to limit them to an essential experience. I have instead sought to explain their dislocations by illustrating their constitution as fragmented subjects. My objective is that readers come away from this study with a sense of the various fragmentations imposed by structural processes on subjects.

This theoretical undertaking, one that I call the analysis of migration from the level of the subject, differs from the intermediate level of analysis but at the same time shares with it the consideration of institutional processes. While the subject level of analysis proposes that dislocations are the determining features of the everyday experience of migration, this is not the case in the intermediate level of analysis. In other words, the dislocations elicited within the institutional processes of migration and not the institutional processes per se characterize the lived experience of migration and settlement. Another difference concerns their analysis of agency: the intermediate level of analysis seeks to establish the agency of the migrant, while the subject level of analysis already assumes the agency of the migrant. This latter approach instead seeks to examine the consequences, meaning the limits and possibilities, of agency.

In this study, I have shown that the key dislocations of migrant Filipina domestic workers are partial citizenship, the pain of family separation, contradictory class mobility, and nonbelonging in the migrant community. Dislocations emerge from the positioning of migrant Filipina domestic workers in institutional processes of global restructuring, including the outflow of labor, the formation of transnational households, the entrance of educated women into the secondary-tier transnational workforce, and the constitution of disenfranchised migrant communities.

As a constituted subject, the migrant Filipina bases "her ways of understanding her relations to the world" on her dislocations and not on the abstract systems that mold these dislocations (Weedon, 1997: 32). As an acting subject, she responds in various ways to these dislocations and the "conscious and unconscious thoughts and emotions" that they elicit within her. These responses are acts of resistance against the dislocations engendered by her positioning in the social processes of migration and global restructuring. They are the "immediate struggles" that she deploys in her everyday practices (Foucault, 1983). She particularly responds not only to temper them but also to ensure that they do not interfere with her primary goal of capital accumulation. Additionally, her structural location in various axes of domination limits her resources and subsequently her possible responses. Thus, her responses cannot transcend the process of her constitution as a subject and the external forces molding her constitution.

As the everyday practices of migrant Filipina domestic workers include manifold acts of resistance against the dislocations of migration, I do not claim to identify all of them in this study. Instead, I have only identified the key actions that were revealed to me in my interviews and substantiated by my observations of domestic workers in the field. In response to their quasi-citizenship, I have shown that they turn to the construction of the Philippines as "home" so as to envision a place of rightful membership in the global labor market. In my discussion of the family, I have shown that parents respond to the formation of transnational households by suppressing the emotional needs of family members in the Philippines and prioritizing the material gains of the family. In response to the limited integration of settlement in Rome, migrant Filipina domestic workers, I found, create a base of solidarity in the community but also plague the community with anomie by turning to competition and the use of capitalist activities for expediting their departure. In Los Angeles, migrant Filipina domestic workers act defensively against the middle class by avoiding them and claming temporary membership in the community. In response to the aggravation of their decline in social status by the mechanisms of control in the workplace—for example, the myth of "like one of the family" and the script of deference and maternalism—migrant Filipinas manipulate these mechanisms through their performance. Performance, however, does not translate into compliance, as performance includes interventions. They manipulate the script tactically through occasional interjections of conscious emotional displays, for instance, interrupting smiling by occasionally frowning or crying. In this way, their unexpected behavior elicits emotions among employers (such as discomfort and guilt), which then make employers more cooperative.

These examples show that migrant Filipina domestic workers utilize the mechanisms of inequality that determine the process of their constitution when they take a turn against their subject formation. These direct reactions against their dislocations are nevertheless rendered political and contribute to the subjection of migrant Filipina domestic workers. They represent acts of resistance against their constitution as subjects. Though acting against their dislocations, migrant Filipina domestic workers do not eliminate these dislocations. Instead, they "recuperate" them.

One example of this recuperation is evident when they resist their partial citizenship by turning to the Philippines as "home," an act that denies them the rightful membership that they have earned from their economic contribution to their host societies. The women's response to the pain of family separation, particularly the repression of emotions, exacerbates intergenerational conflicts. This repression is manifested in the infrequent visits of documented workers to the Philippines. In turn, parents delay ending the pain of family separation in order to avoid a problem that their actions ironically aggravate. Women also aggravate the experience of contradictory class mobility when manipulating emblems of inequality in domestic work, for example, embracing the racial bifurcation of domestics. Such forms of resistance do not confront the sources aggravating this dislocation. Similarly, their resistance against nonbelonging heightens the alienation of migrant Filipina domestic workers in the community. In Rome, microcapitalist ventures result in the commodification of relationships. In Los Angeles, acts of defensive posturing against the middle class do not generate solidarity but instead anomie in the community.

Notably, the actions of domestic workers involve the maintenance of inequalities, particularly the system of global restructuring in which their constitution as subjects is situated. For example, the construction of the Philippines as "home" supports their stunted incorporation into the host society and consequently their construction as "guests" in receiving nations. With the turn that they take against the pain of family separation, commodification rules the transnational family, as relationships are reduced to material goods. Capitalism is thus heightened by the actions of migrant Filipina domestic workers in regard to the dislocation imposed by the formation of the transnational household. Capitalism is further reconstituted in the relationships of domestic workers in the community with the emergence of the hyperreality of making money in Rome and the reduction of the basis of membership in the migrant community of Los Angeles to class. Finally, the mechanisms of control in domestic work, as they are neither eliminated nor reconstituted but instead only manipulated, are consequently maintained.

By analyzing migration from the level of the subject, I have illustrated that migrant Filipina domestic workers "resist" as they "recuperate" power (Butler 1997). This comes, however, not without any concrete benefits in their lives. The material rewards of domestic work are maximized with the formation of transnational families and the manipulation of mechanisms of control in the workplace. Moreover, the everyday practices that constitute their community life serve as immediate struggles against the discomfort that they feel in the host society (for women in Rome) or in the Filipino migrant community (for women in Los Angeles).

By tracing the subjection of migrant Filipina domestic workers, this study has not only established the existence of agency but has also illustrated the "bind of agency" (Butler 1997). In addition, this study has identified the key dislocations constituted within the social processes of migration and dislocations to which migrant Filipina domestic workers are compelled to respond in their everyday practices. At most, migrant Filipina domestic workers deploy tactics that are immediately made available to them in the process of their constitution, a process that they cannot escape but at the same time do not necessarily accept. In conclusion, this study has shown that labor organizers of migrant Filipina domestic workers are not faced with the challenge of compelling these migrant women to engage in political actions. They definitely attempt to do so in their everyday practices. Organizers are instead faced with the problem of transforming the various responses against the dislocations of migration of Filipina domestic workers to political actions, which constitute a lesser recuperation and a greater resistance to power.

APPENDIXES

Characteristics of the Samples

The three main types of domestic work are housecleaning, childcare, and elderly care. In Los Angeles, informants claim that Filipino domestic workers are concentrated in elderly care, but my interviews show Filipinos performing a wider range of domestic jobs. The twenty-six women I interviewed in Los Angeles included eight who cared for the elderly, five housekeepers, and five childcare workers. Of the two unemployed women I interviewed, one had been a housekeeper recently fired by her employers, and one was in the process of relocating to New York, where domestic workers are believed to earn more than their counterparts in Los Angeles. Of the six women who are no longer employed as domestic workers, four had primarily been employed as nannies, one as a provider of elderly care, and one as a housekeeper. While two of these women had only been employed by one family for approximately one year, the other four had stayed in domestic work for a longer period and had worked for at least three families.

In Rome, the types of domestic jobs of Filipina women are as varied as in Los Angeles but are mostly concentrated in general housecleaning. Of the forty-six women interviewed, eight work as an *assistenza* (assistant) of the elderly, twenty-five are housekeepers, and the rest, excluding street vendors and unemployed women, do childcare and housecleaning.

In Los Angeles, employers can be subcategorized into one of three groups: post-1965 professional Filipino immigrants, middle- to upper-middle-class elderly persons, and upper-class families. Among twenty-six interviewees, nine have been employed at one point by families of Filipino professionals. Of the eighteen interviewees currently employed as domestic workers, eight have elderly employers, five are employed as housekeepers or nannies by Filipino families, while the rest are employed as housekeepers or nannies by families from the exclusive neighborhoods of Brentwood, Beverly Hills, and Bel Air. Their employers include politicians, Hollywood producers, stockbrokers, doctors, and lawyers. In Rome, almost all of the women interviewed work for Italian families, the majority of whom are in the middle class. Most employers of Filipino domestic workers are small-business owners and professionals (such as architects, lawyers, and doctors), but they also include Italian cinema producers, elected government officials, and foreign diplomats.

WAGES

The survey of 222 women in Rome gives slightly different results than my interviews. According to the survey, the average monthly income of live-in domestic workers is 1,172,358 lira (U.S.$782) and the average of part-time workers is 1,383,120 lira (U.S.$922). The fuller load of the part-time workers whom I interviewed explains the discrepancy between the two sets of findings, while the conflation of providers of elderly care and live-in workers partially accounts for the slightly higher average wage of those designated as "live-in workers" in the survey.

DURATION OF SETTLEMENT

While a small group of Filipina domestic workers began settling in Italy in the early 1970s, the earliest arriving female migrant I interviewed came in 1977. In Los Angeles, the earliest came in 1972 as a companion of the elderly mother of a professional Filipina migrant. Only 4 of the 26 women interviewed in Los Angeles came in the 1970s, while 11 arrived in the 1980s and 11 in the 1990s. In Italy, the majority of women, 27, came in the 1990s, while 17 entered in the 1980s and only 2 migrated in the 1970s. Of the 27 women entering Italy in the 1990s, 20 arrived between 1990 and 1992. The survey results reflect these flows: of 221 women, 6 arrived in the 1970s, 83 in the 1980s, and 132 in the 1990s; of 79 men, 1 came in the 1970s, 26 in the 1980s, and 52 in the 1990s. In both cities, the large flow of migration in the 1990s strongly suggests the continued outflow of labor from the Philippines (see Table 1). Because most are recent migrants, it is too soon to comment on the outcome of their settlement, that is, whether they are temporary or permanent settlers (Massey et al., 1987). We do know that they cannot be categorized as recurrent migrants because most return to the Philippines infrequently, perhaps because the geographic distance from Rome and Los Angeles deters them from doing so.

AGE AND MARITAL STATUS

In Los Angeles, only five of twenty-six interviewees are never-married single women. The rest of the women are married, widowed, or separated from their husbands. Extremely surprising is the median age of my interviewees in Los

Angeles of fifty-two. The youngest research participant was thirty-three years old, while the oldest was sixty-eight years old. What explains the extremely high median age of domestic workers in Los Angeles? We can surmise that younger Filipino immigrant women are not attracted to domestic work because of its isolating nature. As such, they take advantage of the wider range of labor market opportunities available to them in the United States.

In Rome, the median age of interviewees was thirty-one years old, significantly lower than my sample in Los Angeles. Only 4 women were age twenty-five or younger, the youngest being twenty years old, and 11 women were at least fifty years old, with the oldest being sixty-six years old. While the Philippine embassy in Rome claims that most domestic workers in Italy are young and single, less than half of the women whom I interviewed (19) are never-married single women. Moreover, of these women, 3 are single mothers. The rest of the interviewees are married, widowed, separated, or living in domestic partnership arrangements. Survey results also reflect the age and marital status of the women interviewed for the study. Of the 222 women surveyed in Rome, 116 are married and 106 are single. The median age of these women is thirty-three years old.

EDUCATIONAL ATTAINMENT

Of twenty-six domestic workers interviewed in Los Angeles, eleven women have college diplomas, ten of which are in the field of education. Of these ten women, only two have been able to leave domestic servitude for a job commensurate with their training, as they are now employed as public school teachers. In addition, there are six women with two to three years of college education and another seven with high school degrees, two of whom acquired vocational training in cosmetology. Only two of twenty-six women have not finished high school. In Los Angeles, therefore, the interviews reveal two main subcategories of domestic workers: the highly educated group and the average educated contingent.

The educational attainment of domestic workers in Rome resembles that of their counterparts in Los Angeles. Of forty-six female domestic workers interviewed in Rome, exactly half have attained a college diploma in the Philippines. Of twenty-three college-educated women, one has a master's degree. Most obtained degrees in education, commerce (with a specialization in accounting), or nursing. Also attaining a high level of education are seven women who have some years of college training. An additional twelve women have high school diplomas. Among these, five completed two-year vocational programs in midwifery or secretarial training. Four women only completed an elementary school education, with two of these having had some high school education. Thus, in Rome, domestic workers can be categorized into three main levels of educational attainment: high, average, and low.

The survey results mirror the educational qualifications of my interviewees. Of 221 women reporting their level of educational attainment, 87 are college graduates (39 percent), 73 have achieved some years of college or postsecondary training (33 percent), 49 are high school graduates (22 percent), and 12 only reached the level of the sixth grade (5 percent). The majors of the college-educated women include accounting, education, nursing, engineering, and liberal arts (for example, Asian studies, English literature, and philosophy).

The identification of underemployment among either documented or undocumented women in Rome does not come as a surprise, because of the restrictive migration policies in Italy. Though severe underemployment has been identified as a problem plaguing undocumented women from the Philippines in the United States, it is surprising to find documented migrants in Los Angeles confronted with this problem (Hogeland and Rosen, 1990). First, they have access to a wider range of occupational fields. This access is fostered by the community networks that can be safely assumed to have developed from the diverse range of niches occupied by migrant Filipinos in the labor market. Second, they face less of a language barrier than do their counterparts in Rome and most other migrants in the United States, because English has historically been the official language used in the educational system of the Philippines. The unexpected finding of severe underemployment among documented domestic workers results from their particular process of migration either as older women or as tourists who overextended their visas and later obtained their legal status through the sponsorship of employers. The extended number of years it takes domestic workers to obtain green cards through the labor certification program coupled with the fear of "starting over" keep them resolved on staying with the job with which they are most familiar.

REGIONAL BACKGROUND

In Rome, members of the Filipino community are mostly from the Southern Luzon provinces of Batangas and Mindoro. Large numbers also come from the regions of Northern Luzon (for example, Ilocos and Pangasinan), the Visayas (the central islands), and the city of Manila. The sample of interviewees reflects the regional representation of Filipinos in Rome: nineteen are from Southern Luzon, ten are from provinces in the Visayas, eight are from Northern Luzon, and nine are from Manila and its neighboring cities and towns. The survey also reflects this regional representation, as ninety-three women are from Southern Luzon, forty-eight from the Visayan provinces, thirty-eight from Northern Luzon, and the rest mostly from Manila. Only a few come from the southernmost region of the Philippines.

In the United States, Filipino migrants have historically originated from Ilocos in Northern Luzon (Takaki 1989). While migrant networks have furnished a steady flow of migrants from this region, it is impossible to say which regions in the Philippines are best represented in the Filipino American community after the 1965 Immigration Act. The snowball method used in my study led to interviews representing various regions of the Philippines with a concentration in the central region, as nineteen women originated from various provinces of the Visayas (for example, Bacolod, Iloilo, and Samar). The rest of the women are from Manila and its neighboring towns and cities. Among the women from the Visayas, however, five had actually been residing in a country other than the Philippines, and four women had been living in Manila prior to migration.

APPENDIX B

Tables

TABLE 1
Year of Migration

Year of Migration (Length of Stay)	Italy	United States
1996–93 (3 years or less)	7	7
1992–90 (4–6 years)	20	4
1989–86 (7–10 years)	7	8
1985–80 (11–16 years)	10	3
1979– (17 years or more)	2	4
Total	46	26

TABLE 2
Level of Educational Attainment

Educational Attainment	Rome	Los Angeles
Primary School (Grades 0–6)	2	0
Some High School	2	2
High School Graduate	7	5
Vocational Degree	5	2
Some College	7	6
College Graduate	22	10
Postbaccalaureate	1	1
Total	46	26

TABLE 3
Employment in the Philippines

Jobs*	Los Angeles		Rome	
Students	1	(3.8%)	6	(13.0%)
Small-Business Owners	3	(11.5%)	5	(10.9%)
Teachers	9	(34.6%)	5	(10.9%)
Administrative Assistants (e.g., secretaries, data entry clerks, stenographers)	4	(15.4%)	12	(26.0%)
Nurses and Midwives**	2	(7.7%)	6	(13.0%)
Other Professionals (e.g., police officer, manager, marketing consultant)	0		3	(6.5%)
Manufacturing Workers (e.g., microchip assembly-line workers, garment workers)	0		3	(6.5%)
Sales Clerks	0		3	(6.5%)
Domestic Workers	6	(23%)	1	(2.2%)
Farmers	0		1	(2.2%)
Unemployed	1	(3.8%)	1	(2.2%)
Total	26		46	

* Last jobs held by interviewees in the Philippines.
** In Los Angeles, all are midwives.

TABLE 4
Deployed Overseas Contract Workers, 1985–94

Year	Land-based	Sea-based	Total
1994	565,226	154,376	719,602
1993	550,872	145,758	696,630
1992	549,872	136,806	686,678
1991	489,260	125,759	615,019
1990	334,883	111,212	446,095
1989	355,346	103,280	458,626
1988	385,117	85,913	471,030
1987	382,229	67,042	449,271
1986	323,517	54,697	378,214
1985	320,494	52,290	372,784

SOURCE: *Philippine Statistical Yearbook*, "Processed Overseas Contract Workers" in Chapter 11, "Labor and Employment," 1995: 11–27.

TABLE 5

Most Common Destinations of
Migrant Filipinos

Country	Estimated Populations
United States	1,500,000*
Saudi Arabia	1,300,000
Italy	200,000
Canada	165,000*
UAE	156,000
Hong Kong	150,000
Kuwait	105,500
Japan	100,000
Spain	90,000
Britain	80,000

SOURCE: Kanlungan Centre Foundation, in Karp (1995).

*Mostly permanent settlers and includes native-born Filipinos.

TABLE 6

Major Destinations of Deployed Land-Based Workers

Year	Asia	Middle East	Europe	Americas
1994	194,120	286,387	11,513	12,603
1993	168,205	302,975	13,423	12,228
1992	134,776	340,604	14,590	12,319
1991	132,592	302,825	13,156	13,373
1990	90,768	218,110	6853	9557
1989	86,196	241,081	7830	9962
1988	92,648	267,035	7614	7902
1987	90,434	272,038	5643	5614
1986	72,536	236,434	3693	4035
1985	52,838	253,867	4067	3744

SOURCE: *Philippine Statistical Yearbook*, "Deployed Land-Based Contract Workers by Major World Groupings 1985 to 1994," in Chapter 11, "Labor and Employment," 1995: 11–27.

TABLE 7

Modes of Migration to Rome and Los Angeles

Mode	Rome	Los Angeles
Tourist Visas	11	16*
Family Reunification	3	4
Clandestine Border Crossing		
Illegal Travel Agencies	30	0
From Canada	0	1
Direct Hires	2	5**
Total	46	26

*One woman migrated with the assistance of an illegal travel agency, which arranged for her use of another woman's passport and visa to the United States.

**Sponsorship by Filipino employers.

TABLE 8

Typology of Migrant Families

Structure	Rome	Los Angeles
Nuclear Households		
Traditional	3	3
Nontraditional	2	2
Single Householder	0	1
Transnational Households		
One Parent Abroad	20	12
Two Parents Abroad	7	3
Adult Child(ren) Abroad	14	5
Total	46	26

REFERENCE MATTER

INTRODUCTION: MIGRANT FILIPINA DOMESTIC
WORKERS IN ROME AND LOS ANGELES

1. I use the term *diaspora* to refer to the forced dispersal of a particular group of people from their homeland to a multitude of countries. I recognize that the term has come to mean more in recent years. In cultural studies, "'diaspora' refers to the doubled relationship or dual loyalty that migrants, exiles, and refugees have to places—their connections to the space they currently occupy and their continuing involvement with 'back home'" (Lavie and Swedenburg, 1996: 14). There is a lively debate between these two views. See Clifford (1997) for a thorough overview of various theoretical conceptions of diaspora. Though the experiences of contemporary Filipino migrants fit the two meanings of diaspora, I advocate for a return to its classic definition so as to underscore the dispersal of Filipino labor migrants into more than 130 countries as a unique and particular result of globalization. The fact is the transnational ties of migrant Filipinos are not restricted to the homeland. Ties exist between various Filipino communities. This particular "diasporic" reality is discounted by the view of diaspora as "dual loyalty."

2. Though I use Portes and Rumbaut's (1996) formulation of immigrant incorporation as the foundational backbone of my study, I recognize the limits in their conception. By presenting immigration as a unidirectional path toward assimilation into the host society, their conception does not allow much room for the consideration of the transnational practices and diasporic consciousness that define contemporary immigrant life. However, in a special issue of *Ethnic and Racial Studies* on transnational communities, Portes and his colleagues (1999) do recognize the growing phenomenon of transnational activities as a defining feature of immigrant life.

3. Due to the labor shortage of health professionals, Italy finally recognized the foreign training of nurses under the Martelli Law. Yet not many Filipinos have taken advantage of this change in policy, most likely because community members are not familiar with the process of certification. For example, the long bureaucratic process of certifying their training in the Philippines intimidated the thirteen health workers whom I interviewed in Rome. In 1996, the

Philippine embassy estimated that there were only twenty-five Filipino migrants employed as nurses in Rome.

4. Official population figures of Filipinos in Los Angeles County were not made available until 1950, when they numbered approximately 7000 (Ong and Azores, 1994a).

5. Though comprising a relatively small flow of migration, women and professional workers began to migrate earlier through the War Brides Act of 1945 and the McCarran-Walter Act of 1952 (Chan, 1991; Hing, 1998; Takaki, 1989).

6. Because of the influx of migrants, the Filipino community in Los Angeles more than doubled in size in the 1980s (Sabagh, 1993: 107). In the years 1984, 1987, and 1993, Los Angeles was the most popular destination of migrant Filipinos (Portes and Rumbaut, 1996).

7. Examples are provided by Chow (1994) and Ong and Azores (1994b).

8. For example, prospective providers of elderly care can obtain leads for job openings from Filipina nurses of newly released patients in various hospitals in Los Angeles.

9. I thank Jennifer Lee for helping me advance this argument.

10. According to Wong, "a *diasporic perspective* emphasizes Asian Americans as one element in the global scattering of peoples of Asian origin," while a domestic perspective "stresses the status of Asian Americans as an ethnic/ racial minority within the national boundaries of the U.S." (1995: 2).

11. Jonathan Okamura (1998) also applies the concept of "imagined community" to the Filipino diaspora.

12. As migration scholar Luin Goldring notes, "*Community* involves a sense of shared history and identity, mutually intelligible meanings" (1998: 173).

13. According to Basch et al. (1994), transnational social fields form from family connections, business enterprises that market and sell ethnic commodities, and organizations that promote ties to the homeland.

14. While I had the opportunity to work as a domestic worker, I decided against doing so for a multitude of reasons: (1) the high rate of unemployment in the community obliged me to pass employment referrals that I obtained to the jobless Filipina women I met frequently; (2) because of the racialized construction of Filipinos as domestic workers, I did not have to be a domestic worker for Italians and Filipinos to assume I was one; (3) in-depth interviews describe the routine of domestic work from the perspective of the worker, which had been the main data I had hoped to collect by going "undercover"; and (4) the women seemed vehemently opposed to my doing domestic work. Most informants seemed to want to "protect" me from a job that they describe as very physically demanding. They told me that because I could financially afford not to work, I should not put myself through it. Many informants told me that

instead of being a *ragazza* (girl) I should tutor Italians in English or teach in the (American) International School. They did not seem to understand that I needed to do it for the sake of collecting data. Regardless, it seemed that they considered my being a Filipina educated in the United States (and educated in an internationally respected university) as something special. Many times I was invited to meet employers so that the workers could enjoy seeing the eyes of their employers widen in surprise when they mentioned that I was not a domestic worker but an American scholar from University of California, Berkeley.

15. Prior to every interview, I obtained written consent forms from each "human subject." The consent form explicitly states the terms of the interview, i.e., it is voluntary and I would take special precautions to protect the identity of research participants. Nevertheless, many interviewees in Los Angeles still opted to give me a fictitious name to protect their identity while only one person in Rome did so. So, while my appointment book in Los Angeles contains the real names of interviewees, the required official consent form registers fictitious names of research participants.

16. My decision to use fictitious names is also highly influenced by the personal nature of the interviews, which may cause participants to later regret the use of their names.

17. Because this study does not set out to address domestic work as an occupational issue, I did not consider it necessary to interview employers.

18. See Appendix A for a more detailed discussion of the characteristics of the samples.

19. This fact could partly explain why Filipino women in Los Angeles are inaccessible to interview. On weekends, they spend their precious free time with family or friends.

20. "Part-time" is a term used in the Filipino community in Italy to refer to domestic workers who live in their own apartments. Paid by the hour, part-time workers work for one or more days a week for a number of employers on a prearranged schedule. I include those who work for one employer throughout the week and have a monthly salary in the category of part-time workers. In the community, such workers are described as those who work *lungo orario* (long hours). Unlike "live-in" workers, they reside in their own apartments.

21. Many of my interviewees in Rome obtained their legal status through the November 18, 1995, decree that granted amnesty to undocumented workers. Because the legislative decree had been in progress during my research, we can safely assume that the sixteen remaining undocumented women were eventually able to obtain legal status. Prior to the interviews, I had anticipated finding mostly undocumented workers in Los Angeles. I was thus surprised to learn that many have legal documents. Most of the women acquired legal status

through marriage or the sponsorship of an employer, but some obtained their documents through amnesty programs such as the 1986 Immigration Reform and Control Act.

22. In 1996, U.S.$1 was approximately 1,500 lira.

CHAPTER 1: THE DISLOCATIONS OF MIGRANT FILIPINA DOMESTIC WORKERS

1. There are many studies that document the increasing labor market participation of women in developing countries due to global restructuring. See Nash and Fernandez Kelly (1983) and Ward (1990).

2. Many of the low-wage jobs created in advanced capitalist countries are traditionally considered "women's work," jobs that have been historically relegated to women in a sex- (and race-) segmented labor market. They include domestic work, hotel housekeeping, and subcontracting jobs in garment and electronics manufacturing.

3. As Guarnizo and Smith state, studies of transnationalism "should start from a meso-structural vantage point, the point at which institutions interact with structural and instrumental processes so as to identify the intersections of macro and microstructural processes in the formation of transnational practices and institutions" (1998: 23).

4. Weedon writes, "Discourses, in Foucault's work, are ways of constituting knowledge, together with the social practices, forms of subjectivity and power relations which inhere in such knowledge and the relations between them" (1997: 105).

5. O'Sullivan et al. explain, "Discourses are the product of social, historical and institutional formations, and meanings are produced by these institutionalized discourses" (1994: 93–94).

6. At the same time, one cannot assume that subjects passively accept and conform to their dislocations. As Foucault reminds us, "'the other' (the one over whom power is exercised) [must] be thoroughly recognized and maintained to the very end as a person who acts; and that faced with a relationship of power, a whole field of responses, reactions, and results, and possible interventions may open up" (1983: 220).

CHAPTER 2: THE PHILIPPINES AND THE OUTFLOW OF LABOR

1. The close reading includes almost all of the issues of *Tinig Filipino* published from October 1994 to July 1996. A few back issues had been unavailable from the publisher.

2. Additionally, men comprise the majority of deployed skilled workers (e.g., professionals and technical workers) from the Philippines, even though more women can be found in technical and professional positions in the country (Tyner, 1994).

3. It has been reported that illegal trafficking of Filipina domestic workers

occurs between the Muslim regions of Mindanao (Southern Philippines) and the Middle East (Heyzer et al., 1994).

4. Many studies indicate that mail-order brides are easy victims of money-making life insurance scams and, subject to the control of their husbands, are sometimes forced into prostitution (CIIR, 1987; Rosca, 1995).

5. The study's low figures were based solely on official contract worker figures from the third quarter of 1987 (Heyzer and Wee, 1994: 43).

6. Defined by Goss and Lindquist (1995), migrant institutions are the institutionalized resources that facilitate the process of outmigration. In the case of the Philippines, private recruitment agencies are one example of such an institution.

7. Among those women entering with a tourist visa, there is a subgroup of five migrants who had worked in other countries as domestic workers. For three of these women, it had been their employers' assistance that had secured the approval of their applications at the United States embassy.

8. Of the women entering the United States as "tourists," half claim not to have had any intention of settling. Instead, they were lured into domestic work after learning of the high salaries they could earn, especially caring for the elderly, once they were in the country. The other half had originally intended to settle for a longer period in the United States but had anticipated finding higher-paid employment than domestic work, work that recognized their level of educational attainment in the Philippines. Their undocumented status, however, limited their options in the labor market.

9. Individuals who assist migrants in border crossing are neither referred to as coyotes nor given any particular name in the community.

10. In contrast to other countries in Western Europe, Italy historically has not maintained a very strict border regime because of their economic dependence on tourism (Santel, 1995).

11. Officials at the *Questura* (Central Police) in Italy and the Philippine Overseas Employment Administration must approve the direct hire.

12. The survey results mirror my findings. The average cost of illegal migration among the 107 women who entered Italy illegally from 1990 to 1996 amounted to 152,266 pesos (U.S.$6090).

13. Thirty-seven million (48 percent) were women.

14. In 1980, more than 36 percent of overseas contract workers were college graduates and another 13 percent had completed some college units (Gatmaytan, 1997).

15. In 1980, there were 2.8 million students in the secondary level and 1.1 million university students in the Philippines (Campani, 1993b).

16. To integrate the Philippines into the global economy, the International Monetary Fund and the World Bank, beginning in the 1960s, slowly dismantled the import-substitution industries in the Philippines and injected foreign capi-

tal (i.e., structural adjustment loans) to turn the Philippine economy toward
the path of export-led growth (Basch et al., 1994).

CHAPTER 3: THE INTERNATIONAL DIVISION OF REPRODUCTIVE LABOR

1. By definition, patriarchy refers to the systematic inequality between men
and women in any given society. In a patriarchal society, men carry greater
power and privilege over women.

2. According to Israel-Sobritchea, the concentration of women in service
and sales industries explains their lower earnings than those of men. In the
Philippines, women on average earn "only 35% of the total annual income of
all Filipino workers" (1990: 37).

3. The community first assumes the cause of separation to be a "deficiency"
with the wife (e.g., nagger or lazy) for not being able to hold on to her partner.

4. In the Philippines, for example, "barrenness on the part of the wife may
be a ground for separation or an excuse for the husband's infidelity" (Lopez-
Rodriguez, 1990: 21).

5. In making this assertion, I do not claim that Filipinas are defined racially
as domestic workers. They are more so categorized and identified as nurses. Yet
in the Filipino migrant community, it is known that a visible contingent of recent migrants has turned to domestic work. In a study of undocumented women
in the San Francisco Bay area, Hogeland and Rosen found that 41 percent of
fifty-seven survey participants from the Philippines are care providers, and an
additional 23 percent are employed as housekeepers (1990: 43).

6. In the Philippines, older (female) children, not fathers, are more likely to
look after younger siblings while their mothers work (Chant and McIlwaine,
1995). In addition, daughters are traditionally expected to care for aging parents.

CHAPTER 4: THE TRANSNATIONAL FAMILY

1. Although I use the terms *household* and *family* interchangeably in this
chapter, I generally follow the definition of the *family* as a determinate group
of people usually related by marriage, partnerships, or blood and the *household*
not as a "a determinate set of people but . . . a set of relationships that impose a
mutual obligation to pool resources from a multiplicity of labor forms whether
or not one of those resources is a common residence" (Friedman, 1984: 48).
Moreover, I do not limit my view of a household to the modern conception of
a residential unit inclusive of kin and nonkin (Mintz and Kellog, 1988).

2. Three women in Los Angeles consciously decided not to migrate until
their children were at least twenty-one years of age. The rest of the interviewees are composed mostly of women not living with their children since less than
a handful of women in Rome and Los Angeles have reunited with their children.

3. The complexity of household maintenance is not completely captured in
my typology. Extended kin are ever present and intrinsically woven in the mi-

grant family. However, by placing individual subjects in a type of household, I limit my formulation of the family to the family of orientation for married domestic workers and the family of origin for single domestic workers. For married migrants, core family members include spouses and children. For single migrants, the core family refers to parents and siblings; however, the core families of single migrants do include married brothers and sisters and their children.

4. An example is the family of Trina Jusay. A teacher in the Philippines, Trina Jusay, now a forty-five-year-old domestic worker, followed a female neighbor to Rome in 1981—seven months after the birth of her only daughter and when her two sons were still fairly young, three and six years old. While Trina's husband followed her in 1982, Trina's children migrated much later, the youngest at the age of six in 1987 and the two older children at the ages of sixteen and twelve in 1990. Although Trina's family now manages a nuclear household, her family was only able to attain such a structure after a transnational phase of ten years.

5. My sample also includes four women—three in Los Angeles and one in Rome—whose husbands had worked outside the Philippines, mostly in Saudi Arabia, for more than ten years, during which time the women stayed in the Philippines with their children. In these families, marriages clearly sustained long-distance relationships for extended periods, in some cases for the majority of the couple's married life.

6. See the discussion of divorce in Filipino society in Chapter 3.

7. A nipa hut has a bamboo structure and a nipa roof.

8. Filipinos often refer to themselves as "strangers," a term which they have derived from *stranieri*, meaning foreigners.

9. Awareness of growing anti-immigrant sentiments in Italy is also based on the electoral victories in northern regions of the anti-immigrant party *Lega* beginning in the early 1990s (Foot, 1995).

10. The only ones not falling under this subcategory are single parents and children who have since reunited with their parents abroad but still have siblings left in the Philippines.

11. See Moen and Wethington (1992) for a literature review on family adaptive strategies.

12. For an example of advocates of the traditional nuclear family, see Popenoe (1988). For discussions of the debate on the "legitimate" family, see Cheal (1991), Skolnick (1991), and Thorne and Yalom (1992).

13. See Ong (1999) and Wong (1995).

14. According to French theorist Etienne Balibar, racism is based less on traditional biological constructs of race and more on the exclusion of immigrants as culturally unassimilable Others (Balibar and Wallerstein, 1988). He refers to this trend as "neoracism."

15. See Perea (1997).

CHAPTER 5: INTERGENERATIONAL AND GENDER
RELATIONS IN TRANSNATIONAL FAMILIES

1. While the state grants free public education until high school, the state neither enforces nor mandates the education of children. Moreover, legal protection of children from abuse is not strictly enforced.

2. Matthei and Smith (1998) also observe the tendency of parents in Belizean transnational households to commodify love.

3. Although my interviews only include a limited number of children—six in Rome—who had grown up without their mothers, my assessment of the perspective of children also uses the survey conducted by Victoria Paz Cruz (1987), writings by children published in *Tinig Filipino*, and previous interviews that I had conducted with children who had followed their parents to the United States after a prolonged period of separation.

4. Constable (1999) also recognizes the greater priority given by children to emotional bonds in the family than do their transnational parents in Hong Kong.

CHAPTER 6: CONTRADICTORY CLASS MOBILITY

1. A notable dislocation comparably defining the experience of domestic work is displaced caretaking, the contradiction of caring for someone else's children and/or parents while not caring for one's own. Because I already addressed the impact of this dislocation in discussions of the family and the international transfer of caretaking, my analysis of subjection in the workplace focuses on contradictory class mobility.

2. Due to the greater labor market opportunities of migrants in Los Angeles, it is surprising to see a number of my interviewees having chosen to stay in domestic work. I assume that there are many women who left domestic work for more skilled employment immediately after they obtained legal residency. However, it is still surprising that some women have not used networks with the middle class in the Filipino American community to initiate their access to other opportunities in the labor market.

3. I thank Karen Brodkin for making this observation.

4. Not much attention has been given to describe this experience. At most, other scholars have only speculated that downward mobility "leads us to expect high levels of stress-related symptoms and a highly critical perception of the host society" among migrants (Portes and Rumbaut, 1996: 190).

5. In Los Angeles, migrant Filipina domestic workers may avoid this type of work because of their vulnerability as undocumented workers and the competition posed by the larger pool of Latinas in day work.

6. Part-time workers include an equal representation of single and married

women. Interestingly, the few lesbians in my sample are all part-time workers; their sexual orientation seems to restrict their employment options. While some married women whose husbands also work in Rome are able to hold live-in jobs, employers are less likely to tolerate the alternative lifestyle of lesbian women.

7. Two interviewees in Los Angeles had been trained midwives in the Philippines. This suggests that in the United States not all trained medical workers have been able to utilize their skills after migration.

8. Unable to accept this aggrandizing humiliation, Jerissa fled domestic work for the lesser paying job of a security guard.

9. Explaining her contention, Romero states, "As capitalists middle-class employers—like factory owners—own the means of production and the product of the labor; they constantly rationalize the work and control the labor process. . . . Domestic service must be analyzed as a sphere of capitalist production in which race and gender domination are played out" (1992: 93).

10. Filipina domestic workers tend to feel more comfortable eating with Filipino employers. For example, Marilou had felt more at ease eating with her former Filipino employers. The greater comfort domestic workers have with Filipino families is maybe due to their familiarity with these families' cultural practices, the more informal setting of meals in these families, or the absence of racial difference. However, the greater ease they may have does not translate to a preference for Filipino employers. This is most likely because of the wide discrepancy between the wages offered by white and Filipino employers. Those working for Filipino families receive on average $500 a month.

11. In the United States, legalization would increase their job options and protect them from deportation. In Italy, Filipina domestic workers covet legal status so they can visit their families in the Philippines.

12. See Colen (1989: 172–76) for discussion of the process of employment sponsorship in the United States.

13. See Rollins (1985: 157–73 and 173–203) for a more extensive discussion of "deference and maternalism."

14. Based on Rollins's personal experiences, an employer was wary of hiring her because she seemed "too educated."

15. Because the domestics in Rollins's study are housecleaners and not caregivers, the preference of employers for less-educated "cleaners" would not be surprising in the context of Wrigley's discussion.

16. See Wrigley (1995: 92).

17. This information is based on field research.

18. Robert Smith has also noticed the use of racial bifurcation among Mexican migrants in New York City. Citing Smith, Goldring observes that Mexicans in New York "are doubly bounded by attempts to distance themselves from

African Americans and Puerto Ricans, thereby defining themselves as *not black*, and by being defined by the dominant society as *not white*. Mexicans in California also distance themselves from the bottom of the racialized hierarchy" (1998: 170).

19. De Certeau defines strategies as "the calculus of force-relationships which becomes possible when a subject of will and power (a proprietor, an enterprise, a city, a scientific institution) can be isolated from an environment" (1984: xix). Strategies are acts of resistance by the "strong," meaning those with resources. Examples of strategies are business takeovers and labor unions (because of the power to lobby for workers at the level of the state and relieve strikes with wage compensations). De Certeau defines tactics as "a calculus which cannot count on a 'proper' (a spatial or institutionalized location). . . . It has at its disposal no base where it can capitalize on its advantages, prepare its expansions, and secure independence with respect to circumstances . . . . It is always on the watch for opportunities that must be seized on the wing" (1984: xix). Tactics are acts of resistance by the weak who, without resources, can only inject subversive acts within the circumstances of constraint.

20. I will elaborate on this point in the next chapter. Examples include the practice of greeting every domestic worker that one meets on the streets in Rome and the formation of subcommunities of Filipina domestics in retirement villages in Los Angeles.

CHAPTER 7: THE DISLOCATION OF NONBELONGING

1. My discussion of the community is contained to the geographical places of Rome and Los Angeles. Thus, I do not include in my discussion the "global community" of the Filipina diaspora.

2. The term *anomie*, meaning the breakdown of values or formation of a sense of alienation and dislocation in groups or individuals, was originally used by Sarah Mahler (1995) to describe the migrant community of Peruvian and Salvadoran refugees in Long Island.

3. While I am wary of romanticizing Filipino migrant communities, my discussion is not intent on proving the coethnic exploitation of migrant Filipina domestic workers. Such a depiction would also taint the picture of their community life with a one-sided characterization.

4. According to Mahler (1995), particular factors in the situation of Salvadorans and Peruvian migrants explain the emergence of coethnic antagonism as the primary element of migrant community life in Long Island. For Salvadorans, "disenchantment with compatriots" originated prior to migration with the civil war but is also constituted by their particular experience of migration, for example, the non-recognition of their refugee status. The cause of ethnic antagonism for Peruvians is one that is actually shared by migrant Filipina do-

mestic workers in both Rome and Los Angeles. For Peruvians, downward mobility in economic status triggers embitterment, which, Mahler posits, results in the exploitation of noneducated migrants in the informal economy.

5. Mahler states, "The greatest source of economic mobility among my informants is the exploitation of each other's needs and . . . this has serious negative consequences for their construction of ethnic solidarity and community" (1995: 224).

6. At most, they can seek employment, other than low-wage service work, in the handful of remittance agencies in Rome, as these agencies usually hire their front office staff locally. Managers are, however, only hired in the Philippines.

7. My use of this concept follows an analytic trajectory established by Avery Gordon, who urges a paradigmatic shift in sociology toward the consideration of "haunting," or feeling in general, as a "constitutive feature of social life . . . to describe, analyze and bring to life" (1997: 22).

8. As late as 1989, there were no masses conducted in Tagalog in the entire city of Rome. Migrant Filipinos attended English-language masses, which were dominated by Filipino churchgoers but nevertheless led by Irish and not Filipino priests.

9. While labor unions and left-oriented political parties have engaged in coalitions with various migrant groups to strengthen antiracist movements in Italy, networks have not officially formed between these political forces and the Filipino migrant community. This is possibly explained by the gender constitution of the community being primarily female and those of these political forces being primarily male. Grassroots organizations are also not prominent in the community. For example, the one feminist organization in the community has fewer than twenty-five active members. Even the largest advocacy group for the legal rights of migrant Filipina domestic workers, Life-Asper, is church-sponsored.

10. OWWA coordinates cultural and social activities for Filipino migrant workers in other communities, for example, in Spain and Saudi Arabia.

11. But as my field notes illustrate, public places of gathering are not the most comfortable places to have a meal.

Of the 20 cars parked at Eur Fermi, three are filled with Filipino food. These cars are strategically parked at least five cars apart from each other. I notice that each vendor has her own set of regular customers. Because one of them I realized the first time I ever visited Eur is from my father's hometown (among Filipinos, introductions always include our regional background), I have actually been bound to only patronize her business. Eating here seems uncomfortable. There is really no place to sit down and enjoy one's meal. Yet they still choose to eat here instead of a restaurant or bar. After they eat, they usually stand around for another hour or two. In that time, they usually run into their friends. Having spent hours standing around here, I have to wonder how they can stand around here for hours. As it is the middle of the winter, it is quite cold. Everyone is wearing wool coats and has scarves wrapped around their faces. It was drizzling earlier. It was quite a sight seeing groups of Filipinos eat their meals in this weather. Their ability to balance with one hand a tray carrying a drink in a plastic cup, a bowl of soup, a dish, and a plate of rice and eat with another while holding onto an umbrella was quite impressive.

12. My observations contradict Hagan's concerning the community life of Mayan domestic workers in Houston. Hagan (1994) noticed that, in contrast to men of the Mayan community, women have fairly weak community ties because of their concentration in domestic work. Hagan's observation, however, does mirror the situation of Filipina domestic workers in Los Angeles.

13. This includes married women who escape abusive husbands, as the financial security that they garner from working in Italy frees them from having to depend on their husbands once they return to the Philippines.

14. Some women who told me that they earned significantly more than the average hourly rate did not share this information with women who inquired about their salary. They also told me not to disclose this information to their friends.

15. Not one interviewee admitted that she prefers to solicit ethnic entrepreneurs in order to reduce her movements in the public social space of the dominant society.

16. Personal services are enterprises dominated by gay men in the community. Gay men are noticeably absent in domestic work. They are concentrated in "feminine" entrepreneurial activities such as hairstyling and supplying beauty products (e.g., Avon) to the community. Because their labor market activities do not involve domestic work, gay men are arguably the only members in the community who manage to uphold the "ideal notions of femininity." As it is said that domestic workers do the "dirty" work of the household in order for female employers to uphold "cleanliness" as a marker of femininity, it is interesting that gay men told me that they refuse to clean houses for a living because it is "dirty" work.

17. In contrast, an ethnic economy refers to "the self-employed and their co-ethnic employees" (Light et al., 1994: 66) and is therefore not demarcated spatially.

18. Corroborating their visits to ethnic businesses are the responses to my solicitation for research participants from signs I had posted in ethnic businesses in both the inner city and suburbs.

19. Also deserving of some comment is Ligaya's reference to relatives. In the community, relatives are not necessarily those most insensitive to domestic

workers. Domestic work seems to be treated as a "sensitive" topic. Because relatives are those most likely to give advice on employment possibilities, they are put in the position of being the ones who can be most insensitive to domestic workers. For example, suggestions to seek other kinds of employment can easily be misconstrued to insinuate their lack of success.

Abel, Emily K. 1990. "Family Care of the Frail Elderly." Pp. 65–91 in Abel and Nelson, *Circles of Care*.

Abel, Emily K., and Margaret K. Nelson. 1990. "Circles of Care: An Introductory Essay." Pp. 4–34 in Abel and Nelson, *Circles of Care*.

Abel, Emily, and Margaret K. Nelson, editors. 1990. *Circles of Care: Work and Identity in Women's Lives*. Albany, NY: SUNY Press.

Abella, Manolo. 1992. "International Migration and Development." Pp. 22–40 in Battistella and Paganoni, *Philippine Labor Migration*.

Acgaoili, Gloria. 1995. "Mother, Behold Your Child." *Tinig Filipino* (May): 14.

Agbayani-Siewart, Pauline, and Linda Revilla. 1995. "Filipino Americans." Pp. 134–68 in Pyong Gap Min, editor, *Asian Americans: Contemporary Trends and Issues*. Thousand Oaks, CA: Sage Publications.

Aguilar, Delia. 1988. *The Feminist Challenge: Initial Working Principles Toward Reconceptualizing the Feminist Movement in the Philippines*. Metro Manila, Philippines: Asian Social Institute.

Alaba, Marivic. 1995. "Etiquette—A Must." *Tinig Filipino* (May): 42.

Alarcón, Norma. 1990. "The Theoretical Subject(s) of *This Bridge Called My Back* and Anglo-American Feminism." Pp. 356–69 in Gloria Anzaldúa, editor, *Making Face, Making Soul Haciendo Caras: Creative and Critical Perspectives by Feminists of Color*. San Francisco: Aunt Lute Press.

Alcid, Mary Lou. 1994. "Legal and Organizational Support Mechanisms for Foreign Domestic Workers." Pp. 161–77 in Heyzer, Lycklama á Nijeholt, and Weerakoon, *The Trade in Domestic Workers*.

Amber. 1995. "We Are Still the Best among the Rest." *Tinig Filipino* (May): 22.

Ancona, Giovanni. 1991. "Labour Demand and Immigration in Italy." *Journal of Regional Policy* 11: 143–48.

Andall, Jacqueline. 1992. "Women Migrant Workers in Italy." *Women's Studies International Forum* 15(1): 41–48.

Anderson, Benedict. 1983. *Imagined Communities*. New York: Verso.

Anzaldúa, Gloria. 1987. *Borderlands, La Frontera: The New Mestiza*. San Francisco: Aunt Lute Press.

Appadurai, Arjun. 1996. *Modernity at Large: Cultural Dimensions of Globalization*. Minneapolis: University of Minnesota Press.

Aratan, Clarita U. 1994. "Money or Family." *Tinig Filipino* (December): 34.

Arat-Koc, Sedef. 1997. "From 'Mothers of the Nation' to Migrant Workers." Pp. 53–79 in Bakan and Stasiulis, *Not One of the Family.*

Arevalo, Nina Rea. 1994. "Inay, Pasko Na Naman." *Tinig Filipino* (December): 28.

Ascoli, Ugo. 1985. "Migration of Workers and the Labor Market: Is Italy Becoming a Country of Immigration?" Pp. 185–206 in Rosemarie Rogers, editor, *Guests Come to Stay: The Effects of European Labor Migration on Sending and Receiving Countries.* Boulder, CO, and London: Westview Press.

Asis, Maruja M. B. 1992. "The Overseas Employment Program Policy." Pp. 68–112 in Battistella and Paganoni, *Philippine Labor Migration.*

Atiwa, Betty. 1995. "Going Home for Good—Pleasant and Depressing." *Tinig Filipino* (November): 42.

Bakan, Abigail, and Daiva Stasiulis. 1997a. "Foreign Domestic Worker Policy in Canada and the Social Boundaries of Modern Citizenship." Pp. 29–52 in Bakan and Stasiulis, *Not One of the Family.*

———. 1997b. "Introduction." Pp. 3–7 in Bakan and Stasiulis, *Not One of the Family.*

———., editors. 1997c. *Not One of the Family: Foreign Domestic Workers in Canada.* Toronto: University of Toronto Press.

———. 1994. "Foreign Domestic Worker Policy in Canada and the Social Boundaries of Modern Citizenship." *Science and Society* 58(1): 7–33.

Balangatan, Dolores. 1994. "The Two Sides of Migration." *Tinig Filipino* (October): 10.

Balibar, Etienne, and Immanuel Wallerstein. 1988. *Race, Nation and Class.* London and New York: Verso.

Bamyeh, Mohammed A. 1993. "Transnationalism." *Current Sociology* 41(3): 1–95.

Basch, Linda, Nina Glick-Schiller, and Christina Szanton Blanc. 1994. *Nations Unbound: Transnational Projects, Postcolonial Predicaments, and Deterritorialized Nation-States.* Langhorne, PA: Gordon and Breach Science.

Battistella, Graziano. 1992. "Migration: Opportunity or Loss?" Pp. 113–34 in Battistella and Paganoni, *Philippine Labor Migration.*

Battistella, Graziano, and Anthony Paganoni, editors. 1992. *Philippine Labor Migration: Impact and Policy.* Quezon City, Philippines: Scalabrini Migration Center.

Beck, Ulrich, and Elisabeth Beck-Gernsheim. 1995. *The Normal Chaos of Love.* Cambridge: Polity Press.

Birnbaum, Lucia Chiavola. 1986. *Liberazione della Donne.* Middletown, CT: Wesleyan University Press.

Bonifazi, Corrado. 1992. "Italian Attitudes and Opinions Towards Foreign Migrants and Migration Policies." *Studi Emigrazione/Etudes Migrations* 29(105): 21–41.

Boyd, Monica. 1989. "Family and Personal Networks in International Migration: Recent Developments and New Agendas." *International Migration Review* 23(3): 638–71.

Bozorgmehr, Mehdi, Georges Sabagh, and Ivan Light. 1996. "Los Angeles: Explosive Diversity." Pp. 346–59 in Pedraza and Rumbaut, *Origins and Destinies.*

Brenner, Johanna, and Barbara Laslett. 1991. "Gender, Social Reproduction and Women's Self-Organization: Considering the U.S. Welfare State." *Gender and Society* 5(3): 311–33.

Broad, Robin. 1988. *Unequal Alliance 1979–1986: The World Bank, the International Monetary Fund, and the Philippines.* Quezon City, Philippines: Ateneo de Manila Press.

Bueno, Liza Cepillo. 1994. "Ang Buhay sa Abroad." *Tinig Filipino* (October): 21.

Burbach, Roger, Orlando Nuñez, and Boris Kagarlitsky. 1997. *Globalization and Its Discontents.* London: Pluto Press.

Butler, Judith. 1997. *The Psychic Life of Power: Theories in Subjection.* Stanford, CA: Stanford University Press.

———. 1995. "For A Careful Reading." Pp. 127–44 in Judith Butler, Seyla Benhabi, Drucilla Cornell, and Nancy Fraser, *Feminist Contentions: A Philosophical Exchange.* New York: Routledge.

———. 1992. "Contingent Foundations: Feminism and the Question of 'Postmodernism.'" Pp. 3–21 in Butler and Scott, *Feminists Theorize the Political.*

Butler, Judith, and Joan Scott, editors. 1992. *Feminists Theorize the Political.* New York: Routledge.

Cabugas, Lilibeth. 1994. "Let Go of Worry . . . Today." *Tinig Filipino* (December): 20.

Calavita, Kitty. 1994. "Italy and the New Immigration." Pp. 303–26 in Cornelius, Martin, and Hollifield, *Controlling Immigration.*

Calomay, Annaliza B. 1994. "Isang Kontrata Na Lang, Anak." *Tinig Filipino* (October): 29.

Campani, Giovanna. 1993a. "Immigration and Racism in Southern Europe: The Italian Case." *Ethnic and Racial Studies* 16(3): 507–35.

———. 1993b. "Labour Markets and Family Networks: Filipino Women in Italy." Pp. 191–208 in Hedwig Rudolph and Mirjana Morokvasic, editors, *Bridging States and Markets: International Migration in the Early 1990s.* Berlin: Edition Signa.

Cariño, Benjamin. 1996. "Filipino Americans: Many and Varied." Pp. 293–301 in Pedraza and Rumbaut, *Origins and Destinies.*

Caritas di Roma. 1995. *Immigrazione. Dossier statistico '95*. Roma: Anterem
  Edizioni Ricerca.
Castells, Manuel, and Alejandro Portes. 1985. "World Underneath: The Ori-
  gins, Dynamics and Effects of the Informal Economy." Pp. 11–37 in Portes,
  Castells, and Benton, *The Informal Economy*.
Castles, Stephen, and Mark J. Miller. 1998. *The Age of Migration: Interna-
  tional Population Movements in the Modern World*. 2nd ed. New York and
  London: Guilford Press.
Catholic Institute for International Relations (CIIR). 1987. *The Labour Trade:
  Filipino Migrant Workers Around the Globe*. London: Catholic Institute for
  International Relations.
Catorce, Rodney. 1995. "My Dad Is Away, So What?" *Tinig Filipino* (June): 9.
Center for Women's Resources. 1995. *Economic Growth in 1994: At Whose Ex-
  pense*. Manila: Center for Women's Resources.
Cesarani, David, and Mary Fulbrook, editors. 1996. *Citizenship, Nationality
  and Migration in Europe*. New York: Routledge.
Chan, Sucheng. 1991. *Asian Americans: An Interpretive History*. Boston:
  Twayne.
Chaney, Elsa, and Mary Garcia Castro, editors. 1989. *Muchachas No More:
  Household Workers in Latin America and the Caribbean*. Philadelphia:
  Temple University Press.
Chant, Sylvia. 1997. *Women-headed Households: Diversity and Dynamics in
  the Developing World*. New York: St. Martin's Press.
Chant, Sylvia, and Cathy McIlwaine. 1995. *Women of a Lesser Cost: Female
  Labour, Foreign Exchange and Philippine Development*. London and East
  Haven, CT: Pluto Press.
Chavez, Leo. 1997. "Immigration Reform and Nativism: The Nationalist Re-
  sponse to the Transnational Challenge." Pp. 61–77 in Perea, *Immigrants
  Out!*
————. 1992. *Shadowed Lives: Undocumented Immigrants in American Soci-
  ety*. Fort Worth, TX: Harcourt Brace College Publishers.
Cheal, David. 1991. *Family and the State of Theory*. Toronto and Buffalo, NY:
  University of Toronto Press.
Cheng, Lucie. 1994. "Introduction: Immigration Patterns." Pp. 39–43 in Ong,
  Bonacich, and Cheng, *The New Asian Immigration*.
Cheng, Lucie, and Edna Bonacich. 1984. "Introduction." Pp. 1–56 in Edna
  Bonacich and Lucie Cheng, editors, *Labor Migration Under Capitalism*.
  Berkeley and Los Angeles: University of California Press.
Chin, Christine. 1998. *In Service and Servitude: Foreign Female Domestic
  Workers and the Malaysian "Modernity" Project*. New York: Columbia
  University Press.
Chiswick, Barry R., and Paul W. Miller. 1996. "Language and Earnings Among

Immigrants in Canada: A Survey." Pp. 39–56 in Duleep and Wunnava, *Immigrants and Immigration Policy*.

Chow, Esther Ngan-Ling. 1994. "Asian American Women at Work." Pp. 203–227 in Maxine Baca Zinn and Bonnie Thornton Dill, editors, *Women of Color in U.S. Society*. Philadelphia: Temple University Press.

Clifford, James. 1997. *Routes: Travel and Translation in the Late Twentieth Century*. Cambridge: Harvard University Press.

Cock, Jacklyn. 1980. *Maids and Madams: Domestic Workers under Apartheid*. London: The Women's Press.

Cohen, Robin. 1997. *Global Diasporas: An Introduction*. Seattle: University of Washington Press.

———. 1992. "Migration and the New International Division of Labour." In Malcolm Cross, editor, *Ethnic Minorities and Industrial Change in Europe and North America*. Cambridge: Cambridge University Press.

Colen, Shellee. 1995. "'Like a Mother to Them': Stratified Reproduction and West Indian Childcare Workers and Employers in New York." Pp. 78–102 in Faye D. Ginsburg and Rayna Rapp, editors, *Conceiving the New World Order: The Global Politics of Reproduction*. Berkeley and Los Angeles: University of California Press.

———. 1989. "'Just a Little Respect': West Indian Domestic Workers in New York City." Pp. 171–94 in Chaney and Garcia Castro, *Muchachas No More*.

Constable, Nicole. 1999. "At Home but Not at Home: Filipina Narratives of Ambivalent Returns." *Cultural Anthropology* 14(2): 203–28.

———. 1997. *Maid to Order in Hong Kong: Stories of Filipina Workers*. Ithaca, NY, and London: Cornell University Press.

Cordova, Fred. 1983. *Filipinos: Forgotten Asian Americans*. Dubuque, IA: Kendall/Hunt.

Cornelius, Wayne, Philip Martin, and James Hollifield, editors. 1994. *Controlling Immigration: A Global Perspective*. Stanford, CA: Stanford University Press.

Curry, Julia. 1988. "Labor Migration and Familial Responsibilities: Experiences of Mexican Women." Pp. 47–63 in Margarita Melville, editor, *Mexicanas at Work in the United States*. Houston: Mexican American Studies Program, University of Houston.

Daenzer, Patricia M. 1997. "An Affair Between Nations: International Relations and the Movement of Household Service Workers." Pp. 81–118 in Bakan and Stasiulis, *Not One of the Family*.

Daguio, Liza C. 1995. "Family Still Number One." *Tinig Filipino* (February): 40.

De Certeau, Michel. 1984. *The Practice of Everyday Life*. Berkeley and Los Angeles: University of California Press.

Degay, Brenda. 1995. "Food for Thought." *Tinig Filipino* (February): 30.

Dill, Bonnie Thornton. 1994. *Across the Boundaries of Race and Class: An Ex-*

ploration of Work and Family Among Black Domestic Servants. New York and London: Garland.

————. 1988. "'Making Your Job Good Yourself': Domestic Service and the Construction of Personal Dignity." Pp. 33–52 in Ann Bookman and Sandra Morgen, editors, *Women and the Politics of Empowerment*. Philadelphia: Temple University Press.

Dirlik, Arif. 1996. "The Global in the Local." Pp. 21–45 in Rob Wilson and Wimal Dissanayake, editors, *Global/Local*. Durham, NC: Duke University Press.

Dizard, Jan, and Howard Gatlin. 1990. *The Minimal Family*. Amherst: University of Massachusetts Press.

Domiclong, Minda. 1994. "Brunei Blues." *Tinig Filipino* (October): 42.

Donato, Katherine. 1992. "Understanding U.S. Immigration: Why Some Countries Send Women and Others Send Men." Pp. 159–84 in Donna Gabaccia, editor, *Seeking Common Ground: Multidisciplinary Studies of Immigrant Women in the United States*. Westport, CT: Greenwood Press.

Dreyfus, Hubert, and Paul Rabinow. 1983. *Michel Foucault: Beyond Structuralism and Hermeneutics*. Chicago: University of Chicago Press.

Dulatre, Nora. 1996. "Employers Are Different." *Tinig Filipino* (February): 38.

Duleep, Harriet Orcutt, and Phanindra V. Wunnava, editors. 1996. *Immigrants and Immigration Policy: Individual Skills, Family Ties, and Group*. Greenwich, CT: JAI Press.

Dumale, Thelma. 1995. "We Should Not Blame Our Government." *Tinig Filipino* (May): 35.

Engels, Friedrich. 1972. *The Origins of the Family, Private Property and the State*. New York: International Publishers.

Enloe, Cynthia. 1989. *Bananas, Beaches, and Bases*. Berkeley and Los Angeles: University of California Press.

Espiritu, Yen Le. 1999. "Gender and Labor in Asian Immigrant Families." *American Behavioral Scientist* 42(4): 628–47.

————. 1997. *Asian American Women and Men*. Thousand Oaks, CA: Sage Publications.

————. 1995. *Filipino American Lives*. Philadelphia: Temple University Press.

Eviota, Elizabeth Uy. 1992. *The Political Economy of Gender: Women and the Sexual Division of Labour in the Philippines*. London: Zed Books.

Feagin, Joe. 1997. "Old Poison in New Bottles: The Deep Roots of Modern Nativism." Pp. 13–43 in Perea, *Immigrants Out!*

Foner, Nancy. 1997. "The Immigrant Family: Cultural Legacies and Cultural Changes." *International Migration Review* 31(4): 961–74.

————., editor. 1987. *New Immigrants in New York*. New York: Columbia University Press.

Foot, John. 1995. "The Logic of Contradiction: Migration Control in Italy and

France, 1980–93. Pp. 132–58 in Miles and Thränhardt, *Migration and European Integration.*

Foucault, Michel. 1983. "The Subject and Power." Pp. 208–26 in Dreyfus and Rabinow, *Michel Foucault.*

———. 1980. *Power/Knowledge: Selected Interviews and Other Writings, 1972–1977.* New York: Pantheon.

———. 1979. *Discipline and Punish: The Birth of the Prison.* New York: Vintage Books.

———. 1978. *The History of Sexuality, Volume 1: Introduction.* New York: Vintage Books.

Fraser, Nancy. 1989. *Unruly Practices: Power, Discourse and Gender in Contemporary Social Theory.* Minneapolis: University of Minnesota Press.

Freire, Paulo. 1970. *Pedagogy of the Oppressed.* New York: Continuum Press.

French, Carolyn. 1986. *Filipina Domestic Workers in Hong Kong.* Hong Kong: Centre for Hong Kong Studies.

Friedman, Kathie. 1984. "Households as Income-Pooling Units." Pp. 37–55 in Smith, Wallerstein, and Evers, *Households and the World Economy.*

Friedman-Kasaba, Kathie. 1996. *Memories of Migration: Gender, Ethnicity, and Work in the Lives of Jewish and Italian Women in New York, 1870–1924.* Albany, NY: SUNY Press.

Fuentes, Annette, and Barbara Ehrenreich. 1983. *Women in the Global Factory.* Boston: South End Press.

Gatmaytan, Dan. 1997. "Death and the Maid: Work, Violence, and the Filipina in the International Labor Market." *Harvard Women's Law Journal* 20(Spring): 229–61.

Glazer, Nona. 1993. *Women's Paid and Unpaid Labor: The Work Transfer in Health Care and Retailing.* Philadelphia: Temple University Press.

Glenn, Evelyn Nakano. 1994. "Social Constructions of Mothering: A Thematic Overview." Pp. 1–29 in Glenn, Chang, and Forcey, *Mothering.*

———. 1992. "From Servitude to Service Work: The Historical Continuities of Women's Paid and Unpaid Reproductive Labor." *Signs* 18(1): 1–44.

———. 1991. "Cleaning Up/Kept Down: A Historical Perspective on Racial Inequality in 'Women's Work.'" *Stanford Law Review* 43: 1333–56.

———. 1986. *Issei, Nisei, Warbride.* Philadelphia: Temple University Press.

———. 1983. "Split Household, Small Producer and Dual Wage Earner: An Analysis of Chinese-American Family Strategies." *Journal of Marriage and the Family* (February): 35–46.

Glenn, Evelyn, Grace Chang, and Linda Forcey, editors. 1994. *Mothering: Ideology, Experience and Agency.* New York: Routledge.

Glick-Schiller, Nina, and Georges Fouron. 1998. "Transnational Lives and National Identities: The Identity Politics of Haitian Immigrants." Pp. 130–61 in Smith and Guarnizo, *Transnationalism from Below.*

Glick-Schiller, Nina, Linda Basch, and Cristina Szanton-Blanc. 1995. "From Immigrant to Transmigrant: Theorizing Transnational Migration." *Anthropological Quarterly* 68(1): 48–63.

Goddard, V. A. 1996. *Gender, Family and Work in Naples*. Oxford and Washington, D.C.: Berg.

Goldring, Luin. 1998. "The Power of Status in Transnational Social Fields." Pp. 165–95 in Smith and Guarnizo, *Transnationalism from Below*.

Golini, Antonio, Corrado Bonifazi, and Alessandra Righi. 1993. "A General Framework for the European Migration System in the 1990s." Pp. 67–82 in King, *The New Geography*.

Gonzaga, Junelyn. 1995. "Listen to Our Small Voices." *Tinig Filipino* (December): 13.

Gordon, Avery. 1997. *Ghostly Matters: Haunting and the Sociological Imagination*. Minneapolis: University of Minnesota Press.

Goss, Jon, and Bruce Lindquist. 1995. "Conceptualizing International Labor Migration: A Structuration Perspective." *International Migration Review* 26(2): 317–51.

Grasmuck, Sherri, and Patricia Pessar. 1991. *Between Two Islands: Dominican International Migration*. Berkeley and Los Angeles: University of California Press.

Grasmuck, Sherri, and Ramón Grosfoguel. 1997. "Geopolitics, Economic Niches, and Gendered Social Capital among Recent Caribbean Immigrants in New York City." *Sociological Perspectives* 40(3): 339–63.

Gregson, Nicky, and Michelle Lowe. 1994. *Servicing the Middle Classes: Class, Gender and Waged Domestic Labour in Contemporary Britain*. New York: Routledge.

Grewal, Inderpal. 1994. "Autobiographic Subjects and Diasporic Locations: Meatless Days and Borderlands." Pp. 231–54 in Grewal and Kaplan, *Scattered Hegemonies*.

Grewal, Inderpal, and Caren Kaplan, editors. 1994. *Scattered Hegemonies: Postmodernity and Transnational Feminist Practices*. Minneapolis and London: University of Minnesota Press.

Guarnizo, Luis Eduardo, and Michael Peter Smith. 1998. "The Locations of Transnationalism." Pp. 3–34 in Smith and Guarnizo, *Transnationalism from Below*.

Gurak, Douglas T., and Fe Caces. 1992. "Migration Networks and the Shaping of Migration Systems." Pp. 150–76 in Mary Kritz, Lin Lean Lim, and Hania Zlotnik, editors, *International Migration Systems: A Global Approach*. Oxford: Clarendon Press.

Gutierrez, Bobby. 1995. "Solving the Root Cause of Poverty." *Tinig Filipino* (January): 31.

Hagan, Jacqueline. 1994. *Deciding to Be Legal: A Maya Community in Houston*. Philadelphia: Temple University Press.

Hall, Stuart. 1991a. "Ethnicity: Identity and Difference," *Radical America* 23(4): 9–20.

———. 1991b. "Old and New Identities, Old and New Ethnicities." Pp. 41–68 in Anthony King, editor, *Culture, Globalization, and the World-System*. London: Macmillan Education.

———. 1990. "Cultural Identity and Diaspora." Pp. 222–37 in Jonathan Rutherford, editor, *Identity: Community, Culture, and Difference*. London: Lawrence and Wishart.

———. 1988. "Minimal Selves." Pp. 44–46 in *Identity: The Real Me, ICA Document 6*. London: Institute of Contemporary Arts.

Hannerz, Ulf. 1996. *Transnational Connections*. New York: Routledge.

Harris, Nigel. 1995. *The New Untouchables: Immigration and the New World Worker*. New York: Penguin.

Harvey, David. 1989. *The Condition of Postmodernity*. New York: Basil Blackwell.

Heyzer, Noeleen, and Vivienne Wee. 1994. "Domestic Workers in Transient Overseas Employment: Who Benefits, Who Profits?" Pp. 31–102 in Heyzer, Lycklama á Nijeholt, and Weerakoon, *The Trade in Domestic Workers*.

Heyzer, Noeleen, Geertje Lycklama á Nijeholt, and Nedra Weerakoon, editors. 1994. *The Trade in Domestic Workers: Causes, Mechanisms, and Consequences of International Labor Migration*. London: Zed Books.

High Court of Singapore. 1993. "Criminal Case No. 23 of 1992 and Court of Criminal Appeal No. 6 of 1993, Public Prosecutor v. Flor Contemplacion." *Diwaliwan* (July 1995): 10–11.

Hing, Bill Ong. 1998. "Asian Immigrants: Social Forces Unleashed after 1965." Pp. 144–82 in David Jacobson, editor, *The Immigration Reader: America in a Multidisciplinary Perspective*. Oxford: Blackwell Publishers.

Hochschild, Arlie. 1989. *The Second Shift*. New York: Avon Books.

———. 1983. *The Managed Heart: Commercialization of Human Feeling*. Berkeley and Los Angeles: University of California Press.

Hogeland, Chris, and Karen Rosen. 1990. *Dreams Lost Dreams Found: Undocumented Women in the Land of Opportunity*. San Francisco: San Francisco Coalition for Immigrant Rights and Services.

Hondagneu-Sotelo, Pierrette. 1999. "Introduction: Gender and Contemporary U.S. Immigration." *American Behavioral Scientist* 42(4): 565–76.

———. 1996. "Immigrant Women and Paid Domestic Work: Research, Theory and Activism." Pp. 105–22 in Heidi Gottfried, editor, *Feminism and Social Change: Bridging Theory and Practice*. Urbana and Chicago: University of Illinois Press.

———. 1994. *Gendered Transitions: Mexican Experiences of Migration.* Berkeley and Los Angeles: University of California Press.

Hondagneu-Sotelo, Pierrette, and Ernistine Avila. 1997. "'I'm Here, but I'm There': The Meanings of Latina Transnational Motherhood." *Gender and Society* 11(5): 548–71.

Horn, Pamela. 1986. *The Rise and Fall of the Victorian Servant.* Wolfeboro Falls, NH: Alan Sutton.

Hunter, Tera. 1997. *To 'Joy My Freedom: Southern Black Women's Lives and Labors after the Civil War.* Cambridge and London: Harvard University Press.

Ilago, Delia C. 1995. "Let's Avoid Trouble in Hong Kong." *Tinig Filipino* (February): 43.

Israel-Sobritchea, Carolyn. 1990. "The Ideology of Female Domesticity: Its Impact on the Status of Filipino Women." *Review of Women's Studies* 1(1): 26–41.

Jones, Jacqueline. 1985. *Labor of Love, Labor of Sorrow: Black Women, Work and the Family, from Slavery to the Present.* New York: Vintage Books.

Kandiyoti, Deniz. 1996. "Contemporary Feminist Scholarship and Middle East Studies." Pp. 3–27 in Deniz Kandiyoti, editor, *Gendering the Middle East: Emerging Perspectives.* Syracuse, NY: Syracuse University Press.

Kaplan, Caren. 1994. "The Politics of Location as Transnational Feminist Critical Practice." Pp. 137–52 in Grewal and Kaplan, *Scattered Hegemonies.*

Kaplan, Elaine Bell. 1987. "'I Don't Do No Windows': Competition between the Domestic Worker and the Housewife." Pp. 92–105 in Valerie Miner and Helen E. Longino, editors, *Competition: A Feminist Taboo?* New York: Feminist Press.

Karp, Jonathan. 1995. "A New Kind of Hero." *Far Eastern Economic Review* 158: 42–45.

Katzman, David. 1978. *Seven Days a Week: Women and Domestic Service in Industrializing America.* New York: Oxford University Press.

Kearney, Michael. 1995. "The Local and the Global: The Anthropology of Globalization and Transnationalism." *Annual Review of Anthropology* 24: 547–65.

Kelley, Robin. 1994. *Race Rebels: Culture, Politics, and the Black Working Class.* New York: Free Press.

Kessler Harris, Alice. 1981. *Out to Work.* New York and London: Oxford University Press.

Khandelwal, Madhulika S. 1996. "Indian Networks in the United States: Class and Transnational Identities." Pp. 115–31 in Duleep and Wunnava, *Immigrants and Immigration Policy.*

Kibria, Nazli. 1993. *Family Tightrope: The Changing Lives of Vietnamese Americans.* Princeton, NJ: Princeton University Press.

King, Anthony D., editor. *Re-Presenting the City: Ethnicity, Capital and Culture in the Twenty-First Century Metropolis*. London: Macmillan Press.

King, Russell, editor. *The New Geography of European Migrants*. London: Belhaven Press.

King, Russell, and Krysia Rybaczuk. 1993. "Southern Europe and the International Division of Labor: From Emigration to Immigration." Pp. 175–206 in King, *The New Geography*.

Koptiuch, Kristin. 1996. "'Cultural Defense' and Criminological Displacement: Gender, Race and (Trans)Nation in the Legal Surveillance of US Diaspora Asians." Pp. 215–33 in Lavie and Swedenburg, *Displacement*.

Kritz, Mary, C. B. Keely, and S. Tomasi, *Global Trends in Migration*. New York: Center for Migration Studies.

Laguerre, Michel. 1994. "Headquarters and Subsidiaries: Haitian Immigrant Family Households in New York City." Pp. 47–61 in Ronald Taylor, editor, *Minority Families in the United States*. Englewood Cliffs, NJ: Prentice Hall.

Lamphere, Louise. 1984."On the Shop Floor: Multi-Ethnic Unity against the Conglomerate." Pp. 247–63 in Sacks and Remy, *My Troubles*.

Lamphere, Louise, Patricia Zavella, and Felipe Gonzales, with Peter Evans. 1993. *Sunbelt Working Mothers: Reconciling Family and Factory*. Ithaca, NY: Cornell University Press.

Lamprea, Jehcel. 1995. "The Inequality of the Sexes." *Tinig Filipino* (March): 11.

Lan, Pei-Chia. 1999. Bounded Commodity in a Global Market: Migrant Workers in Taiwan. Paper presented at the 1999 Annual Meeting of the Society for the Study of Social Problems, Chicago, August 6–8.

Lavie, Smadar, and Ted Swedenburg. 1996. "Introduction: Displacement, Diaspora and Geographies of Identity." Pp. 1–25 in Lavie and Swedenburg, *Displacement*.

———., editors. 1996. *Displacement, Diaspora and Geographies of Identity*. Durham, NC, and London: Duke University Press.

Layosa, Linda. 1995a. "Economy Menders." *Tinig Filipino* (June): 7.

———. 1995b. "A Salute to Filipino Women." *Tinig Filipino* (March): 6–7.

———. 1994. "Families are Forever." *Tinig Filipino* (December): 12–13.

Licuanan, Patricia. 1994. "The Socio-economic Impact of Domestic Worker Migration: Individual, Family, Community, Country." Pp. 103–16 in Heyzer, Lycklama á Nijeholt, and Weerakoon, *The Trade in Domestic Workers*.

Light, Ivan, Georges Sabagh, Mehdi Bozorgmehr, and Claudia Der-Martirosian. 1994. "Beyond the Ethnic Enclave Economy." *Social Problems* 41(1): 65–79.

Liu, John, and Lucie Cheng. 1994. "Pacific Rim Development and the Duality of Post-1965 Immigration to the United States." Pp. 74–99 in Ong, Bonacich, and Cheng, *The New Asian Immigration*.

Lopez-Rodriguez, Luz. 1990. "Patriarchy and Women's Subordination in the Philippines." *Review of Women's Studies* 1(1): 15–25.

Lorde, Audre. 1984. *Sister Outsider*. Trumansburg, NY: Crossing Press.

Lowe, Lisa. 1996. *Immigrant Acts: On Asian American Cultural Politics*. Durham, NC, and London: Duke University Press.

Lowell, B. Lindsay. 1996. "Review and Policy Commentary—Skilled and Family-Based Immigration." Pp. 353–71 in Duleep and Wunnava, *Immigrants and Immigration Policy*.

Luciani, Giacomo, editor, *Migration Policies in Europe and the United States*. Dordrecht, Boston, and London: Kluwer Academic Publishers.

Lycklama á Nijeholt, Geertje. 1994. "The Changing International Division of Labour and Domestic Workers: A Macro Overview." Pp. 3–29 in Heyzer, Lycklama á Nijeholt, and Weerakoon, *The Trade in Domestic Workers*.

Mahler, Sarah. 1999. "Engendering Transnational Migration: A Case Study of Salvadorans." *American Behavioral Scientist* 42(4): 690–719.

———. 1998. "Theoretical and Empirical Contributions Toward a Research Agenda for Transnationalism." Pp. 64–100 in Smith and Guarnizo, *Transnationalism from Below*.

———. 1995. *American Dreaming: Immigrant Life on the Margins*. Princeton, NJ: Princeton University Press.

Manlal-lan, Edna. 1994. "Do Maids Need Tests?" *Tinig Filipino* (October): 37.

Mariano, Jocelyn. 1995. "Child Abuse and OCWs." *Tinig Filipino* (October): 26–27.

Martin, Philip. 1995. "Proposition 187 in California." *International Migration Review* 29(1): 255–63.

———. 1993a. "Migration and Trade: The Case of the Philippines." *International Migration Review* 27 (3): 639–45.

———. 1993b. "The Migration Issue." Pp. 1–16 in King, *The New Geography*.

Martiniello, Marco. 1992. "Italy—The Late Discovery of Immigration." Pp. 195–218 in *Europe — A New Immigration Continent: Policies and Politics in Comparative Perspective*, Münster and Hamburg: Lit Verlag.

Massey, Doreen. 1994. *Space, Place and Gender*. Minneapolis: University of Minnesota Press.

Massey, Douglas, Rafael Alarcón, Jorge Durand, and Humberto Gonzales. 1987. *Return to Aztlan: The Social Process of International Migration from Western Mexico*. Berkeley and Los Angeles: University of California Press.

Matthei, Linda Miller, and David A. Smith. 1998. "Belizean 'Boyz 'n the Hood.'" Pp. 270–90 in Smith and Guarnizo, *Transnationalism from Below*.

Medick, Hans, and David Warren Sabean. 1984. "Interest and Emotion in Family Kinship Studies: A Critique of Social History and Anthropology." Pp. 9–27 in Hans Medick and David Warren Sabean, editors, *Interest and Emotion: Essays on the Study of Family and Kinship*. Cambridge: Cambridge University Press.

Medina, Belinda. 1991. *The Filipino Family: A Text with Selected Readings*. Quezon City, Philippines: University of the Philippines Press.

Melendy, Brett H. 1974. "Filipinos in the United States." *Pacific Historical Review* 43(4): 520–47.

Menjivar, Cecilia. 1999. "The Intersection of Work and Gender: Central American Immigrant Women and Employment in California." *American Behavioral Scientist* 42(4): 601–27.

Meyer, Donald. 1987. *The Rise of Women in America, Russia, Sweden, and Italy*. Middletown, CT: Wesleyan University Press.

Migrante. 1996. "Press Statement," March 13. Manila: Migrante.

Miles, Robert. 1993a. "Introduction—Europe 1993: The Significance of Changing Patterns of Migration." *Ethnic and Racial Studies* 16(3): 459–66.

———. 1993b. *Racism after 'Race Relations.'* New York and London: Routledge.

Miles, Robert, and Dietrich Thränhardt, editors. 1995. *Migration and European Integration: The Dynamics of Inclusion and Exclusion*. Madison and Teaneck, NJ: Farleigh Dickinson University Press.

Mintz, Steven, and Susan Kellog. 1988. *Domestic Revolutions: A Social History of American Family Life*. New York: Free Press.

Miyoshi, Masao. 1993. "A Borderless World? From Colonialism to Transnationalism and the Decline of the Nation State." *Critical Inquiry* 19: 726–51.

Mobido, Jack. 1995. "Justice for Flor, Justice for All OCWs." *Tinig Filipino* (May): 12–13.

Modell, John, and Edna Bonacich. 1980. *The Economic Basis of Ethnic Solidarity: Small Business in the Japanese American Community*. Berkeley and Los Angeles: University of California Press.

Moen, Phyllis, and Elaine Wethington. 1992. "The Concept of Family Adaptive Strategies." *Annual Review of Sociology* 18: 233–51.

Mohanty, Chandra. 1997. "Women Workers and Capitalist Scripts: Ideologies of Domination, Common Interests, and the Politics of Solidarity." Pp. 3–29 in M. Jacqui Alexander and Chandra Mohanty, editors, *Feminist Genealogies, Colonial Legacies, and Democratic Futures*. New York: Routledge.

———. 1991. "Under Western Eyes: Feminist Scholarship and Colonial Discourses." Pp. 51–80 in Chandra Talpade Mohanty, Ann Russo, and Lourdes Torres, editors, *Third World Women and the Politics of Feminism*. Bloomington: University of Indiana Press.

Montanari, Armando, and Antonio Cortese. 1993 "Third World Immigrants in Italy." Pp. 275–92 in Russell King, editor, *Mass Migrations in Europe: The Legacy and the Future*. London and New York: Belhaven Press.

Morokvasic, Mirjana. 1984. "Birds of Passage Are Also Women . . . " *International Migration Review* 18(4): 886–907.

Mufti, Aamir, and Ella Shohat. 1997. "Introduction." Pp. 1–11 in Anne Mc-
    Clintock, Aamir Mufti, and Ella Shoha, editors, *Dangerous Liaisons: Gen-
    der, Nation, and Postcolonial Perspectives*. Minneapolis: University of Min-
    nesota Press.
Nash, June, and Maria Patricia Fernandez Kelly, editors. 1983. *Women, Men
    and the International Division of Labor*. Albany, NY: SUNY Press.
Nelson, Margaret K. 1990. "Mothering Other's Children: The Experiences of
    Family Day Care Providers." Pp. 210–32 in Abel and Nelson, *Circles of Care*.
O'Connor, Julia S. 1996. "From Women in the Welfare State to Gendering
    Welfare State Regimes." *Current Sociology* 44(2): 1–130.
Okamura, Jonathan. 1998. *Imagining the Filipino American Diaspora: Trans-
    national Relations, Identities and Communities*. New York: Garland.
Ong, Aihwa. 1999. *Flexible Citizenship: The Culture Logic of Transnationality*.
    Durham, NC: Duke University Press.
———. 1996. "Cultural Citizenship as Subject-Making: Immigrants Negotiate
    Racial and Cultural Boundaries in the United States." *Contemporary An-
    thropology* 37(5): 737–62.
———. 1991. "The Gender and Labor Politics of Postmodernity." *Annual Re-
    view of Anthropology* 20: 279–301.
———. 1987. *Spirits of Resistance and Capitalist Discipline: Factory Women
    in Malaysia*. Albany, NY: SUNY Press.
Ong, Paul, and Tania Azores. 1994a. "Asian Immigrants in Los Angeles: Diver-
    sity and Divisions." Pp. 100–129 in Ong, Bonacich, and Cheng, *The New
    Asian Immigration*.
———. 1994b. "The Migration and Incorporation of Filipino Nurses." Pp. 164–
    195 in Ong, Bonacich, and Cheng, *The New Asian Immigration*.
Ong, Paul, Edna Bonacich, and Lucie Cheng. 1994. "The Political Economy of
    Capitalist Restructuring and the New Asian Immigration." Pp. 3–35 in
    Ong, Bonacich, and Cheng, *The New Asian Immigration*.
———., editors. 1994. *The New Asian Immigration in Los Angeles and Global
    Restructuring*. Philadelphia: Temple University Press.
Osteria, Trinidad. 1994. *Filipino Female Labor Migration to Japan: Economic
    Causes and Consequences*. Manila: De la Salle University Press.
O'Sullivan, Tim, et al. 1994. *Key Concepts in Communication and Cultural
    Studies*. New York and London: Routledge.
Overbeek, Henk. 1995. "Towards a New International Migration Regime:
    Globalization, Migration, and the Internationalization of the State." Pp. 15–
    36 in Miles and Thränhardt, *Migration and European Integration*.
Paganoni, Anthony, editor. 1984. *Migration from the Philippines*. Quezon
    City, Philippines: Scalabrini Migration Center.
Palmer, Phyllis. 1989. *Domesticity and Dirt: Housewives and Domestic Ser-*

vants in the United States, 1920–1945. Philadelphia: Temple University Press.

Paz Cruz, Victoria. 1987. *Seasonal Orphans and Solo Parents: The Impacts of Overseas Migration*. Quezon City, Philippines: Scalabrini Migration Center.

Paz Cruz, Victoria, and Anthony Paganoni. 1989. *Filipinas in Migration: Big Bills and Small Change*. Quezon City, Philippines: Scalabrini Migration Center.

Pedraza, Silvia. 1994. "Introduction from the Special Issue Editor: The Sociology of Immigration, Race, and Ethnicity in America." *Social Problems* 41(1): 1–8.

———. 1991. "Women and Migration: The Social Consequences of Gender." *Annual Review of Sociology* 17: 303–25.

Pedraza, Silvia, and Rubén Rumbaut, editors. 1996. *Origins and Destinies: Immigration, Race and Ethnicity in America*. Belmont, CA: Wadsworth Press.

Pedraza-Bailey, Silvia. 1990. "Immigration Research: A Conceptual Map." *Social Science History* 14(1): 43–67.

Pelegrin, Lea. 1994. "Home for Good." *Tinig Filipino* (October): 7–8.

Perea, Juan, editor. 1997. *Immigrants Out! The New Nativism and the Anti-Immigrant Impulse in the United States*. New York: New York University Press.

Pessar, Patricia R. 1999. "Engendering Migration Studies: The Case of New Immigrants in the United States." *American Behavioral Scientist* 42(4): 577–600.

———. 1995. "On the Homefront and in the Workplace: Integrating Immigrant Women into Feminist Discourse." *Anthropological Quarterly* 68(1): 37–47.

Peterson, Jean Treloggen. 1993. "Generalized Extended Family Exchange: A Case from the Philippines." *Journal of Marriage and the Family* 55 (August): 570–84.

Philippine Embassy of Rome. 1995. "Official Report of the Philippine Embassy of Rome."

Philippine National Statistical Coordination Board. 1999. *Women and Men in the Philippines*. Makati City, Philippines: Philippine National Statistical Coordination Board.

Pido, J. Antonio. 1986. *The Filipinos in America: Macro/Micro Dimensions of Immigration and Integration*. New York: Center for Migration Studies.

Pile, Steve. 1997. "Introduction: Opposition, Political Identities, and Spaces of Resistance." Pp. 1–32 in Steve Pile and Michael Keith, editors, *Geographies of Resistance*. New York: Routledge.

Pineda Ofrereo, Rosalinda. 1994. "The Philippine Garment Industry." Pp. 162–79 in Edna Bonacich, Lucie Cheng, Norma Chinchilla, Nora Hamilton, and

Paul Ong, editors, *Global Production: The Apparel Industry in the Pacific Rim*. Philadelphia: Temple University Press.

Plandano, Veronica. 1995. "Bayan, Kailan Pa?" *Tinig Filipino* (October): 60.

Poponoe, David. 1988. *Disturbing the Nest*. New York: Aldine de Gruvter.

Portes, Alejandro. 1997. "Immigration Theory for a New Century: Some Problems and Opportunities." *International Migration Review* 31(4): 799–825.

———. 1995. "Economic Sociology and the Sociology of Immigration: A Conceptual Overview." Pp. 1–41 in Alejandro Portes, editor, *The Economic Sociology of Immigration: Essays on Networks, Ethnicity, and Entrepreneurship*. New York: Russell Sage Foundation.

———. 1989. "Contemporary Immigration: Theoretical Perspectives on Its Determinants and Modes of Incorporation." *International Migration Review* 23(3): 606–30.

———. 1983. "International Labor Migration and National Development." Pp. 71–91 in Mary Kritz, editor, *U.S. Immigration and Refugee Policy*. New York: D. C. Heath.

———. 1981. "Modes of Structural Incorporation and Present Theories of Labor Migration." Pp. 279–97 in Kritz, Keely, and Tomasi, *Global Trends in Migration*.

Portes, Alejandro, and Alex Stepick. 1993. *City on the Edge: The Transformation of Miami*. Berkeley and Los Angeles: University of California Press.

Portes, Alejandro, and John Walton. 1981. *Labor, Class, and the International System*. New York: Academic Press.

Portes, Alejandro, and R. L. Bach. 1985. *Latin Journey: Cuban and Mexican Immigration to the United States*. Berkeley and Los Angeles: University of California Press.

Portes, Alejandro, and Rubén Rumbaut. 1996. *Immigrant America: A Portrait*. 2nd ed. Berkeley and Los Angeles: University of California Press.

Portes, Alejandro, Luis E. Guarnizo, and Patricia Landolt. 1999. "Introduction: Pitfalls and Promise of an Emergent Research Field." *Ethnic and Racial Studies* 22(2): 217–37.

Portes, Alejandro, Manuel Castells, and Lauren A. Benton, editors. 1985. *The Informal Economy: Studies in Advanced and Less Developed Countries*. Baltimore and London: Johns Hopkins University Press.

Presidenza del Consiglio dei Ministri. 1990. *Norme Urgenti In Materia Di Asilo Politico, Ingresso E Soggiorno Dei Cittadini Extracomunitari E Di Regolarizzazione Di Cittadini Extracommunitari Ed Apolidid Giá Nel Territorio Dello Stato*. Italia: Instituto Poligrafico E Zecca Dello Stato.

Pugliese, Enrico. 1996. "Italy Between Emigration and Immigration and the Problems of Citizenship." Pp. 106–21 in Cesarani and Fulbrook, *Citizenship*.

Q. Bella. 1995. "Heroes or Martyrs." *Tinig Filipino* (November): 22–23.

Reich, Robert. 1991. *The Work of Nations*. New York: Vintage Books.

Reimers, David. 1996. "Third World Immigration to the United States." Pp. 309–21 in Duleep and Wunnava, *Immigrants and Immigration Policy.*

———. 1985. *Still the Golden Door: The Third World Comes to America.* New York: Columbia University Press.

Repak, Terry. 1995. *Waiting on Washington: Central American Workers in the Nation's Capitol.* Philadelphia: Temple University Press.

———. 1994. "Labor Recruitment and the Lure of Capital: Central American Migrants in Washington, DC." *Gender and Society* 8(4): 507–24.

Republic of the Philippines. 1995. *Philippine Statistical Yearbook.* Makati, Philippines: National Statistical Coordination Board.

Reskin, Barbara, and Irene Padavic. 1994. *Women and Men at Work.* Thousand Oaks, CA: Pine Forge Press.

Rivera, Ma. Theresa L. 1995. "Let's Persevere Under Trial." *Tinig Filipino* (April 1995): 24.

Rivera-Batiz, Francisco L. 1996. "English Language Proficiency, Quantitative Skills, and the Economic Progress of Immigrants." Pp. 57–77 in Duleep and Wunnava, *Immigrants and Immigration Policy.*

Rollins, Judith. 1985. *Between Women: Domestics and Their Employers.* Philadelphia: Temple University Press.

Romero, Mary. 1992. *Maid in the U.S.A.* New York and London: Routledge.

Rosca, Ninotchka. 1995. "The Philippines' Shameful Export." *Nation* 260(15): 522–27.

Rothman, Barbara Katz. 1989a. *Recreating Motherhood: Ideology and Technology in a Patriarchal Society.* New York and London: W. W. Norton.

———. 1989b. "Women as Fathers: Motherhood and Child Care under a Modified Patriarchy." *Gender and Society* 3(1): 89–104.

Rouse, Roger. 1992. "Making Sense of Settlement: Class Transformations, Cultural Struggle, and Transnationalism among Mexican Migrants in the United States." Pp. 25–52 in *Towards a Transnational Perspective.* Vol. 645 of the *Annals of the New York Academy of Sciences.*

———. 1991. "Mexican Migration and the Social Space of Postmodernism." *Diaspora* 1(1): 8–23.

Rubin, Gayle. 1996. "The Traffic in Women: Notes on the 'Political Economy' of Sex." Pp. 105–51 in Joan Scott, editor, *Feminism and History.* Oxford and New York: Oxford University Press.

Rubin, Lillian. 1976. *Worlds of Pain: Life in the Working-Class Family.* New York: Basic Books.

Ruddick, Sara. 1992. "Thinking About Fathers." Pp. 176–90 in Thorne and Yalom, *Rethinking the Family.*

Ruzza, Carlo, and Oliver Schmidtke. 1996. "The Northern League: Changing Friends and Foes, and Its Political Opportunity Structure." Pp. 179–208 in Cesarani and Fulbrook, *Citizenship.*

Sabagh, Georges. 1993. "Los Angeles, a World of New Immigrants: An Image of Things To Come." Pp. 97–126 in Luciani, *Migration Policies.*

Sacks, Karen, and Dorothy Remy, editors. 1984. *My Troubles Are Going to Have Trouble With Me: Everyday Trials and Triumphs of Women Workers.* New Brunswick, NJ: Rutgers University Press.

Safa, Helen. 1995. *The Myth of the Male Breadwinner.* Boulder, CO: Westview Press.

Sandoval, Chela. 1991. "U.S. Third World Feminism: The Theory and Method of Oppositional Consciousness in the Postmodern World." *Genders* 10(Spring): 1–24.

Santel, Bernhard. 1995. "Loss of Control: The Build-up of a European Migration and Asylum Regime." Pp. 75–91 in Miles and Thränhardt, *Migration and European Integration.*

Santillan, Imelda Soriao. 1995. "Katarungan, Ikaw Ay Nasaan?" *Tinig Filipino* (May): 13.

Sarmiento, J. N. 1991. "The Asian Experience in International Migration." *International Migration Review* 29(2): 195–201.

Sassen, Saskia. 1998. "Cracked Casings: Notes Towards an Analytics of Studying Transnational Processes." Working paper. New York: Russell Sage Foundation and the Social Science Research Council Committee on Sovereignty.

———. 1996a. "Analytic Borderlands: Race, Gender and Representation in the New City." Pp. 183–202 in King, *Re-Presenting the City.*

———. 1996b. *Losing Control? Sovereignty in an Age of Globalization.* New York: Columbia University Press.

———. 1996c. "New Employment Regimes in Cities: The Impact on Immigrant Workers." *New Community* 22(4): 579–94.

———. 1996d "Rebuilding the Global City: Economy, Ethnicity and Space." Pp. 23–42 in King, *Re-Presenting the City.*

———. 1994. *Cities in a World Economy.* Thousand Oaks, CA: Pine Forge Press.

———. 1993. "The Impact of Economic Internationalization on Immigration: Comparing the U.S. and Japan." *International Migration* 31(1): 73–99.

———. 1989. "New York City's Informal Economy." Pp. 60–77 in Portes, Castells, and Benton, *The Informal Economy.*

———. 1988. *The Mobility of Labor and Capital: A Study in International Investment and Labor.* New York: Cambridge University Press.

———. 1984. "Notes on the Incorporation of Third World Women into Wage Labor through Immigration and Offshore Production." *International Migration Review* 18(4): 1144–67.

Scott, James. 1990. *Domination and the Arts of Resistance.* New Haven, CT: Yale University Press.

Scott, Joan. 1992. "Experience." Pp. 22–40 in Butler and Scott, *Feminists Theorize the Political*.

———. 1988. *Gender and the Politics of History*. New York: Columbia University Press.

Silverman, Gary. 1995. "Mothers to the World." *Far Eastern Economic Review* 158: 48.

Simon, Rita, and Margo DeLey. 1984. "The Work Experiences of Undocumented Mexican Women Migrants in Los Angeles." *International Migration Review* 18(4): 1212–29.

Skolnick, Arlene. 1991. *Embattled Paradise: The American Family in an Age of Uncertainty*. New York: Basic Books.

Smith, Joan, Immanuel Wallerstein, and Hans-Dieter Evers, editors. 1984. *Households and the World Economy*. Beverly Hills, CA: Sage Publications.

Smith, Michael Peter, and Luis Eduardo Guarnizo, editors. 1998. *Transnationalism from Below*. New Brunswick, NJ, and London: Transaction.

Smith, Paul. 1988. *Discerning the Subject*. Minneapolis: University of Minnesota Press.

Smith, Robert C. 1998. "Transnational Localities: Community, Technology and the Politics of Membership within the Context of Mexico and U.S. Migration." Pp. 196–238 in Smith and Guarnizo, *Transnationalism from Below*.

Sorensen, Ninna Nyberg. 1998. "Narrating Identity across Dominican Worlds." Pp. 241–69 in Smith and Guarnizo, *Transnationalism from Below*.

Soysal, Yasemin Nuhoglu. 1994. *Limits of Citizenship: Migrants and Postnational Membership in Europe*. Chicago and London: University of Chicago Press.

Specter, Michael. 1998. "The Baby Bust." *New York Times*, July 10.

Stacey, Judith. 1991. *Brave New Families: Stories of Domestic Upheaval in Late Twentieth Century America*. New York: Basic Books.

Stack, Carol. 1974. *All Our Kin*. New York: Harper and Row.

Stack, Carol, and Linda Burton. 1994. "Kinscripts: Reflections on Family, Generation, and Culture." Pp. 33–44 in Glenn, Chang, and Forcey, *Mothering*.

Stasiulis, Daiva, and Abigail Bakan. 1997. "Regulation and Resistance: Strategies of Migrant Domestic Workers in Canada and Internationally." *Asian and Pacific Migration Journal* 6(1): 31–57.

Stepick, Alex. 1991. "The Haitian Informal Sector in Miami." *City and Society* 5(June): 10–22.

———. 1989. "Miami's Two Informal Sectors." Pp. 111–31 in Portes, Castells, and Benton, *The Informal Economy*.

Tade, Juliet. 1995. "From Bad to Good Employers." *Tinig Filipino* (May): 24.

Tadiar, Neferti Xina. 1997. "Domestic Bodies of the Philippines." *Sojourn* 12(2): 153–91.

Takaki, Ronald. 1989. *Strangers from a Different Shore*. Boston: Little Brown.

Thorne, Barrie. 1992. "Feminism and the Family: Two Decades of Thought." Pp. 3–30 in Thorne and Yalom, *Rethinking the Family*.

Thorne, Barrie, and Marilyn Yalom, editors. 1992. *Rethinking the Family: Some Feminist Questions*. Rev. ed. Boston: Northeastern University Press.

Tinig Balita Staff. 1995. "Ala-Ala ng isang Ina." *Tinig Balita* (May): 7.

Tolentino, Roland. 1996. "Bodies, Letters, Catalogs: Filipinas in Transnational Space." *Social Text* 48 (14:3): 49–76.

Toribio, Eddie. 1994. "Parenting via Long Distance." *Tinig Filipino* (October): 34.

Toro-Morn, Maura I. 1995. "Gender, Class, Family and Migration: Puerto Rican Women in Chicago." *Gender and Society* 9(6): 712–26.

Trinh T. Minh-ha. 1989. *Woman Native Other*. Bloomington: University of Indiana Press.

Tyner, James. 1999. "The Global Context of Gendered Labor Migration from the Philippines to the United States." *American Behavioral Scientist* 42(4): 671–89.

———. 1994. "The Social Construction of Gendered Migration from the Philippines." *Asian and Pacific Migration Journal* 3(4): 589–615.

United States Bureau of the Census. 1993. *1990 Census of the Population, Asians and Pacific Islanders in the United States*. Washington, D.C.: Government Printing Office.

USA Today. 1995. "Death Sentence." *USA Today*, September 18.

Velasco, Pura. M. 1997. "'We Can Still Fight Back': Organizing Domestic Workers in Toronto." Pp. 157–64 in Bakan and Stasiulis, *Not One of the Family*.

Venturini, Alessandra. 1991. "Italy in the Context of European Migration." *Regional Development Dialogue* 12(3): 93–112.

Veugelers, John. 1994. "Recent Immigration Politics in Italy: A Short Story." Pp. 33–49 in Martin Baldwin-Edwards and Martin Schain, editors, *The Politics of Immigration in Western Europe*. Portland, OR: Frank Cass.

Villaruz, Bing Cerdenola. 1995. "Should I Go or Should I Stay?" *Tinig Filipino* (October): 62.

Vista, Rosalie D. 1995. "My Life in Singapore." *Tinig Filipino* (1995): 30.

Waldinger, Roger. 1996. *Still the Promised City? African Americans and New Immigrants in Postindustrial New York*. Cambridge and London: Harvard University Press.

———. 1994. "The Making of an Immigrant Niche." *International Migration Review* 28(1): 3–30.

Waldinger, Roger, and Mehdi Bozorgmehr, editors. 1996. *Ethnic Los Angeles*. New York: Russell Sage Foundation.

Walkerdine, Valerie, and Helen Lucey. 1989. *Democracy in the Kitchen: Regulating Mothers and Socialising Daughters*. London: Virago Press.

Wallace, Michelle. 1990. *Invisibility Blues: From Pop to Theory*. New York: Verso.

Wallerstein, Immanuel. 1984. "Household-Structures and Labor-Force Formation in the Capitalist World-Economy." Pp. 17–22 in Smith, Wallerstein, and Evers, *Households and the World Economy*.

Ward, Kathryn, editor. 1990. *Women Workers and Global Restructuring*. Ithaca, NY: Cornell University Press.

Weedon, Chris. 1997. *Feminist Practice and Poststructuralist Theory*. 2nd ed. Oxford and Cambridge: Blackwell.

White, Paul. 1993. "The Social Geography of Immigrants in European Cities: The Geography of Arrival." Pp. 47–66 in King, *The New Geography*.

Williams, Raymond. 1977. *Marxism and Literature*. Oxford and New York: Oxford University Press.

Wilson, William Julius. 1996. *When Work Disappears: The World of the New Urban Poor*. New York: Vintage Books.

———. 1987. *The Truly Disadvantaged: The Inner City, the Underclass, and Public Policy*. Chicago: University of Chicago Press.

Wong, Sau-ling. 1995. "Denationalization Reconsidered: Asian American Cultural Criticism at a Theoretical Crossroads." *Amerasia Journal* 21(1 & 2): 1–27.

———. 1994. "Diverted Mothering: Representations of Caregivers of Color in the Age of 'Multiculturalism.'" Pp. 67–91 in Glenn, Chang, and Forcey, *Mothering*.

Wrigley, Julia. 1995. *Other People's Children: An Intimate Account of the Dilemmas Facing Middle-Class Parents and the Women They Hire to Raise their Children*. New York: Basic Books.

———. 1991. "Feminist and Domestic Workers." *Feminist Studies* 17(2): 317–29.

Yamanaka, Keiko, and Kent McClelland. 1994. "Earning the Model-Minority Image: Diverse Strategies of Economic Adaptation by Asian American Women." *Ethnic and Racial Studies* 17(1): 79–114.

Yawan, Ruth. 1995. "Through the Eyes of a Child." *Tinig Filipino* (April): 13.

Yeoh, Brenda S. A., Shirlena Huang, and Joaquin Gonzalez III. 1999. "Migrant Female Domestic Workers: Debating the Economic, Social and Political Impacts in Singapore." *International Migration Review* 33(1): 114–36.

Young, Grace Esther. 1987. "The Myth of Being 'Like a Daughter.'" *Latin American Perspectives* 14(3): 365–80.

Yuval-Davis, Nira. 1991. "The Citizenship Debate: Women, Ethnic Processes, and the State." *Feminist Review* 39(Winter): 58–68.

Zlotnick, Hania. 1995. "The South-to-North Migration of Women." *International Migration Review* 29(1): 229–54.

———. 1990. "International Migration Policies and the Status of Female Migrants." *International Migration Review* 24(2): 372–81.

Zolberg, Aristide R. 1993. "Are the Industrial Countries Under Siege?" Pp. 53–81 in Luciani, *Migration Policies.*

———. 1983. "International Migrations in Political Perspective." Pp. 3–27 in Kritz, Keely, and Tomasi, *Global Trends in Migration.*

INDEX

In this index "f" after a number indicates a separate reference on the next page, and "ff" indicates separate references on the next two pages. A continuous discussion over two or more pages is indicated by a span of numbers. *Passim* is used for a cluster of references in close but not consecutive sequence.

Advanced capitalist nations, 10, 15, 25, 105, 248; Women in the labor force, 69–72. *See also* Economic bloc of postindustrial nations
African Americans, 76, 108, 164, 175, 278n18
African migrants, 2, 8, 176, 179
Agency, 23, 24, 34, 115, 251. *See also* Bind of agency
Albanian refugees, 43, 209
Andall, Jacqueline, 71
Anderson, Benedict, 11–12
Appadarai, Arjun, 12
Arevalo, Nina Rea, 133, 147
Au pair, 176
Australia, 50, 58

Bakan, Abigail, and Daiva Stasiulis, 9, 48, 50
Balibar, Etienne, 275n14
Balila, Luisa, 95–99, 122
Bangladesh, 51
Basch, Linda, Nina Glick-Schiller, and Christina Szanton Blanc, 13, 81–82
Batung, Maria, 102–4
Bind of agency, 34–35, 60, 254
Butler, Judith, 34–35, 250

Canada, 9, 50, 58, 59, 91
Care, 71, 73, 117–19, 132, 142, 143, 276; displaced caretaking, 122, 182–83, 276
Caribbean domestic workers, 76
Catorce, Rodney, 140, 148

Central American refugees, 30
Chant, Sylvia, and Cathy McIlwaine, 67
Characteristics of the samples, 18–20, 257–61
Children, 49, 92–93, 114–15, 138–49; care of 76–78, 86–90 *passim*, 96–99, 106, 112, 117–19; education, 89–90, 94–95, 123–24, 106. *See also* Transnational parenting
Chinese migrants, 81, 179
Citizenship, 107, 243. *See also* Partial citizenship
Civil Rights movement, 7, 38
Colen, Shellee, 166
Colonialism. See Roman Catholic Church; United States
Commodification, 71, 73, 94, 249, 253; of love, 122–23, 130, 131, 134; of mothering. *See* International division of reproductive labor
Community, 270n12, 197, 213, 226; anomie, 198, 202, 212–15, 228, 237, 239, 241, 242, 245
—in Los Angeles: 7, 227–28, 241; geography, 229, 231–35; pockets of gathering, 233, 234–35; solidarity, 233f, 238–39, 241
—in Rome: 187, 198–200, 205, 215–26, 227; ethnic economy, 209, 214–26; geography, 201–4; pockets of gathering, 202–4, 211; public and private domains, 204–10; residences of migrant Filipina, 221–24; solidarity, 198, 202, 210–12, 221, 225

305

Centers & Solidarity. New Filipino Immigrants in Southern California